Baruch: My Own Story

Bernard Baruch

To the memory of

MY MOTHER, MY FATHER, *and* MY WIFE

Preface

It was my children who first urged me to write the story of my life. As they grew up, they often would ask, "Can a young man or woman starting in life still do the things you did?" or "Is there anything fixed and lasting in this constantly changing world?"

Others have wanted me to tell the story of my career in Wall Street—hoping, I suspect, that it might reveal some short cut, some sure-fire formula for becoming rich. Still others have been more concerned with my judgments of the seven Presidents whom I have known, from Woodrow Wilson to Dwight D. Eisenhower.

Then there have been those—and I must confess they have had the greatest effect—who have urged me to review my experiences through two world wars and two peacemakings to determine whether my observations would yield any guiding thoughts to the problems of survival that confront the world today.

Actually, I began writing these memoirs in the late 1930's, but their completion was always being delayed. With the rise of Hitler, I devoted much of my time to trying to get this country to arm as the best safeguard against war. When World War Two broke out, all my energies were drawn into helping to speed the mobilization of our nation's resources for victory and trying to prevent a repetition of the mistakes we had made in World War One. When the war ended, I found myself struggling with the difficulties of its aftermath and with such problems as the international control of atomic energy.

These duties not only left no time for work on my memoirs, but gave me much more to write about. The fresh insights these experiences yielded also required my rewriting much of what I had written.

My original intention was not to publish my autobiography until it was completed. But a narrative that begins with the Reconstruction period and extends past the splitting of the atom is not easily compressed into a single volume. Also, I have always felt a man's memoirs should be published while he is still alive so that those who might object to what is written would be able to confront the writer with their views.

And so, at eighty-seven, it seemed to me that I should wait no longer to publish this first volume. It will be followed not too long from now, I hope, with a final volume, on which I am now working.

There may even be some special advantage in paying extra attention to my formative years. None of us ever really outgrows his or her childhood. How we meet the problems of adult life usually does not differ greatly from how we met the problems of growing up.

As a boy I was shy and fearful, with a dread of speaking in public. I had an ungovernable temper. As I grew older I liked to gamble—a horse race, ball game, or prize fight still thrills me and makes me feel young again.

Whatever I saw others accomplish, I was driven to try to do myself. Only after much effort did I learn how to control my feelings, and do what I could do best, leaving what I could not do well to others.

If there was any "key" to this process of growing up, it lay in the systematic efforts I made to subject myself to critical self-appraisal. And as I came to know myself, I acquired a better understanding of other people.

My years in Wall Street and business, in fact, became one long course of education in human nature. Nearly always the problem that arose in the Stock Exchange or in other business dealings was how to disentangle the impersonal facts of a situation from the elements of human psychology which came with these facts. When I left Wall Street to go into public life I found myself confronted with this same eternal riddle—

how to balance the nature of things in this world in which we live with the nature of mankind.

Human nature, of course, changes far more slowly than do our external surroundings. When new situations arise some persons dig their heels dogmatically into the past and declare that we must hold rigidly to the old rules.

Others treat each new situation as if it requires a *de novo* approach, relying on trial and error as if the past had no value.

To govern ourselves effectively, both these extremes must be rejected. The real problem is to know when to stand by the old truths and when to strike out in new, experimental ways. In these memoirs I have tried to set forth the philosophy through which I have sought to harmonize a readiness to risk something new with precautions against repeating the errors of the past.

Some of the things I have done may arouse disapproval. Still, I have told of my failings and mistakes, if only because I have found that failure is a far better teacher than success.

In preparing these memoirs I am indebted to my friends Harold Epstein, Samuel Lubell, and Herbert Bayard Swope for their help. Robert Lescher of Henry Holt and Company also contributed valuable editorial suggestions.

Contents

1. A Confederate Surgeon

THE TWO-STORY FRAME HOUSE in which I was born on August 19, 1870, stood on the main street of Camden, South Carolina. Still, living there was almost like living in the open country. Directly behind the house were a vegetable garden, stables, and barn. Beyond them stretched three acres of land which Father had turned into a kind of experimental "farm." One year I remember it was set out in sugar cane, on whose cultivation Father bestowed as much pains as if it were a plantation of money-making cotton.

Father used to spend time on his "farm" which Mother thought should have been devoted to his medical practice. Yet he was one of the most successful physicians in the state. He was only thirty-three when the South Carolina Medical Association elected him president. He also served as head of the State Board of Health and was active in the troubled and sometimes bloody politics of the Reconstruction.

Recently I was reading through one of his early case books. Those scribbled pages mirrored his role in the community. He treated Negroes and whites alike for all their ailments and accidents, from the lad who caught a fish-hook in his leg to the poor old Negro who, on the death of his former master, refused to eat or drink for eighteen days and starved to death.

Father often took me along in his two-seater buggy when he made his rounds through the countryside. Sometimes I would hold the reins while he read or dozed. Once we stopped at a crude cabin. I waited in the buggy while Father went inside. Soon he came hurrying out. Taking an ax, he smashed in the wooden shutters, exclaiming, "That man is dying for lack of fresh air!"

1.

Father's work on his experimental "farm" reflected an interest in bettering the community which he displayed through his whole life. When we moved to New York about six months after my tenth birthday, he pioneered in establishing public baths in overcrowded tenement districts. In South Carolina, when we lived there, the state had not yet set up its own agricultural service to experiment with better farming methods. But Father saw the need for such experimentation and, although he had no prior agricultural training, soon became expert at it.

Alongside the medical books in his office were heaped a stack of yellow-backed farm journals. He tested the theories he drew from them on his own three acres. His yields of cotton, corn, oats, and sugar cane took first prizes at the County Fair.

He gave away seeds and was never too busy to help a farmer solve a particular problem. Once Father bought a few acres of lowland to show it could be drained with tile. This was, I believe, the first experiment of its kind in our part of the country.

Father was a man worth looking at—six feet tall, erect and military, with a dark beard and mild, unwavering blue eyes. His dress was rather formal. Never do I recall seeing him in his shirt sleeves. Yet he had a kindly manner, and a soft voice which had no trace of accent to suggest his foreign birth.

2

Simon Baruch—as Father was named—was born in the village of Schwersenz, near Posen, then part of Germany, on July 29, 1840. He rarely spoke of his forebears. When the matter came up he would say that it was not so important where you came from as where you were going.

Not until I was twenty and Father took me to Europe to visit his parents did I learn anything of the Baruch ancestry. My grandfather, Bernhard Baruch, whose name I bear, had an old family relic, a skull, on which was recorded the family genealogy. It appeared that the Baruchs were of a rabbinical family and of Portuguese-Spanish origin, although somewhere along the line there must have been an admixture of Polish or Russian stock.

Grandfather also claimed descent from Baruch the Scribe, who edited the prophecies of Jeremiah and whose name is given to one of the Books of the Apocrypha. On this claim Father himself was silent.

Grandfather Baruch and I became great friends. He could not speak English, but since I knew German fairly well we got along famously. He was six feet or more, with fine brown hair, rosy cheeks, and dark eyes magnified by thick spectacles. Something of a scholar and dreamer, he liked to sit in a beer garden, smoking cigars and talking. We spent most of our time that way while Father stayed at home with his mother.

Grandmother Baruch was a different type—hard-working, saving, exacting, and practical. She was short, with very blue eyes which Father and I inherited. Her hair was parted in the middle and drawn down severely on either side of her head. Her maiden name was Theresa Gruen, and I believe she was of Polish descent.

Father had come to the United States in 1855 to avoid conscription into the Prussian Army. He was fifteen years old and a student at the Royal Gymnasium in Posen when, with some secrecy, he set out for America. It took a bit of courage since he knew only one person here, Mannes Baum, also a native of Schwersenz, who owned a small general store in Camden.

Mannes Baum became Father's protector. Young Simon went to work for Mannes as a bookkeeper, teaching himself English by reading American history with a translating dictionary beside him. Mr. Baum's wife—she was Mother's aunt and it was through her that Father and Mother met—quickly appreciated the promise of this bright boy. She persuaded Mannes to send him to South Carolina Medical College in

Charleston, and later to the Medical College of Virginia in Richmond.

Father never forgot the kindness of Mannes Baum. Mannes was given me for a middle name. I am proud to bear it. A little fellow, Mannes had "the courage of Julius Caesar," as a local expression went.

Father liked to tell how a bully came to the store to make Mannes retract some statement. When Mannes refused, the man began to beat him with the iron head of a hoe. His scalp cut and bleeding, Mannes still refused to retract. The tough threw him down, pressed his thumbs against Mannes' eyes, and threatened to gouge them out.

"Now do you take it back?" demanded the bully.

"No!" shouted Mannes Baum.

The assailant started to put his threat into execution. Mannes squirmed. The gouger's thumbs slipped and Mannes got one of them between his teeth and held on until the bully howled for him to let go. It might have been a case of a thumb for an eye, but the tough decided not to accept even that modification of the Mosaic Law.

In telling me that story Father had an object in view. The code of defending one's honor, with a duel if necessary, still prevailed in South Carolina at that time. Praising Mannes Baum's bravery, Father counseled, "Son, never stand an insult."

It was Mannes Baum who gave Father the uniform and sword that he donned on April 4, 1862, when he joined the Third Battalion, South Carolina Infantry. Father had just graduated from medical school and was appointed an Assistant Surgeon "without even having lanced a boil," as he used to say.

Enlisting in the Confederate Army was the natural, human thing for Father to do. Like so many others, including Robert E. Lee, who neither owned slaves nor approved of slavery, Father felt his first allegiance to be to his adopted state. Moreover, nearly all the youth he knew in Camden were enlisting.

Before marching north with his unit, Father admonished

his seventeen-year-old brother, Herman, who had come over from Germany, to keep out of the war. Nine months later they met. Herman was a Confederate cavalryman. When Father rebuked him, Herman explained, "I could no longer stand it. I could not look into the faces of the ladies."

As a surgeon, Father saw the saddest, most grisly side of the war. He did not talk much of his experiences. When my three brothers and I asked him to "tell us of the war," he usually would send us to our studies or assign us some chore.

But there were times when Father, with his four sons crowded around him, would reminisce. One favorite story was how he tried to stem the Confederate retreat at Cedar Creek, which was made memorable by General Sheridan's ride from Winchester.

"I saw General Early waving a flag and imploring the men to stop the rout," Father recalled. "Galloping toward the front I yelled, 'Rally, men, for God's sake, rally!' Yankee shells were bursting in every direction. One exploded over my head. The mare I was riding took the bit in her teeth and ran away with me. The men yelled after me, 'Why in hell don't *you* rally?' "

Another story we liked to hear was of Father's first experience as a battlefield surgeon at the Second Battle of Manassas. Father had reported to the field hospital, arriving just as a veteran surgeon was about to perform an amputation. Correctly gauging Father's inexperience, the surgeon held out the scalpel and said ironically, "Perhaps you would like to operate, Doctor." Father accepted the challenge and performed the operation—his first. He did it well enough to earn the surgeon's praise.

Although Father was present at some of the bloodiest battles of the war, he often commented on the chivalry which both sides displayed. When World War One broke out, he remarked that the Civil War was, by comparison, a "gentleman's war." One instance of battlefield chivalry made so deep an impression that he recalled it on his deathbed in 1921.

Among the Union dead at the Battle of the Wilderness was

Major General James S. Wadsworth, whose grandson became U.S. Senator from New York. He had been shot in the head. General Lee sent word to the Union lines that he would be pleased to return the body of so gallant a foe. As the ambulance, flying a flag of truce, carried General Wadsworth's body through the Confederate lines, tattered men in gray bared their heads.

3

In all his reminiscences of the war, Father never displayed any bitterness toward the North. This may have reflected the treatment he received each time he was taken prisoner.

He first was captured at the battle of Antietam. In a preliminary onslaught at South Mountain, the Third South Carolina Battalion had been severely mauled and its commanding officer, Colonel George S. James, was killed. While the Confederates streamed back in retreat, Father was ordered to take charge of the wounded in a churchyard in Boonsboro. An operating table was hastily contrived from a door balanced across two barrels, and a seriously wounded man was placed upon it. The patient was receiving chloroform and Father had just picked up his instruments when a hail of bullets interrupted proceedings. The wounded man was carried into the church, where the operation was performed.

By the time Father finished, the road outside was filled with Union cavalry. Father and his orderlies continued their work while the cannonading at Sharpsburg, a few miles away, shook the earth. A Union surgeon came by and asked Father if he needed help. This unexpected offer of aid made such a profound impression on Father that more than fifty years later he still remembered the man's name. It was J. P. Daly.

Assistant Surgeon Baruch was now a military prisoner. But he knew he soon would be free since it was the policy of both armies to exchange doctors as speedily as possible. He remained at Boonsboro for almost two months—two of the most agreeable months he spent in the Army, he always said. Then he and several other medical officers were taken aboard a train for Baltimore. En route, the prisoners received word that they would be met at the depot by Southern sympathizers and lodged at the homes of prominent citizens until they were exchanged.

But the Yankee lieutenant in charge didn't like these fraternizing arrangements and marched his prisoners to the provost marshal. The provost marshal proved less punctilious. He gave Father and a fellow officer freedom of the city in exchange for their pledge to report at headquarters the following day. The two young Confederates were taken to the home of a wealthy citizen and were entertained at a dance which lasted until two in the morning.

After breakfast, at the request of a number of young ladies, they rode in an open carriage to a photographer's studio, where each posed for his picture. A copy of this photograph, which Father's female admirers paid for, hung in our Camden home when I was a boy. The following day the captured Confederate surgeons were on their way to Virginia to be exchanged.

Father was captured a second time ten months later at Gettysburg. When I was a grown man, Father and I visited Gettysburg and he described the battle as he had witnessed it. As he talked, Father gestured with his black hat, while his long white hair waved in the wind. It was a stirring picture that he drew of General Pickett's forces moving against the Peach Orchard. Nearly all the wounded, Father recalled, were hit in the side by the enfilading Yankee fire because of an order changing the direction of the Confederate charge.

The Confederate field hospital had been set up in Black Horse Tavern. Father pointed out the spot along Marsh Creek where orderlies had drawn water for the surgeons. He told me he spent two days and two nights operating or in constant vigil over the wounded.

Then, as the Confederate Army began its heart-breaking

retreat, an order came from General Lee for Father and two other doctors to remain at the hospital until further notice—an order which meant capture by the enemy.

While waiting for the Union troops to appear, Father and the two other doctors busied themselves by roasting a peacock which had been parading in a nearby meadow. It was the first good meal they had had in three days. No sooner had they picked the last bone clean than a line of Union cavalry appeared.

The treatment Father received from the Yankees overwhelmed him. Almost immediately a clerical-looking gentleman named Dr. Winslow called on Father with an offer of emergency supplies. Then he directed Father to the Sanitary Commission warehouse in Gettysburg, where supplies overflowed onto the street—a rare sight to a Southerner, serving in an army that lived from hand to mouth.

The clerk advised Father to apply at the quartermaster's for a wagon. Dubiously Father went to quartermaster headquarters, where once again he was surprised by the reception.

"Take a seat, Doctor," said one young officer politely. "Here is a New York *Herald* from which you may learn what has become of General Lee. Read it until one of our wagons arrives."

Soon a mule-drawn wagon was placed at Father's disposal. He filled it with enough medical and commissary supplies to last a month. Among these were a barrel of eggs packed in sawdust, some wines, lemons, and butter packed in ice.

Two Maryland women and an elderly English nurse came to care for the wounded. A Baltimore physician brought Father a fine set of surgical instruments with Father's name engraved on the case. These Father later sent to Camden to have something to begin his practice with when the war was over.

Six weeks were passed in this captivity. Then suddenly Father was put aboard a cattle car with other Confederate prisoners and was shipped to Fort McHenry in Baltimore. It developed that Father and other Confederate doctors were being held as hostages.

A Dr. Rucker, a Union sympathizer in Charleston, West Virginia, had been convicted of murder and had been sentenced to be hanged. His wife had appealed to Federal authorities, claiming that her husband had not obtained a fair trial. Washington had halted the exchange of Confederate medical officers until Dr. Rucker was released.

Imprisonment at Fort McHenry was not as irksome as might be imagined, Father used to assure us. In fact, he often referred to it as a "summer spent at a seaside resort." He and the other doctors had the freedom of the grounds inside the fort. They played football and chess, conducted language classes and debates. Best of all for their morale, young ladies visited the fort daily to cheer the captives, who would bargain for fresh paper collars to improve their appearance.

A sergeant of the guard was bribed to allow some of the prisoners to visit Baltimore in the evenings. This worked well until several doctors failed to return for morning roll call. The other prisoners tried answering to their names but the ruse soon was discovered. Confinement became more rigorous until the remaining officers gave their word not to attempt to escape. After two months the deadlock between the two governments was broken by the escape of Dr. Rucker. The prisoners at Fort McHenry were sent South.

While at Fort McHenry Father wrote a medical paper, later published under the title of *Two Penetrating Bayonet Wounds of the Chest*. During World War One, Surgeon General Merritte W. Ireland of the United States Army told me that this work was still of value to military surgeons.

4

One other story Father told was of his last—and most arduous—war experience. In July, 1864, he was promoted to Surgeon. The following March he was sent to Thomasville,

North Carolina, to prepare hospital facilities for the Confederate forces which were trying to contain the northward push of General Sherman's army.

Organizing a detachment of half-duty men, Surgeon Baruch directed the conversion of two small factory buildings and a hotel into hospital wards. When word came that 280 wounded were on the way from the Battle of Averyboro, Father sent out an armed guard to impress into service every man and grown boy in the neighborhood. They were put to work tearing out pews from two churches, to provide extra space for the casualties, and gathering pine straw and pine knots. The straw was stuffed into sacks for mattresses. The pine knots were lighted and used to show the way to the makeshift hospitals when the wounded arrived by train in the night.

Their plight was piteous. They lay moaning and cursing in the cars on loose cotton clotted with blood.

Earlier in the day Father had gone from house to house asking women to bake bread and prepare rye coffee and bacon for the wounded. He saw that every man who could eat was fed and all were made as comfortable as possible. After two hours of sleep he began operating.

Neither he nor the two doctors assisting him stopped until every wound had been dressed. It was the most exhausting experience Father had known in the entire war. When it was over he telegraphed the medical director of the district. His head throbbing wildly, he asked to be temporarily relieved from duty. Then he fainted.

What had felled Father, it turned out, was typhoid fever, which he had contracted but had been unaware of while performing his operations. Two weeks later when he regained consciousness the war was over. While Father lay delirious, the Union troops advanced beyond the hospital area—and Father had been "captured" and formally paroled without knowing a thing about it.

As soon as he could travel he returned to Mannes Baum's home in Camden, the only home Father had ever known in America. The typhoid attack had left him so weak that he arrived on crutches. Like tens of thousands of other Confederates he was destitute. To help him start as a country practitioner he had counted on the medical instruments which were given him by the friend in Baltimore. But they had been carried away by Sherman's raiders.

The war left one indelible influence which remained with Father for the rest of his life. Let the band strike up "Dixie," and, no matter where he was, he would jump up and give the rebel yell.

As soon as the tune started Mother knew what was coming and so did we boys. Mother would catch him by the coattails and plead, "Shush, Doctor, shush." But it never did any good. I have seen Father, ordinarily a model of reserve and dignity, leap up in the Metropolitan Opera House and let loose that piercing yell.

2. Some Colonial Ancestors

WHILE ON FATHER'S SIDE I am the son of an immigrant, on Mother's I am descended from a family which came to America in the 1690's.

The first of Mother's ancestors to reach these shores was Isaac Rodriguez Marques, whose name also is spelled in old documents as Marquiz, Marquis, and Marquise. Arriving in New York sometime before 1700, he established himself as a shipowner whose vessels did business with three continents. He was a contemporary of the legendary Captain William Kidd, who was hanged for piracy on what many now believe to have been perjured testimony. Kidd's widow lived across the street from Isaac Marques. She was accepted in the best circles and eventually remarried a well-to-do, respected citizen.

Marques' choice of the city and his calling suggest a keen business judgment. New York at that time extended only two or three streets north of its wooden wall. Still, it was a bustling place of 3500 inhabitants. Its boom-town character was largely the result of the liberal attitude to maritime affairs, including piracy, taken by the Royal Governor of the colony, Benjamin Fletcher.

He welcomed every mariner, including the noted pirate Thomas Tew, whom Fletcher entertained at the Executive Residence and pronounced "an agreeable and companionable man." Tew reciprocated by virtually abandoning Newport as his home port in favor of New York.

Under Governor Fletcher, New York came to rival Newport and Charleston as a remarkably convenient place to dispose of seaborne commerce, with no embarrassing questions asked as to a cargo's origin. It has been said that under

Fletcher's administration nearly every shipowner operating out of the city was suspected of piracy.

It would be colorful if I could claim descent from a pirate. Alas, the documentation I have assembled prevents my doing this. All available evidence indicates that Isaac Marques kept his salt-water ventures on the starboard side of the law.

One bit of circumstantial data supporting this conclusion arises from the fact that a year after he became a freeman of the city, piracy suddenly went out of fashion. This was due to the arrival of a new governor, the Earl of Bellomont, who, reversing Fletcher's policies, launched a vigorous anti-pirate drive. One victim of this campaign was Captain Kidd.

Bellomont's reforms upset the carefully built-up business organizations of some of New York's foremost citizens, including several friends of my ancestor. But Marques himself does not seem to have been affected, if one may judge from the growth of his fortune and the fact that his name nowhere appears in the black books of the crusading Bellomont.

There is no record of the exact date or place of birth of Isaac Rodriguez Marques. One family tradition makes him a native of Denmark, another of Jamaica, which is more likely. At any rate he was descended from Spanish-Portuguese Jews.

The earliest document relating to my first American ancestor that I have been able to find is dated September 17, 1697. On that day Isaac mounted the City Hall steps, stood before the Mayor and Aldermen of the Corporation, and, after due examination and the payment of five pounds, was made a freeman of the city. This gave him the right to vote in local elections. It also required him to serve in the militia.

How long Marques resided in New York before he accepted the privileges and obligations of a freeman is not clear, but he probably did not delay this step for long. Although one could live in the city without being a citizen, the statutes provided that "no person or persons whatsoever other . . . than free Citizens shall . . . use any Art trade Mystery or Manual Occupation within Said City . . . or Sell or expose for sale any manner of Merchandise." And by this time Isaac Marques was busily engaged in the "art" and "mystery" of seafaring.

He is said to have owned three ships. I have found record of only one, the *Dolphin*, which appeared to have two regular runs—one, New York to England and back; the second, New York to England, then to the African slave coast, the West Indies, and home, the famous triangular trade route. Sometimes the run was made directly from Africa to New York, for slave labor was being widely introduced into the colony.

It is worth observing that on at least one voyage the *Dolphin* carried a surgeon, showing a regard for the health of crew and human cargo which was not common among merchantmen and slavers. It is also worth noting that whatever wealth came to Marques from the cruel traffic in slaves was paid for over and over again through the suffering and loss of life and fortune by his descendants both in the North and South during the Civil War.

A year after he became a freeman, Isaac's wife, Rachel, was delivered of a son, Jacob. There already was a daughter, Easter—so spelled in Isaac's own hand.

As he prospered, Marques purchased for £550 what the deed describes as "a large brick house" on Queen Street, the grounds of which ran through to the East River. The portion of this property on which the house stood is now 132 Pearl Street.

The records I have studied give some intriguing glimpses into the regulations that governed New York in those days. "In the dark time of the moon," as the ordinance read, Queen Street was to be lighted by lanterns suspended from poles in front of every seventh house, the cost being prorated among the residents. At night a watchman patrolled the thoroughfare with a bell, announcing the weather and the hour. Chimneys and hearths were officially inspected at intervals as a safeguard against fire.

His surviving papers indicate that Isaac moved in a wealthy and influential circle. His Queen Street home stood only a block from the mansion of Abraham DePeyster, a former mayor. Nicholas Roosevelt, the sugar importer, served as alderman of the ward.

The witnesses signing Isaac's will were Ebenezer Willson, a mayor of the city, Rip Van Dam, the first native-born American to act as governor of the colony, and William Peartree, who rose from seaman to master of a ship, traded in slaves, and later became mayor of New York, establishing the city's first free school.

Abraham de Lucena, rabbi of the synagogue on Beaver Street, and Luiz Gomez, another leading Jewish citizen, seem to have been especially trusted friends of my ancestor, for he named them in his will to assist his wife in managing his estate.

This will, dated October 17, 1706, opens with a curious flourish: "Being . . . bound on a Voyage to Jamaica in the West Indies and Considering the certainty of death and the uncertain Time of the Coming of the same . . ."

The will then spells out Isaac's testament. He directed that a slave be purchased as a maid for his mother, who also shared in his estate. The remainder of the estate was to be divided equally among the wife and two children, Easter and Jacob. Easter was also to have "Fifty pounds to Buy her a Jewel at her age of Eighteene yeares or marriage with her mothers consent."

With this will the documentary record of Isaac Marques comes to an abrupt end. Nor have I been able to learn anything more of his children, Easter and Jacob, or his wife, Rachel.

I have often thought of Isaac Marques, particularly as I stood at the rail of a ship coming into New York harbor. Looking out across the bay I have marveled at the astonishing physical transformation in New York's skyline from the wooden walls which Isaac Marques saw when he landed here.

And yet how unchanging has been the symbolic meaning of the country behind that skyline. To Isaac Marques it was a land of freedom and opportunity and so it has remained for more than two and a half centuries.

That what this country stands for has remained unchanged for so long—even in the face of so vast a physical transformation—is evidence, I believe, of how enduring is the American national character. Our material life has been revolutionized again and again but we have remained freedom's shore.

2

After Isaac Rodriguez Marques, the next ancestor I have a record of was Isaac Marks, as he spelled the name. He is listed as a son of Isaac Rodriguez, but since he was born in 1732 he was more likely a grandson.

During the Revolutionary War, Isaac Marks followed the Continental Army when it evacuated New York City and moved to Albany. There he joined the Fourth Albany County Regiment of militia.

It was Isaac's son, Samuel, who established Mother's side of our family in South Carolina. He was born in New York City in 1762. As a grown man he moved to Charleston, South Carolina, where he became the proprietor of a small store. One of his children, Deborah, who married Rabbi Hartwig Cohen of Charleston, was my maternal great-grandmother.

Great-grandmother Cohen was past eighty when I knew her. She was a fastidious old lady with neat shawls and "half-hands," as they called the fingerless gloves women wore at the time.

Like most old people she had a more distinct recollection of remote events than of recent ones. Eleven years old at the time, I was a rapt listener to these recollections. Her most cherished memory was of dancing with Lafayette at a Charleston ball during his tour of the country in 1825. The War of 1812 belonged to her childhood memories. Just as vivid were the stories she had heard from her mother, who as a girl had lived in New York under the British military occupation during the Revolution.

When I think of this great-grandmother of mine, I am struck by how truly young this country is. Through my own eyes and the stories she told, I have enjoyed a virtual eye-witness account of much of this country's history since it gained independence.

My grandmother, Sarah Cohen, a daughter of Deborah Marks and Rabbi Hartwig Cohen, was courted by Saling Wolfe, a young merchant and planter of Winnsboro, in the "upcountry" of South Carolina. They were married in November, 1845. Their marriage contract, which was drawn up in Hebrew, followed the forms of the synagogue in noting the bride's dowry and the groom's obligations:

"On the fourth day of the Week, twenty-six days in the month of Cheshvan Five Thousand Six Hundred and Six, corresponding with the Seventieth Year of the Independence of the United States of America as we reckon in the City of Charleston, South Carolina—Zeaib the Son of Isaac (Saling Wolfe) asked Sarah the Daughter of Zebee of Priestly Descent (Sarah Cohen) to become his wife, according to the Law of Moses and Israel. . . . Now the said Sarah having agreed to become his wife brought to him her portion in Silver and Gold Ornamental Dresses, bedding and furniture to the amount of One Thousand Dollars, to which the aforesaid Bridegroom added of his property the sum of Two Thousand Dollars binding himself and his heirs, assignees & Executors from this day and forever to pay to Zebee the Son of Yecheal of priestly descent (Hartwig Cohen) and to Jehudah the son of Isaiah (L. I. Moses) Trustees for the said Bride, the aforesaid portion and the sum added amounting to Three Thousand Dollars current money of this City, with the most valuable property . . . which he possessed under the Canopy of Heaven or should acquire hereafter . . ."

Thirteen children were born to Sarah and Saling Wolfe, of whom three died in early childhood. My mother, Isabelle

17.

Wolfe, who was born on March 4, 1850, was the third child and first daughter. A line in the family Bible recording her birth reads, "God grant her a blessing." I like to think that this line prophesied Mother's marriage to Father since the name "Baruch" is the Hebrew word for "blessed."

Grandfather Wolfe was a wealthy slaveholder when the Civil War broke out. The war ruined him as it did the entire social structure in which he moved. What little remained of his fortune after four years of war was destroyed by Sherman's raiders.

To save some of his valuables, Grandfather Wolfe hid his silver in the well. When the Yankees appeared and began to ransack the house, some of the colored people standing near the well began to wail: "Oh, dey's goin' to find de silver plate," and of course they did. The house, the other buildings, and the cotton were put to the torch and the cattle driven off.

The local Episcopal minister and a number of ladies, including my grandmother, appealed to General Sherman to stop these wanton destructions. But word came back that nothing could be done.

When, as a child, I knew my grandfather, he was struggling to rebuild his fortune. He had several plantations which were regaining their former prosperity. But old debts which hung over from the war took practically everything he had. For all his gallant struggle, he died at eighty-four, a poor man. While ill, he was permitted to get out of bed and sit before the fire with the chair tilted so that he could warm his feet. The chair fell over, throwing him into the fire. The burns proved fatal. Nothing remained of his former wealth, as I later learned, but a wardrobe drawer full of Confederate money.

I have fond memories of childhood visits to my grandparents' home, which was rebuilt after the war. Every morning Grandfather, looking like an English country squire, would mount his horse, Morgan, and ride out to inspect his crops. Sometimes he let my brothers and me help distribute the weekly rations of sugar, coffee, bacon, and rice to the Negro hands. Our reward was a handful of brown sugar.

My keenest memory is of the railroad—the old Charlotte, Columbia & Augusta line—which ran back of the house and at whose passing trains I threw stones. As I watched the brakeman walking to and fro on the careening cars, I thought how wonderful it would be to grow up and run a railroad. This ambition to own a railroad remained with me through my entire financial career. Several times I started to buy control of a railroad but realization of this dream always eluded me.

One tale set around Mother's old home is a family favorite. Before the Civil War Father had been a guest in the home of Saling Wolfe and had become interested in the oldest Wolfe daughter, Isabelle. During the war they saw each other when Father was home on furlough. On one such visit Belle painted a portrait of the young surgeon.

When Sherman's raiders were setting fire to Saling Wolfe's house, Mother, who was about fifteen, rescued this portrait. She was carrying the picture across the yard when a Yankee soldier wrenched it from her hand and ripped it with his bayonet. When she protested, he slapped her.

A Yankee officer, Captain Cantine by name, rushed up and beat the cowardly soldier with the flat of his sword. Naturally Miss Belle appreciated this chivalrous act. Before the Union troops left Winnsboro a romance was budding.

When Simon Baruch returned from the war, he found his own romance with Belle in danger. She and Captain Cantine were exchanging letters, a correspondence which lasted for some time. But Simon Baruch soon took command of the situation. In 1867, after starting as a country doctor, he and Belle Wolfe were married.

There were four children, all sons. Hartwig, the oldest, was born in 1868; I, two years later; Herman in 1872; and Sailing in 1874.

During World War One, when I was chairman of the War Industries Board, a visitor presented himself at my office in Washington with a request that I help him get overseas to the fighting front. He carried a letter of introduction in Mother's handwriting.

"The bearer of this," said my mother's letter, "is a son of Captain Cantine. I know you will do what you can for him."

3. A Country Boy

UP TO THE TIME of Sherman's raid, Mother's family had been so well off that she had never even dressed herself. But until Father's practice was firmly established, she taught piano and singing at twenty-five cents a lesson. She also sold milk and butter from the herd of Jersey cows which was one of Father's prides.

One habit of luxury Mother retained, however. She always had breakfast in bed. Each morning my three brothers and I would present ourselves before her for inspection. "Let me see your fingers. Let me see your ears. Did you clean your teeth?" Frequently these examinations meant another trip to the wash basin.

In those days, Camden was a town of about 2000, with Negroes making up about half the population. During the Revolutionary War, Camden was occupied by Lord Cornwallis. One of Camden's tourist sights was the grave of a woman named Ellen Glasgow, who had followed her sweetheart, General Cornwallis, to America. When the waters of the nearby Wateree River flooded over, the Negroes used to say that Ellen's ghost had the power to stop the flood short of her grave.

Camden also took pride in the fact that it gave six generals to what then was called the Confederate War. The war brought economic hardship to Camden, as it did to all of the South. Still, I cannot recall that our family ever suffered real economic adversity.

We lived in a large, comfortable house and had about as much of material things as any of our neighbors. A good part of Father's income came in the form of goods and services— a cord of wood, a bale of cotton, a load of corn, chickens, a colt or calf, a day's work on his farm. We raised our own vegetables, fruit, and berries, which were dried or preserved for winter use. In our yard grew damson plums, walnuts, and a mulberry tree. When the mulberry tree didn't bear, Minerva, our Negro nurse, would tell us to beat it with a switch so that next year we would be sure to have mulberries.

We made our own sugar—I never knew sugar was any color but brown until we moved North. In the fall everyone gathered hickory nuts and walnuts. Candy, oranges, bananas, and raisins we received only on occasions like Christmas. Cloth, shoes, coffee, tea, salt, and spices were about all we bought regularly. Books, magazines, and the Charleston *News and Courier* were treasured articles to be passed from house to house.

Strawberry festivals and the visit of the circus were the big excitements. There was also a local dramatic organization which staged Shakespearean readings and plays at the Camden town hall. In one performance of *Kathleen Mavourneen*, by William Travers, Mother was playing the lead while Uncle Nathan Baruch had the part of the villain. In one climactic scene, the villain threatens the heroine with a knife. The sight of Mother cowering while Uncle Nathan brandished his dagger proved too much for me. I jumped from my seat crying, "Oh, Uncle Nathan, don't hurt Mama!" The players were thrown somewhat off their lines and I was hustled out of the theater.

As a child I was shy and sensitive, something of a mama's boy. I always sat at Mother's right at the dinner table, and I remember how fiercely I fought for this privilege. When I married, I asked my wife to sit where my mother would have sat—with me to her right.

When Mother taught us elocution, my brother Hartwig, who was two years older than I, displayed considerable talent. Eventually, in fact, he became an actor. But for me, getting up to recite was an agonizing ordeal.

I never have forgotten one disastrous evening at Mannes Baum's house. Mother took me by the hand and, leading me to the center of the room, urged, "Now say something, dear."

I was scared to death but started off in a singsong voice. So deeply etched into my memory is the incident that I still can quote the opening lines of the piece I was trying to recite. They were from "Hohenlinden," by Thomas Campbell, a Scotch poet:

> On Linden when the sun was low,
> All bloodless lay the untrodden snow;
> And dark as winter was the flow
> Of Iser, rolling rapidly.

I got no further than that when Father lifted a finger to the side of his nose and made a mimicking noise that sounded like:

A-toodle-dah!

That finished me. I rushed from the room, ran back to our house through the night, of which I was afraid, and cried myself to sleep.

In later years Father often told me how much he regretted his little joke. That episode nearly destroyed any hope I ever had of mastering the art of public speaking. For years afterward I never could rise to my feet to say anything without remembering "A-toodle-dah!"

Once I told President Woodrow Wilson about this. At first he consoled me by saying, "There are too many men who like to speak and too few to do things. Most of them the world does not care to hear. I wouldn't advise even you to try to learn."

I couldn't agree. I believe it is almost as important for a man to be able to express his views as to have them.

Later President Wilson helped me improve my speech delivery. During the Peace Conference in Paris, he took enough time one evening to show me how to gesture graciously rather than abruptly. "Do it this way," he explained, gesturing slowly with his hand, "not this way," illustrating his point with an abrupt thrust.

Other friends also helped. I had a habit of speaking through almost clenched lips. Herbert Bayard Swope would often say, "For heaven's sake, open your mouth!" In 1939 I was asked to deliver a short radio tribute on the death of Pope Pius XI. As I talked, Swope stood in front of me making facial gestures to remind me to "open your mouth."

2

I was four or five years old when I started at a school kept by Mr. and Mrs. William Wallace. It was about a mile from home, and Harty and I walked, carrying our lunches in a tin box with the food wrapped in a doily. In those days a "napkin" was something you put on babies, and for a long time I thought of it as not a nice word.

Mrs. Wallace conducted what would now be called kindergarten. The "classroom" was the kitchen of her house. I learned my letters lying on my stomach on the floor while she sat nursing her baby or preparing the noonday meal. Mr. Wallace presided over the upper grades, or the school proper, in another building equipped with long benches and crude desks which opened at the top.

Mr. Wallace was an excellent teacher, although some of his methods would hardly be tolerated today. Inattention brought a ruler down across the offender's knuckles or opened palm. Persistent negligence or other serious offenses meant a sound thrashing. In a corner of the room stood a number of switches ready for use. I do not remember that those switches ever were used on me, but it was at Wallace's school that I first felt the switch that is wielded by one's conscience.

One afternoon as class ended I saw a boy leave half of a red-and-white peppermint stick in his desk. Store candy was so rare a treat that I was tempted beyond my strength. With a crony I plotted to get that candy.

When the school was empty we stole back, crawled under the building, forced up a loose plank in the floor with our hands and squirmed through. We took the candy and went off under a tree and ate it.

A feeling of guilt came over me almost at once. The sweet peppermint taste in my mouth seemed bitter. Curiously, again and again in later life this trivial episode came back to me.

Once, when I was just starting in Wall Street, James R. Keene, one of the master speculators of his time, asked me to look into the underwriting of a new company, Brooklyn Gas. My investigation convinced me that it would be a good investment. Then a young man connected with the syndicate selling the securities offered me a $1500 "commission" to turn in a favorable report.

Fifteen hundred dollars was a lot of money to me at the time. But the memory of the red-and-white peppermint stick rose before me and I couldn't take it. In fact, it made me fear that there might be something wrong with the stock so I went over my ground again. And in my report to Mr. Keene, I told him of the offer of the "commission."

The Wallace school ground was also a tough arena for testing one's character. You had to fight or be known as a coward. My brother Harty was a scrapper by instinct. But it took me a long time to learn to fight skillfully and with a cool head.

My main trouble was that I lost my temper too quickly. I was fat, freckle-faced, and relatively short as a boy—"Bunch" was my nickname—and inevitably seemed to get licked in every scrap. The humiliation of being beaten did not improve either my self-confidence or my temper.

Once when Harty took my fishing pole and started up the street with it, I ran after him, picked up a stone and angrily threw it at him. When I saw the stone was going to hit him I called out a warning. Harty turned around just in time to get the stone on the mouth. It left a scar on his lip which he bore to the end of his days.

On another occasion, while visiting Grandfather Wolfe, I flew into a tantrum at the breakfast table. I got so angry over something—just what I can't recall—that I lunged across the table, grabbed a piece of meat and stuffed it down my throat. I did no harm to myself, but I "caught it" from my grandmother.

The boys of Camden were divided into two gangs, an "uptown" gang to which we belonged, and a "downtown" gang which was considered tougher than we were. Behind this division there may have been some deeper social conflict of which I was unaware, since, as I recall, we "uptown" boys had to wash our feet every night while the "downtowners" seldom washed theirs.

The rivalry between the two groups was intense. The annual baseball game between the two sections of town was always an exciting event. We played in a field behind the old jail. In one game I tried to beat a throw to third base. I didn't make it but collided with the baseman and he dropped the ball. That started a fight in which I got my usual licking.

There was a Huckleberry Finn or Tom Sawyer quality in how we lived. In fact, whenever I read Mark Twain or saw the cartoons of Clare Briggs or H. T. Webster's "Life's Darkest Moment," I would feel a sense of nostalgia for my boyhood.

Every spring the Wateree River would flood the Camden countryside. The floods were calamities to the grownups but we boys enjoyed them. We built rafts to explore the inundated country for miles about. We always regretted the fall of the waters.

The best place to fish and swim was Factory Pond, which furnished the power for Malone's mill, a cotton compress and corn mill, and was also used for baptisms. During the long summers we were in the water every day. A shirt and a pair of pants were our only clothes and these were unbuttoned on the run as we neared the pond. Without stopping, we would jump out of our clothes and plunk into the water like so many bull frogs.

Strung out across the pond were First Stump, Second Stump, Third Stump, and Flat Stump. I remember what a thrill it was the first time I swam to First Stump and back. Then I tackled Second Stump. I had worked up to Third Stump when our family left South Carolina.

Nearly all the boys in town would collect birds' eggs, which we would trade with each other. Harty was particularly good at shinning up trees, although Mother didn't take kindly to our robbing birds' nests. Harty and I also used to hunt small game in the woods with muzzle-loading shotguns.

I must have been six or seven when I first learned to shoot. We had an arrangement with Father through which we earned a little money by picking cotton alongside the Negro hands on Father's farm. With our earnings we bought ammunition. We carried the shot in an old leather pouch and the powder in a cow's horn which was scraped so thin that you could see through it.

With us when we hunted usually went Sharp, a white English mastiff that a patient had given Father. Sharp really belonged to Harty, but he was a companion to us all, the finest comrade any boys ever had. He swam with us and followed us to school. He was a great ratter. It was fun watching Sharp's huge paws fling out the dirt as he dug for rats under the corncrib. When we moved North, Father gave Sharp to friends. Our parting remains one of my most poignant memories.

Despite our full quota of escapades and scrapes, our parents rarely disciplined us beyond a reprimand. I cannot remember ever being spanked by either Father or Mother. Father was inclined to be more strict but whenever he seemed on the verge of punishing us Mother would restrain him. I can hear her saying, "Now Doctor, don't be hard on the boys or they won't love you."

But this is not to say that we never knew the beneficial effects of a sound spanking. Our Negro nurse, Minerva, would not have favored progressive education. When she was an old woman, she would visit me at my South Carolina plantation and delight in telling my Northern guests how she used to paddle me for my bad behavior.

It is true that I stood in awe of Minerva's right hand, and so did my brothers, but what impressed me most were the stories she told and the songs she sang to us.

Minerva was steeped in the superstitions of the primitive Negro. To her the woods, waters, and fields, in fact our own yard and garden, were peopled with "hants" and ghosts. She once explained that the reason Negroes didn't like glass windows in their cabins was because the "hants" could look in.

It was from Minerva that I heard of Brer Rabbit, Brer Fox, Brer Terrapin, and other characters which Joel Chandler Harris was to put into his Uncle Remus books.

Minerva used to sing a doleful song about a lion, named Bolem, that had lost its tail. I can still hear her voice chanting mournfully:

> Bolem, Bolem, where me tail?
> Bolem, Bolem, where me tail?

Then the disembodied tail would answer:

> Bolem, Bolem, here me am.
> Bolem, Bolem, here me am.

Bolem's tragic and never-ending search for his tail was a real thing to me. Many were the times the thought of Bolem's wandering tail kept me awake at night.

I loved Minerva as she loved me. To the last, she never failed to greet me with a big hug and kiss, for I was always her "chile."

She had a good many children of her own, although she never had a husband. She would tell Mother, "Miss Belle, I done made another mistake." We used to play with her children and the children of other Negroes in our neighborhood. I remember particularly Minerva's son Frank. He could beat us all at fishing and hunting and could snare birds, an achievement I admired. What a cruel thing it was when I grew old enough to appreciate the gulf which separated the white and black races! I couldn't understand why Frank wasn't as good as anybody.

3

One autumn day, when I was about five or six, Harty and I were rummaging about the attic of our house. We were looking for a place to store the nuts which, like squirrels, we gathered every fall. We came across a horsehide-covered trunk which looked promising. Opening it, we found Father's Confederate uniform. Digging deeper into the trunk, we pulled out a white hood and long robe with a crimson cross on its breast—the regalia of a Knight of the Ku Klux Klan.

Today, of course, the KKK is an odious symbol of bigotry and hate, reflecting its activities during the 1920's, when it acquired considerable power, particularly outside the South. I have good reason to know the character of the modern Klan since I was a target for its hatred.

But to children in the Reconstruction South, the original Klan, led by General Nathan Bedford Forrest, seemed a heroic band fighting to free the South from the debaucheries of carpetbag rule. To my brother and me the thought that Father was a member of that band exalted him in our youthful eyes.

So intent were we in our examination of those garments that we did not hear Mother's footstep on the garret stairs. She gave us a mighty scolding and swore us to secrecy. It was really an important secret. The Klan had been outlawed by the Federal government. Large rewards were offered for the conviction of its members, and spies were scattered through the South in an effort to discover who those members were. We came down from the attic feeling we had grown a foot taller.

Harsh as were the economic effects of the war, the political effects of eight years of carpetbag rule proved more galling and lasting. Even today, when the South is prospering, the carpetbag legacy of political and racial bitterness hangs on.

The carpetbaggers maintained power largely through the control that they and their scalawag allies exerted over the vote of the Negro. This use of the ignorant Negro as a tool of oppression aggravated all the racial wounds and sores of slavery and the war. In the end it hurt the Negro most and probably set back progress in racial relations by a quarter of a century.

Through much of my childhood no white man who had served in the Confederate Army was allowed to vote—while all Negroes could vote, even though few could write their names. Our state senator was a Negro, as was the county auditor and school commissioner—although at the county level never more than a third of the officials were Negroes. Still, the declared intention of the Black Republicans in Washington was to make this state of affairs perpetual.

So oppressive was this state of affairs that even a man like my father could write a fellow veteran of the Confederate Army that death was preferable to living under such conditions. "There is one recourse when all is lost. I mean the sword," Father wrote in a letter which was quoted by Claude Bowers in *The Tragic Era*. "What boots it to live under such tyranny, such moral and physical oppression when we can be much happier in the consciousness of dying for such a cause?"

The issue was to be decided by the contest for the governorship in 1876 between General Wade Hampton and the carpetbag incumbent, Daniel H. Chamberlain. I remember distinctly one Hampton mass meeting in Camden when barrels of resin were lighted at the street corners. There was a campaign chant in which we boys joined:

> Hampton eat the egg,
> Chamberlain eat the shell,
> Hampton go to Heaven,
> Chamberlain go to Hell.

The song was all the more appealing because that was the first time I was permitted to use the word "Hell" with impunity.

In later years Father told us many stories of how Hampton carried the election in the face of a preponderant black majority. One device was to distribute tickets to a circus that was playing out-of-town on election day. Another method was to beat the carpetbaggers at their own game by capitalizing on the Negroes' simplicity.

In those days a separate ballot box was assigned to each candidate. Most Negroes could not read the labels on the boxes but were coached to recognize the Republican boxes by their position in the line. With a crowd of Negroes around the polls, some Hampton man would fire a shot into the air. In the ensuing commotion, the Hampton and Chamberlain boxes would be switched. The Negroes would then be rushed up to vote as quickly as possible. As a result many dropped their ballots into Hampton's box.

On another election day, when I was about ten years old, Father was absent from home, either on professional or political business—probably both, for in those times there often was work for a doctor after a political rally. We heard a great din about the house. Mother became alarmed. She told Harty and me to get our guns.

We got them—one a single-barreled and one a double-barreled muzzle-loader. Mother told us to load them and to take a position on the second-floor porch.

"But do not shoot," she cautioned, "unless I tell you to shoot."

We stood there, our hearts pounding, each with a gun almost as tall as himself, watching the crowd of colored people milling about the street. Drunk on cheap whiskey, they were on their way to the polls or to a rally.

I have a blurred memory of what happened next. I recall seeing a Negro fall from behind a tree. Suddenly everyone fled. We ran down to where the man lay to see what had happened. His head had been split as with an ax. Mother brought a basin of water and dressed the wound. I do not know what became of him, but he could not have lived long with his head as it was. Casualties of this nature were not uncommon, and it was the Negro who suffered most.

It was against the background of such happenings that we saw Father's membership in the Klan. That membership did not reflect any love of violence or any bitterness in his nature. Once Father was called to the deathbed of a scalawag Southerner. When Father came home he remarked that no friends or loving relatives had come to visit the dying man and how sad it was "to see men made completely callous to the call of humanity by political differences."

Nor did Father have any prejudice against the Negro or any grudge against the North. He blamed the Civil War on the extremists of both sides who would not use reason to settle their differences. He considered Abraham Lincoln a great man who might have reunited the country had he lived.

Still, the Reconstruction rule was oppression to Father and he fought to free the South of it. It is tragic that the Negro got trapped in this struggle, which has embittered race relations to this day.

4

Like all boys I had my childhood heroes. They seem to have been drawn less from books than from among my relatives and a few figures in the community.

I was brought up to believe that Robert E. Lee was the epitome of all virtues. Father often quoted a maxim of Lee's as a guide to my own conduct:

"Do your duty in all things. You could not do more. You would not wish to do less."

Generals Beauregard, Stonewall Jackson, and Jeb Stuart were other shining figures, as were Marion, Sumter, and Picken from the Revolutionary War. Not even George Washington loomed as large in my mind as those soldiers of the swamp.

Beyond these soldierly figures, my favorites were Mannes Baum, my uncles Herman and Joe Baruch, and Fischel Cohen, my great-uncle.

Uncle Herman, who had gone to war because he could not stand the reproach in the eyes of the ladies, was a bon vivant and a free spender. After working for Mannes Baum, whose mercantile establishment had grown to be the largest in Camden, Herman opened his own store. He would regale us with tales of high times on buying trips to New York. But what interested us more was that he never returned without gifts for every member of the family.

Uncle Joe, Father's youngest brother, had served in a Uhlan cavalry regiment in Germany. He was "considerable of an athlete," as we used to say, and taught us to perform on the horizontal and parallel bars, which he put up in our back yard. My tomboy Aunt Sarah, Mother's youngest sister, who used to visit us from Winnsboro, would compete with us on the bars. I remember how shocked everyone was when she hung by her toes.

I adored my great-uncle Fischel Cohen, the only son of Rabbi Hartwig Cohen. He had been a telegraph operator on General Beauregard's staff and would tell, by the hour, humorous stories of his wartime experiences.

"Yes," he used to say, "I was a brave man in the war—always where the bullets were thickest—under the ammunition wagon."

Uncle Fischel played the banjo and had a whole line of songs. The refrain of one ran:

> I would rather be a home guard private,
> Than a brigadier brought home to die.

I recall many happy evenings with Fischel strumming his banjo, Mother at the piano, and a roomful of friends singing Southern songs. One which I have not heard for seventy-odd years ended every verse with the line: "And the bells went ringing for Sarah!"

Mother, being a talented amateur actress, was eager that her sons should play and sing. In this we uniformly disappointed her. Only Harty and Sailing learned any musical instrument and that was the banjo. I have never been able even to whistle a tune.

One local personality I admired, although secretly, was Boggan Cash of the celebrated dueling Cashes from Chesterfield County. His father, Colonel E. B. C. Cash, had commanded a regiment in Father's brigade. Young Boggan was not old enough for the Civil War, but he did all he could to make up for that lost opportunity to display his marksmanship.

Dueling was fairly common in the South Carolina of my childhood. Camden, in particular, seems to have been a center for it. I remember watching Boggan Cash at target practice, wheeling and firing at an iron man which had been set up on the bank of Factory Pond. Sometimes he would get one of the older boys to call, "Ready, fire!" for him.

One duel in which the Cashes were involved had a profound effect on my life in that it led to Father's leaving South Carolina.

The trouble began when a brother of Mrs. Cash assaulted another man in the course of a drunken orgy. To avoid a court judgment, Mrs. Cash's brother transferred some property to his sister's name. Colonel William M. Shannon, as an attorney for the man who had been assaulted, instituted an action against Mrs. Cash's brother on grounds of constructive fraud.

Declaring that this suit was an affront to Mrs. Cash, Colonel Cash and his son, Boggan, began a campaign of insult which Colonel Shannon, a man of peace, bore patiently for a year. The situation finally became intolerable and Colonel Shannon challenged Colonel Cash to a duel.

The Shannon family and ours were intimate. Shannon had been a leader in the revival of country fairs as a means of stimulating better farming methods. Mother often pointed him out to us as a model of courtesy.

The duel was arranged for July 5, 1880, at Du Bose's Bridge in Darlington County. Hoping to avert any shooting, Father, without Shannon's knowledge, advised the sheriff of the hour and place of the meeting. The sheriff promised to be on hand in time to prevent hostilities.

First to reach the appointed spot was Colonel Shannon, attended by Dr. Burnett, his physician, a second, and a few friends, including Father. A few minutes later Colonel Cash arrived. There was no sign of the sheriff.

The seconds paced off the ground, decided by lot the choice of position and the giving of the signal. Still no sheriff.

The principals took their stations. At the word of command Shannon fired quickly. The bullet tore up the earth in front of Colonel Cash. Cash aimed deliberately and fired. Shannon fell. When he was reached he was beyond help.

A few minutes later the sheriff galloped up.

This was one of the last fatal duels in the United States. Its repercussions were many, for Camden had no more highly respected citizen than William M. Shannon. I remember a group of grim-looking men, armed with rifles and shotguns, riding up to our house to see Father. Among them I recognized a young fellow who was engaged to Colonel Shannon's daughter.

Father invited them into his office. Presently the men emerged, mounted their horses, and rode slowly away. Father had persuaded them not to take the law into their own hands and kill Cash. Public sentiment avenged Colonel Shannon's death. Cash, who had been a man of distinction in his community, was ostracized and left to a fate similar to Aaron Burr's.

This tragedy also resulted in legislation which outlawed duels in South Carolina and disqualified from public office anyone who had taken part in one. At the inauguration of James F. Byrnes as governor in 1951, I was amused to hear him take a solemn oath that he had never engaged in a duel.

For some time Mother had been urging Father to go North where opportunities would be greater. But Father held back until the Cash-Shannon duel, which he had tried to prevent and which was such a shock to him.

In the winter of 1880 Father sold his practice and the house with its little "farm." Together with his savings, the sale brought his total financial assets to $18,000, the fruit of sixteen years as a country doctor.

Father went on ahead to New York City. Mother followed with her four boys. The first leg of the journey was made in our old carriage to Winnsboro, where we took the train North. In the hamper of food we carried aboard the train were some of Grandmother Wolfe's cookies. When the hamper was emptied we left the train to eat at the regular meal stops. Our best meal was in Richmond, and to this day that city suggests good food to me. We arrived on the New Jersey side of the Hudson River at dusk and took the ferry across the river.

4. The Big City

NEW YORK CITY was a strange new world for us four country boys. At first it overwhelmed and terrified me. At the time, of course, I was going on eleven and still extremely shy. Also, an incident that took place while we still lived in South Carolina had left the impression that New York was not too friendly a place.

A New York lady who was a relative of the family had come to Camden for a visit. We boys had our faces scrubbed and were sent to pay our respects. We wondered what a New York lady looked like.

My recollection is that the visitor stared at us through a lorgnette. It was summer and we were barefooted. The New York lady looked at our feet and threw us a dime, remarking, "Buy yourself some shoes." She intended it as a joke, but the humor was lost on us. We bolted home.

In Camden we had worn shoes only when the weather demanded it or on the Jewish Sabbath. In New York, of course, we had to wear shoes every day, which often made us feel that the sidewalks of the city were a poor substitute for the woods around Camden.

Among the other first impressions of the big city that I still recall was my amazement at the sight of the elevated trains with their puffing steam locomotives, and the wonder with which I saw water pouring from a tap into the kitchen sink or tub. One of the delights of New York was that we did not have to carry water from a well for a bath, as in the South.

I don't know how I could have stood those first days in New York if it had not been for the stalwart example set by Harty. Nothing ever daunted Harty and he waded into the big, tough city as if it were just another big, tough boy who was trying to pick a fight with him.

Our new lodgings were quite cramped compared with our spacious Camden home. Father had rented two rooms on the top floor of a four-story brownstone boardinghouse at 144 West 57th Street. Mother, Father, Herman, and Sailing occupied one room. Harty and I shared the other. During our first Northern winter we would huddle against the wall, behind which was a warm chimney.

We took our meals where we lodged. Some years later I became something of a vaudeville addict and would go into uncontrollable laughter at some of the comedians and their jokes. But I never was able to laugh at a boardinghouse joke. It always reminded me of those first days in New York.

Our landlady did her best to make us comfortable. Her name was Miss or Mrs. Jacobs—at my age the distinction didn't seem too important. I do remember that she was a large woman with a row of curls across her forehead.

She took a fancy to us boys. There were always raisins or fruit on the table, and she often slipped sweets into our pockets. Her kindness did much to smooth over a time of anxiety for all of us.

Not long after our arrival Father fell ill. His complaint was diagnosed as heart trouble and he was told that he did not have long to live. His first impulse was to return South. Fortunately he went to a second doctor, the distinguished Alfred Loomis, who diagnosed the trouble as indigestion induced by worry over getting a foothold in New York. Father's affliction disappeared as soon as a few more patients began to call.

Meanwhile, Mother had enrolled us at P.S. 69, then on 54th Street, between Sixth and Seventh avenues. The principal was Mathew Elgas, whom I remember fondly. He escorted me personally to my teacher—one of my happiest memories. Katherine Devereux Blake was her name and more than any other one person she helped overcome the confusion that New York stirred in me. Her first words, as I recall them, were, "Bernard, I am so happy to see you. I am sure the other boys are pleased too."

She sat me in front and seemed to pay no attention to me. But at noon, and again at the end of the day, she asked, "Will some boy volunteer to take Bernard home and call for him until he knows his way to and from school?" A chubby lad, named Clarence Housman, quickly volunteered. Fourteen years later I became his partner in Wall Street.

Katherine Blake gave me the first prize I ever won. A copy of *Oliver Twist*, it still is in my library, bearing the inscription: "Awarded to Bernard Baruch for Gentlemanly Deportment and General Excellence. June 1881."

I kept in touch with her until her death in 1950 and delivered a eulogy to her in John Haynes Holmes' Community Church. I never think of her without feeling how unappreciative our society generally is of our schoolteachers.

It is our teachers—especially those who deal with the very young—who have made the character and conscience of America what it is today. We continue to look to them to instill in future generations a sense of decency and a determination to do one's very best. Yet not so long ago I remember reading that a group of high school students had voted teaching the profession they would like least to enter.

Teachers should be given salaries which will enable them to live comfortably. Their enormous contribution to society should be recognized with public honors. I have urged that "Oscars" be awarded annually to our most deserving teachers. Some such tangible honor is certainly as appropriate as the prizes that are awarded regularly to actors and actresses, writers, ball players, and so many others.

2

As we came to know New York City more intimately, some of the differences between it and Camden tended to disappear. We found, for example, that the city did provide room in which boys could play. The ground on 59th Street, where the Plaza Hotel now stands, consisted of vacant lots, except for the shack of a squatter who owned a mean little dog. The north side of 57th Street between Sixth and Seventh avenues was also vacant lots, save for a few buildings on Sixth Avenue and a blacksmith shop run by a man named Gardner. His son was in my class in school. We used to watch his father work and envy him those muscles.

These vacant lots were the roving grounds—and battle-grounds—for the neighborhood gangs. In fact, we soon found ourselves in an atmosphere which reminded us of the fights in Camden between the "uptowners" and "downtowners." The "52nd Street gang" was the toughest in our neighborhood.

As in Camden, it fell to Harty to bear the brunt of the fighting that upheld our standing. He bested several members of the 52nd Street gang, including a good-looking Irish boy named Johnston, who used to lick all the little fellows, me included. The last time Harty whipped Johnston was on the stairs inside the school. When Johnston complained to the teacher, Harty was suspended. He then transferred to another school. But that fight ended our troubles with Johnston.

The summers were particularly happy for us since they were spent "up north" in Washington Heights, then still largely rural. Dr. William Frothingham engaged my father to take over his practice for the summer months—an arrangement which continued for several years. We lived in the Frothingham residence, a comfortable house at 157th Street and St. Nicholas Avenue.

My room, I recall, was in the rear, looking out over the area where the Polo Grounds now stands. Then it was a tangled mass of woods, blackberries, honeysuckle, shrubs—and poison ivy, as I learned when I got too close to it.

For fifty cents we could hire a flat-bottomed boat, ideal for getting up the shallow creeks and salt marshes of the Harlem River, which then were thick with soft-shelled crabs.

One particular river expedition nearly proved my last. Harty and I had spent the morning fishing and crabbing. After eating a picnic lunch, we joined some boys who were sitting on the trestle of the New York Central Railroad, which ran along the Harlem River. We entertained our new friends with imaginary stories of our adventures among the wild people of the South Sea Islands.

As we rowed back home we laughed long and loud over how, as we imagined, we had fooled those boys. I was sitting in the back of the boat, balanced on the gunwales. Suddenly we collided with another boat. An oar hit me, knocking me head first into the shallow river.

For what seemed years I struggled to extricate myself from the muddy bottom. To this day I remember the thoughts that rushed through my mind: first, that I was being punished for being such a terrible liar with those South Sea tales; second, that I should never have killed that black cat—everyone knows that brings bad luck; and third, how anguished my mother would be over my tragic end.

About this time I came to the surface, my face smeared with the soft black mud. The men in the boat that had collided with ours were probing for me with their oars, while Harty crouched on the edge of our boat ready to jump in after me. They started to laugh at my appearance, but stopped when they saw how sick I was from the water I had swallowed. They pulled us to the shore, put me over a barrel, and rolled the water out of me.

On our way back home the only thought Harty and I had was whether Mother would discover my clothes were wet. We were late getting home, and in the relief of seeing us Mother did not ask any questions.

3

New York was filling up with pleasant associations for our parents as well. Father was steadily building the reputation which was to bring him considerable medical recognition. He achieved perhaps his greatest renown as the father of scientific hydrotherapy in the United States, becoming the first professor of hydrotherapy in the country. But before that he pioneered in public baths for the poor and was one of the first doctors to diagnose a case of perforating appendicitis on which surgery was successfully performed.

It happened during Christmas week of 1887. While visiting New York, a son of Samuel Wittkowsky, who was Uncle Herman's partner, was taken ill with what then was termed "inflammation of the bowels." Father called in two consulting surgeons, H. B. Sands and William T. Bull, and recommended removing the boy's appendix. Dr. Sands protested that the boy would die if they did. "He will die if we don't," replied Father.

The inflamed appendix was removed—the date was December 30, 1887—and the boy got well.

In an address before the New York Academy of Medicine in 1889, Dr. A. J. Wyeth, an eminent surgeon, recalled the incident and declared, "The profession and humanity owe more to Dr. Baruch than to any other individual for the development of the surgery of appendicitis."

While handling Dr. Frothingham's practice, Father took charge of the New York Juvenile Asylum. This may have sparked his interest in public baths. At the time the city maintained what were called "floating baths" on the North River. These were wooden barges with the central portion cut open, in which youths could swim in the summer. As it happened, though, the city's sewage was also being emptied in the North River, which led Father to define Manhattan Island as "a body of land surrounded by sewage."

As chairman of the Committee on Hygiene of the New York County Medical Society, Father began a long crusade which led to the erection of the first municipal baths in both New York City and Chicago. The Rivington Street baths, which were opened in 1901, were later renamed in Father's honor.

Mother also interested herself in civic affairs. She was a

good speaker and was in considerable demand by various clubs and charitable organizations. She belonged to the New York Chapter of the Daughters of the American Revolution and of the Daughters of the Confederacy. She also interested herself in every kind of charity—Jewish, Protestant, and Catholic. The denominational background did not concern her as long as it was a worthy cause.

One summer Mother became acquainted with Mrs. J. Hood Wright, the wife of a Drexel, Morgan & Company partner. When Mrs. Wright organized a society fair to finance the founding of the J. Hood Wright Hospital, she found an able assistant in Mother. The J. Hood Wright Hospital later became Knickerbocker Hospital and Father became a visiting physician there.

New York also gave Mother the satisfaction of being able to worship in a synagogue. Camden had not had one and Mother's only opportunity to attend services had been on occasional trips to Charleston.

In New York Mother not only went to the synagogue but often attended church services with her Gentile friends as well. She liked to listen to the preaching of the Reverend Thomas Dixon, the fiery Southerner who wrote *The Clansman*. She often went to Brooklyn to hear Henry Ward Beecher.

There was a ribald song about the Reverend Beecher and his involvement in a scandal, which the children in the street gangs used to sing. I remember one day one of my brothers came into the house chanting:

Henry Ward Beecher, the Sunday School teacher . . .

My brother stopped abruptly when he saw the look on Father's face.

Once I recall hearing Mother being asked how, as a Jewess, she could go into a church where the worship of Christ was part of the creed. She replied, "If He was not divine, all His actions, His life and His death were."

4

One winter day Harty, two boys named Drucker, and I were playing near Gardner's blacksmith shop when some boys from another gang started a snow fight. Pretty soon our adversaries were throwing rocks, and since we were outnumbered we retreated to the stoop of the boardinghouse. Our pursuers didn't come up the steps but stood in the gutter calling us names.

That was the first time I ever heard the word "sheenie." Because of our Southern accent some boys had mimicked our speech, which always meant a fight, but "sheenie" was a new jibe. Neither Harty nor I knew what it meant until the Druckers explained that it was an insult hurled at Jews.

I can see the leader of our tormentors now—a stoutish, heavy lad with blue eyes, dark eyelashes, and a baby complexion. Harty started down the steps after him and they ganged him. I went to the rescue but was knocked down. Harty called to me to run upstairs and get his wagon spoke, which stood just inside the hall. I got it and Harty began to lay about him. He soon had them standing at a distance.

Calling them cowards, he offered to fight any two of them. One big boy stepped out and said he would fight Harty alone. My brother gave him such a beating that Harty's name became a byword in the neighborhood. No one in that gang ever called us "sheenie" again.

That fight was my introduction to a prejudice against Jews which was new to me but which I was to experience many times in my later life.

In South Carolina we never had suffered discrimination because we were Jews. We were one of five or six Jewish families who lived in Camden. The De Leons and Levys had settled there before the Revolution; the Baums and Wittkowskys came later. They were all respected citizens. The

De Leons in particular were a numerous and distinguished clan which furnished the Confederacy with a surgeon-general and a diplomatic agent to France. Old General De Leon I never saw, for he was one of the Confederate officers who refused to accept the terms of surrender and fled to Mexico. In later years he returned by invitation of President Grant and finished his days practicing medicine in the West.

Since Camden had no synagogue, Mother would read prayers to us at home. On Saturdays we wore our best clothes and shoes and were not permitted outside the yard of our own home. This was something of a hardship because Saturday was the "big day" in Camden, when everyone came into town from the farms for miles around.

Out of respect for our neighbors, Mother made us dress up and "behave ourselves" on Sundays as well.

If anything, the differences in religion bred a sense of mutual respect. How high was the community's regard for my Father was brought home to me rather vividly when I returned to Camden around 1913, more than thirty years after we had left. A Negro driver was taking me from the railroad station. As we passed the house in which we had lived, the Negro remarked, "A doctor used to live there. The Yankees paid him all kinds of money to come North. After he left, the people around here died like flies."

Mother had been brought up in a strictly kosher home and the observance of the Jewish holidays meant more to her than it did to Father. In South Carolina Father had headed the Hebrew Benevolent Association, and I still have a copy of the letter of resignation he wrote when he was leaving for New York. In the letter he urged continued teaching of the "high morality" of Judaism and the Bible. But although Father was a highly moral person, I remember his telling me, "I don't believe there is an avenging God standing over people with a sword."

One day Father called my brothers and me into his study. After closing the door, he asked us to promise that when he lay dying we would not allow Mother to send for a rabbi to say any final Jewish prayer. "There is no use trying to fool God at this late date," Father explained.

When he was eighty-one, Father had a stroke and knew he was dying. Mother was also ill—she died six months later—and could not move from her bed. She lay in a room on the second floor while Father lay in a room on the third floor.

Mother called us in and asked us to send for Frederick Mendes, the rabbi of the West 82nd Street synagogue, to say a final prayer with Father. Strangely enough, only a few days earlier Father had reminded us of our earlier promise, adding, "The last thing I can do for you boys is to show you how to die."

We had to say, "No, Mother, you know the promise we made." Mother turned over on her side and cried softly to herself.

Father had been afraid that while dying he might get hysterical or delirious, but he had control of his faculties almost to the end. My younger brother, Herman, who was a doctor, sat on the edge of the bed and tested Father by saying, "I'm Harty. I'm Harty." Father had lost the power of speech but his eyes turned to Harty, showing he still recognized us. Father had asked to be cremated. When Mother died we placed Father's ashes at her feet in her coffin as she had asked us to do.

In my earlier years I took after Mother in the matter of religious observance, more so than my brothers. I studied Hebrew under Dr. Mendes and could read it well enough to follow the prayers. I attended synagogue and Sunday school. Until after graduation from college, I kept every Jewish holy day and fasted scrupulously on the Day of Atonement.

In college, although I was popular enough with my classmates to be elected to several class offices, I never was admitted to the so-called "secret societies"—what now are known as fraternities. I had to endure similar discriminations in Wall Street, and even in public life at one time.

After I achieved some prominence, in fact, I became a favored target for professional anti-Semites. Henry Ford's *Dearborn Independent* once devoted considerable space to me as a leader of what was called an "international Jewish conspiracy." These attacks later were echoed by the KKK, Father Charles E. Coughlin, Gerald L. K. Smith, Dudley Pelley, to say nothing of Joseph Goebbels and Adolf Hitler.

These attacks never hurt me as much as did the discriminations my children suffered. My two daughters were brought up in the Episcopalian faith of their mother. Yet they were refused admission to the same dancing school their mother had attended. Even when the pastor of their church intervened, they were denied admission to several private schools for girls.

It was not easy to explain to my children why they were suffering such senseless discriminations. Instead of allowing these things to embitter and frustrate them, I told them to take these discriminations as spurs to more strenuous achievement—which is how I myself have met the problem of prejudice.

Above all, I have told my children not to be blinded to the greatness of America by the pettiness of some of the people in it. The men who wrote the Declaration of Independence were wise in this regard. When they came to define what they conceived as man's unalienable rights, they chose their words carefully—"life, liberty and the *pursuit* of happiness."

Not "happiness" but "the pursuit of happiness." They made no promises of Utopia. They promised only the *opportunity* to better one's living.

It would be wonderful if laws could be passed which would wipe out bigotry and prejudice. But human nature is not changed so easily. The key to progress in racial and religious understanding lies in the recognition that the individual gains for his or her own attainments.

The priceless heritage which America has given us—the heritage which *is* America—is this opportunity of being able to better oneself through one's own striving. No form of government can give a person more than that. And as long as that heritage remains ours, we will continue our progress toward better religious and racial understanding as more and more each of us comes to be recognized for his own or her own worth.

5. College Days

I WAS ONLY FOURTEEN YEARS old when I entered the College of the City of New York. This was not, I should hasten to add, evidence of any special precociousness on my part. It was simply that in those days there were no public high schools and one could go directly into college from grammar school if one met the entrance requirements.

My heart had been set on Yale. To help pay my way through, I planned to work as a waiter. But Mother felt that I was too young to leave home.

CCNY, as it was called then and now, was located at 23rd Street and Lexington Avenue. The old college building has long been torn down, but the School of Business and Public Administration now occupies the same site. We were living at 49 East 60th Street, and usually I walked the thirty-odd blocks to and from college.

This added a dime a day to my weekly allowance of twenty-five cents. When I became a senior, Father raised my allowance to fifty cents. But on one morning that I walked to college it definitely was not to save a dime—that was the day of the famous blizzard of 1888. The streetcars weren't running, and I had to go on foot. I made my way through the snow drifts by walking under the Third Avenue El, which had served as something of a shield against the blizzard. Not many students or teachers were in attendance that day.

I always brought lunch from home and during my first years in college wore Father's discarded clothes. By this time I was shooting up in height as if I had swallowed the beans that made Jack's beanstalk. Soon I was too long in the legs to get into Father's trousers, but Mother still made over his coats for me.

Then as now, CCNY was a college where a boy who wanted an education could get a good one free. We paid no tuition and were given our books, notebooks, and even pencils. In return, we were required to study. Entrance requirements were high; standards were strict, with examinations held twice a term; and those who could not keep up were dropped.

I entered a class of about three hundred, of whom fifty were graduated, although many of those dropping out were economic rather than academic casualties.

Many of the boys had jobs after school. Gano "Ginkie" Dunn, who became an electrical engineer with a list of distinctions which would fill a page of type, worked himself through school and supported a widowed mother as a night telegrapher at the Park Avenue Hotel. I kept Father's books and superintended collection of his accounts.

At first I enrolled in the Scientific Course, where emphasis was laid on sciences and modern languages. However, I soon switched to the Classical Course, which stressed the classical languages. I had to employ a tutor to catch up.

The whole college course extended over five years—the first or sub-freshman year serving in place of high school and as a transition to the higher realms of knowledge. There were no "snap" courses and virtually no elective system.

In public school I had graduated second in my class but in college I largely wasted my opportunities. My worst subjects were drawing and science. Almost my only memory of the chemistry class was of making some sulfuric acid into a foul-smelling concoction and dropping it into another student's pocket. The "ologies"—biology, zoology and geology—were taught by Professor William Stratford, who was six feet four inches tall, with handsome features and a flowing blond mustache. I felt that he played favorites and that I was not one of them. So resentful was I of Stratford that a question from him put what little knowledge I may have had out of my head.

The professor who made the deepest impression on me was

George B. Newcomb of the Political Economy Department. He wore gold-rimmed glasses and looked like an old-fashioned Englishman. In a squeaky voice, which he tried to improve by sucking sugar, he used to say, "Those gentlemen who wish to play chess may sit on the back seats. Those gentlemen who wish to hear me may have the front seats."

Although I was a chess player, I always took a front seat and missed little of what the professor said.

Much of my later success can be attributed to what I learned from him. Professor Newcomb never would have agreed with some popular present-day economic theories. He plugged away at the law of supply and demand and taught us to believe in it. It was in his class that I first heard:

"When prices go up two processes will set in—an increased production and a decreased consumption. The effect will be a gradual fall in prices. If prices get too low two processes will set in—decreased production because a man will not continue to produce at a loss and, second, increased consumption. These two forces will tend to establish the normal balance."

Ten years later I became rich by remembering those words.

Professor Newcomb taught not only political economy, but philosophy, logic, ethics, and psychology—all in one course. Today these subjects would be fragmented among several professors. I believe there was considerable advantage in being taught all these subjects by the same man. Too many educators seem to have forgotten that you cannot teach good economics, good politics, good ethics, or good logic unless they are considered together as parts of one whole.

Colleges as a rule teach economics badly. With overspecialization has also come a tendency to mistake information for education, to turn out "quiz experts" who are crammed full of useful detail but who have not been trained how to think.

I also believe it a mistake that Greek and Latin are no longer subjects that all students must take. At CCNY I read most of the Greek and Latin classics in the original and could carry on a conversation in Latin. My study of both languages gave me an appreciation of the cultural background of our civilization which I never would have had otherwise.

During Mayor Purroy Mitchel's administration, while I was a trustee of CCNY, a movement was started to turn the college into an industrial school. One day the trustees were called to City Hall to meet the mayor. My mind was still absorbed in the operation I had left in Wall Street and I was gazing out of the window when I heard someone say, "The first step will be to do away with Latin and Greek."

I whirled around in my chair and asked, "What is this about?"

It was explained to me.

Then I started to make a speech. Someone tried to quiet me but I was not to be quieted. The value of an education, I argued, did not lie in the facts that you stored in your head. It lay in the discipline you acquired and the general philosophy of life you gained from becoming acquainted with the great minds of the past. Education should open up new vistas of intellectual interest. To deprive CCNY students of the study of Greek and Latin would impoverish their minds and spirits.

I suppose no one at the meeting expected a man engaged in money making to voice such an objection. In any case, my speech stopped the plan to make CCNY an industrial college. On all proposals to "liberalize" the curriculum I usually turned out to be the most reactionary of the trustees. I even opposed the introduction of the elective system, maintaining that unpopular courses are good for young people because of their disciplinary value. In life we do not always do what we wish. But the elective system rolled over me like a locomotive.

If I were a trustee today, I would fight to cut out snap courses and would try to restore the "dead languages" to their old importance.

Another bit of "old-fashioned" pedagogy which prevailed in my student days and which could be revived with considerable advantage was the practice of delivering orations before the student body.

Every morning we filed into assembly. General Alexander Stewart Webb, the college president, would begin by reading from the Bible. A sophomore then would climb the rostrum to deliver a "declamation"—a recitation of poetry or prose; a junior and a senior would follow with an "oration" which he had written for the occasion.

The terrors of my first sophomore "declamation" almost equaled those of the "A-toodle-dah" incident. For my junior oration I wore striped trousers, a black coat and vest. My knees trembled and my heart pounded as I mounted the platform, bowed first to President Webb and the faculty, and then to the student body. It was not easy to hold one's poise while some of the students tried to make you laugh by grimacing and making funny gestures.

All I can recall from that first oration of mine is the opening line: "There is no joy without alloy." I can't remember whether it was a quotation I picked up somewhere or an original phrase, but I do know that it is true.

2

From all this one should not conclude that we did not have plenty of fun in school and out.

It was while I was in college that I first became a vaudeville fan. For twenty-five cents one could get into the top balcony of a theater. We would line up before the box office, shove in our quarters, and then fly up the stairs in hopes of getting seats in the front row.

Niblo's Garden and a playhouse on West Twenty-third Street are ones I remember particularly. As new theaters were built further uptown and the family finances improved, we visited them as well. Mother and Father were always trying to expose us to the first-rank Shakespearean actors of the day. But, sad to say, I remember less of these Shakespearean dramas than I do about *The Black Crook*.

That was the first play in which I saw women in tights. You were supposed to be quite a fellow when you had seen *The Black Crook*.

Few if any of us took much interest in national politics, although I have a vague recollection of being paid fifty cents to carry a torch in a Grover Cleveland parade. We were, of course, quite intense over college politics. In the first half of my senior year, I was elected president of the class; in the second half, I was elected secretary. Dick Lydon, my closest chum and later a Justice of the New York Supreme Court, alternated with me in these offices. I was also chairman of the senior class day program.

The Greek-letter societies or fraternities played an important part at the college. Although many Jews made their mark at the college, the line was drawn against them by these societies. Each year my name would be proposed and a row would ensue over my nomination, but I never was elected. It may be worth noting, particularly for those who regard the South as less tolerant than the North, that my brother Herman was readily admitted to a fraternity while he attended the University of Virginia.

Next to the "secret societies," the "rage" during my college days were the literary and debating societies. I belonged to two, Eiponia, which was limited to seniors, and Phrenocosmia.

The members of Eiponia would meet at each other's homes to hear papers on Hawthorne or Emerson or Thoreau after which the critic appointed for the occasion would rip into the efforts of the speaker. The records show that I delivered a paper on William Dean Howells and a critique on another Eiponian's paper on Oliver Wendell Holmes.

Phrenocosmia, the debating society, was even more scornful of "superficial" subjects. Among the "issues" debated in my senior year were:

"Resolved: that the end justifies the means."

"Resolved: that Bacon wrote the plays of Shakespeare."
"Resolved: that trusts are inimical to the best interests of the United States."

I cannot recall ever taking part in any debate. Pleased as I was to be known as a member of the debating society, I still was so terrified at the thought of speaking in public that I avoided every opportunity for actual debate.

Although I had lost much of my shyness, I still felt uncomfortable at parties or in large gatherings. Once our family went to the wedding of a distant cousin. After fidgeting about for a time, I slipped out of the drawing room and went down into the basement to hide until the affair was over.

Nor will I ever forget my sense of panic at my first big party. It marked the debut of Marie, the oldest of Dick Lydon's three lovely sisters. Dick was often at my house and I at his, and I knew the Lydon girls well; but the idea of attending a formal party put me into a nervous sweat. Dick, knowing of my bashfulness, told Mother of the invitation and suggested that she make sure I came. I could have murdered Dick—for, sure enough, Mother told me she wanted me to go.

I reminded her that I had no evening clothes. Father's dress suit, she replied, would do very well. This was my last or next to the last year in college, and although Father was six feet tall, by this time I was even taller.

On the evening of the party Mother laid out Father's suit, a shirt, collar, and white tie. I worked into them. The trousers were too short. They were what we boys called "high waters." Mother took a few safety pins and by piecing out the suspenders made the pants at least a little longer, so that they came down over my shoe tops. The vest also was too short. Mother pinned it to my shirt in such a way that this deficiency would not be too noticeable.

My long, bony hands hung far out of the coat sleeves. Mother couldn't think of anything that could be done about *that*. Every time my arms moved, the coat also hiked up in the back, and this could not be remedied either. When I looked in the mirror, heavy beads of perspiration glistened on my forehead. My face was as white as a sheet.

After a final check to make sure that all the safety pins were holding, Mother led me by the hand to the front hall, pulled my head down, and kissed me.

"You are the handsomest boy in the world," she said.

That helped a little.

"Remember," she added, "the blood of princes flows through your veins." (Mother always said that she was descended from King David. And if she said something, it must be so.) "No one is any better than you, but you are no better than anyone else until you prove it."

I slipped on my overcoat. Mother patted me on the back and assured me that everyone would be glad to see me. I closed the door and started briskly on my way. But I had not gone far before my courage began to ooze away. When I reached the Lydon house, all aglow with light and with a canopy over the front door, I was terrified. Several times I walked past the house before I could muster enough spunk to enter.

As I was let in, I noticed the attire of the servant who admitted me. How much better his clothes fit than mine!

"Gentlemen, second floor rear," he directed.

I found the room and shed my overcoat. I was alone. Apparently all the other guests were downstairs, from where I heard music and laughter. After glancing in a mirror at my white face and ill-fitting clothes, I simply could not make my feet take me down.

I do not know how long I had remained in the dressing room when I heard a girl's voice:

"Bernie Baruch! What *are* you doing here?"

It was Bessie Lydon, Dick's second sister.

Grasping my hand, she dragged me down the stairway. I felt myself shedding safety pins all the way. I was still in a trance when Bessie introduced me to a beautiful creature who seemed to float through the air in a cloud of light blue.

That, at any rate, was the impression she left upon my confused mind.

The next thing I knew, I was dancing. More safety pins tinkled to the floor, but no one seemed to notice. Although I was an awkward dancer at that time, I got through the number pretty well. And after that I had a good time.

What a tremendous supper I ate! I was hungry, having been able to eat little for days in contemplation of the dreadful ordeal.

Perhaps I have exaggerated the grotesqueness of my appearance that evening, but certainly it must have been obvious that my clothes did not fit me. Yet those charming people made me forget it and helped me enjoy myself for the first time in a large social party.

Never afterwards have I seen a person, young or old, in strange company and embarrassed on that account, without recalling that incident. Always I try to do something to put the embarrassed person at ease.

3

Along with shyness, my main personal difficulty was with my temper. Often my mother, seeing the anger rising in me, would reach out and put a restraining hand on my shoulder. She often counseled me, "Keep your tongue between your teeth unless you have something pleasant to say."

My temper may have had its roots in the fact that I was always getting licked as a child. In any case, my self-control did seem to improve steadily as my physical confidence grew.

While I was at college, I kept a set of parallel bars in my bedroom, on which I exercised every day. I also spent a good deal of time in the gym at the YMHA, then on Forty-second Street.

One of the popular sports of that day was the seven-day "Go As You Please Races" in which the contestants were free to run, trot, or walk as they chose. I often tried to emulate the winners by walking, running, and trotting around Central Park.

By my senior year I was a fairly good athlete. I had attained my full growth of six feet three inches and weighed about one hundred and seventy pounds. Curiously, most of my weight was in the upper half of my body. My legs were as thin as pipe stems and the contrast between them and my rather broad chest always called forth cries of amusement when I appeared in a baseball suit or running shorts.

I was a member of the college lacrosse team and also of the tug-of-war team, where I made up in spirit what I lacked in weight. For a time I also fancied myself something of a heel-and-toe walker and a sprinter. But when I found that my best time for running 100 yards was thirteen seconds, I gave that up.

My anger still flared quickly. At college one day I was going up a flight of stairs when a student in front of me cursed me, making some reference to my mother. I swung and knocked him down. Both of us were summoned before President Webb, who had commanded a Union brigade at Gettysburg and who seemed to us the epitome of military discipline.

The student I had hit was bleeding. Staring at me sternly, General Webb exclaimed, "A gentleman and the son of a gentleman engaging in a brawl!"

"Yes, sir," I replied angrily. "I tried to kill him. He called my mother a vile name."

General Webb ordered me to step into his inside office. Presently he entered and said:

"You are the kind of young man who ought to go to West Point, but I shall have to suspend you."

Following General Webb's suggestion, I decided to try for an appointment to the Military Academy. Father checked me over physically. To our surprise when he held a clock near my left ear, I could not hear the ticking. I was almost totally deaf in that ear.

I then remembered a baseball game we had played against

Manhattan College, I believe it was, on a lot on what is now Morningside Heights. In the ninth inning there were two or three men on base and I represented the winning run. Some of the boys began to yell, "Home run, Shorty! Home run!"

I hit the first ball right on the nose. I can feel the impact yet. The runners got safely home. I got to home plate at the same moment that the ball arrived in the catcher's hands. I ran into him. He dropped the ball. The umpire yelled, "Safe!"

A fight started and someone clouted me on the left ear with a bat. Although I did not know it then, the blow damaged my eardrum and, of course, ended any prospect of going to West Point.

During both the First and Second World Wars, while working with military officers in Washington on mobilization problems, I would tell this story of how I might have been a general if it hadn't been for that ball game.

By the time I was graduated from CCNY, what with having been a class politician and something of an athlete, I began to fancy myself as something of a man about town.

After leaving college I continued my body-building program by becoming a regular patron at a gymnasium run by John Woods. Situated over a livery stable on 28th Street between Fifth and Madison avenues, Woods' gym was the equivalent of an athletic club and was highly popular. Among the patrons were some of the leading actors of the day, lawyers, brokers, clergymen, prize fighters, and professional athletes of all kinds.

At Woods' I played a good deal of handball. But most of my energies went into boxing. Among the "pros" who worked out at Woods' were Bob Fitzsimmons, Joe Choynski, Billy Smith, Sailor Sharkey, and Tom Ryan. I would watch them by the hour, trying to pick up pointers. If in a gracious mood, the pros might show us our shortcomings and how to overcome our awkwardness.

Fitzsimmons told me that my main trouble was that I didn't hit hard enough. "When you hit a man in the jaw," he advised, "try to knock his block off. When you hit him in the belly try to drive that glove clean through him." Fitzsimmons also used to caution me, "Don't get mad while you are fighting."

One bout in Woods' gym remains one of my most thrilling memories. It was with a red-haired policeman whose beat was along Fifth Avenue. He was about as tall as I was but outweighed me by many pounds. He was also a good boxer.

Pretty soon he was batting me all over the ring. Bleeding from the nose and mouth, I hung on, employing every trick and device I had learned, but nothing seemed to do any good.

My senses were beginning to swim and possibly my adversary got a little bit careless. Anyway, he uncovered for an instant and I shot a left into his stomach with every ounce I could put behind it, following with a right that was flush on the jaw.

When that big policeman crumpled to the canvas I never was more surprised in my life. In those days a fighter was not ordered to his corner after a knockdown. With shoulders heaving from exhaustion, I stood over my man waiting for him to get up. But he did not stir until a bucket of water was emptied over his face. I felt a slap on my back and turned to face freckled, grinning Bob Fitzsimmons.

"The prize ring lost a good man in you," he said, laughing. "You were getting a licking but you hung on. That's what you always want to do. You know how you feel and maybe you feel pretty bad. But you don't know how the other fellow feels. Maybe he is worse off than you are."

"A fight is never over until one man is out," he emphasized. "As long as you ain't that man you have a chance. *To be a champion you have to learn to take it or you can't give it.*"

I have tried to carry that philosophy into fields far removed from the boxing ring. It has not always brought me out on top but it has won a good many fights which otherwise I would have lost. To reach the top in any endeavor, you must learn to take the bitter with the sweet—the ridicule and taunts of other boys, the sneers, threats, and sleepless opposition of other men, and the anguish of your own disappointments.

To this day I have remained an ardent prize-fight fan. In my younger years I collected pictures of the outstanding boxers, and even after I was married I kept a boxing ring in the basement of my house, where I would practice at the punching bag.

I have always done some physical exercising, which undoubtedly has helped me stay in good health. But the main benefit I drew from my boxing was the ability to control my temper and the added self-confidence I drew from my improved physique. I have been told—and I agree—that it is easier to be conciliatory and understanding when you know that, if this fails, you will be there with the sock.

When I was about twenty-two I posed for a photograph showing me with a mustache and curly black, almost kinky hair, and with muscular arms folded across a bare chest. That photograph still stands on my living room table, and when I look at it I am reminded of how I had changed from the fat little boy who first came to New York.

6. *Looking for a Job*

As WITH MANY FAMILIES, the early dreams of my parents for their children were not fully realized. Mother and Father had wanted all four of their sons to get a college education, but only two of us proved sufficiently interested—Herman and myself.

When he was twelve or thirteen, Sailing, the baby of the family, was sent to a military academy. But he had to leave school after a fight with one of the other students. He tried his hand at various jobs and businesses—from being a floor-walker to running a clothing factory—but eventually followed me into Wall Street.

Herman was to have been a lawyer. He became a doctor instead, earning a Phi Beta Kappa key and finishing near the top of his class in the College of Physicians and Surgeons of Columbia University. He practiced medicine for some years, then went into Wall Street, and eventually became ambassador first to Portugal and then to Holland. He died in 1953 at the age of eighty-one.

Mother intended Harty to be a rabbi. He had been named for Great-grandfather Hartwig Cohen, who was a rabbi. As a child Harty had been desperately ill, and Mother, in praying for him, had vowed that if Harty recovered he would become a rabbi. But Harty wound up on the stage.

A handsome six-footer, Harty looked like a stage hero. He had the physique and strength of a Tarzan. He could do somersaults, perform like a professional on the horizontal and parallel bars, and was a heavy-weight lifter. Once I saw him pick up a man and throw him through the swinging doors of a café on Broadway, near 42nd Street.

Even at the age of seventy-nine, Harty was strong enough

to have a leg amputated. He died five years later, only two weeks before my brother Herman.

I remember Harty's stage debut. In fact, I helped make it possible. The experience was hardly something to brag about and I rarely talked of it. During World War One, however, President Wilson surprised me by relating the story and it was evident he thought it quite funny.

John Golden, the theatrical producer and a close friend of Harty, had told the President the tale of what Golden liked to describe as "Bernie Baruch's dramatic exit, if not spectacular entrance as a theatrical producer."

I was about a year out of college and still the awed younger brother where Harty was concerned. He was studying at the dramatic school of Dion Boucicault, where he met an older woman who impressed him as being a great actress. She set Harty afire with visions of the bright future that awaited them both. All they needed was someone to back a show and give them the opportunity to display their talents to a waiting world.

Harty and his actress friend came to me with their project. The lady personified the glamour of the theater and alas, I was in my impressionable years. Moreover, she was an authentic disciple of Mark Twain's Colonel Mulberry Sellers. Swiftly she sketched for me how the backers of artists got rich. A theater contained so many hundreds of seats. With tickets at so much a seat, this would yield so many dollars. Expenses for a performance were only so much. The rest went into the producer's pocket. Simplicity itself.

My salary at the time was $5 per week but somehow I raised some money. We were to open with *East Lynne* at the opera house in Centerville, New Jersey. A cast was assembled but there were no rehearsals. Apparently rehearsals had been brushed aside as an unnecessary detail for so fine a company of artists.

On opening night I got off from work as soon as I could and joined the cast at the ferry slip. After we had crossed to New Jersey, I distributed the railroad tickets to the cast.

When I came to the leading man, he asked for $10. Since the request was delivered in the nature of an ultimatum, he got the ten.

The curtain rose that lovely spring evening on an audience that comfortably filled three full rows. I had been assured that every member of our company was an artist. At least the leading man who played the part of the city slicker had not been miscast—he got his pay in advance. We even had a real, live baby which the heroine was to carry on the stage in the third act. Not every *East Lynne* company had a real baby. It turned out, however, that this real baby did not do us much good. The show lasted only two acts.

Perhaps the actors were artists, as represented. If so, they were not artists who knew the lines of *East Lynne*. During Act One, the audience was alternately angry and amused. During the second act it was only angry.

Although small, this audience outnumbered the performers, so I asked the fellow at the box office to give the patrons their money back. Like the Duke in *Huckleberry Finn*, I went backstage and told the troupe that fortunately I had bought round-trip tickets and it was only a short walk through a dark street to the depot.

I think we were at the railroad station before the audience realized there would be no third act. A train had just pulled in. We climbed aboard without even noticing which way it was going. Luckily it was headed for New York.

Harty was not discouraged by this debacle. He continued to study under Boucicault and at the Boston Lyceum, which was where he met John Golden, then also an aspiring actor. They became such close friends that Mother used to call Golden "my fifth son."

After several small parts in road shows, Harty made his New York première under the name of Nathanial Hartwig in *The Corsican Brothers*, in which Robert Mantell played the lead. Later Harty joined the company of Marie Wainwright and became her leading man in a good repertoire which included *Camille, The School for Scandal,* and several Shake-spearean plays.

Harty also played opposite Olga Nethersole in *Carmen* and helped make the "Nethersole kiss" famous. Harty's big scene came when, as Don José, he stood by the bar and Car-men danced before him. Harty would sweep Miss Nethersole into his arms and carry her upstairs with his lips glued to hers in what was billed as the longest kiss on any stage. In a later play, *Sappho,* Miss Nethersole managed an even longer em-brace, which caused the police to raid the show, but by then Harty had abandoned the stage for Wall Street.

2

In my own case the family plan called for me to follow in Father's footsteps and become a doctor. Mother, however, soon changed her mind on this. Her decision was reached in a somewhat unorthodox fashion.

Not long after we moved to New York, my Uncle Her-man's business partner, Samuel Wittkowsky, came up from South Carolina on a buying trip. While talking with Mother about the careers we boys would follow, Mr. Wittkowsky suggested that Mother take me to a Dr. Fowler, a phrenolo-gist, whose office, I believe, was opposite A. T. Stewart's store, later John Wanamaker's.

I remember Dr. Fowler as a man with gold eyeglasses and an impressive bearing. He examined my head and then, pass-ing his fingers over the bulges above my eyebrows, asked:

"And what do you propose to do with this young man?"

Mother replied, "I am thinking of making him a doctor."

"He will make a good doctor," Dr. Fowler agreed, "but my advice to you is to take him where they are doing big things—finance or politics."

Mother later told me that as a result of this interview, she made up her mind that I should not be a doctor.

On being graduated from CCNY in 1889, I actually began

reading medicine with the idea of entering medical school in the fall. But I was not at ease with this decision. When the subject of my future would come up, Mother would recall what the phrenologist had said. Father, of course, recognized that this was her way of urging me toward a business career. He would merely say, "Son, don't become a doctor unless you love the work."

Following my mother's urging, I started to look for work. It proved a disillusioning experience. Like the average college graduate, I was loath to start at the bottom. After wearing thin much shoe leather in answering "Help Wanted" advertisements, and waiting vainly for replies to my own advertisements, I made a list of Father's patients with the idea of striking one of them for a job.

The first person I called on was Daniel Guggenheim of the famous Guggenheim family. At nineteen, I probably was a foot taller than Mr. Dan, which only increased my self-consciousness.

A smile, a wonderful smile, from Mr. Dan restored some measure of my composure. After putting me at ease, Mr. Dan told me that the Guggenheim family was going into mining and smelting and asked, "How would you like to go to Mexico for us as an ore buyer?"

But Mother put her foot down on my going to Mexico. Even though she continually fired our ambitions, she wanted us boys at home.

She thought of us living near her. Walking along Fifth Avenue one day, she pointed out the William C. Whitney mansion at the corner of 57th Street to me and said:

"You will be living there some day."

Many years later when I told her I had bought property on the corner of 86th Street and Fifth Avenue, she recalled this conversation.

And so I tried another of Father's patients, Charles Tatum, of Whitall, Tatum & Company at 86 Barclay Street, wholesale dealers in glassware for druggists. Mr. Tatum, a Philadelphia Quaker, took me on as an office apprentice in the late summer or early autumn of 1889. My salary on this, my first job, was three dollars a week.

One day Mr. Tatum asked me to go over to "Mr. Morgan's office" to pick up some securities. "Mr. Morgan's office" was the banking house of Drexel, Morgan & Company. I entered the old building in Wall Street, where the present Morgan edifice stands, and without any delay or formalities was taken before Mr. Morgan himself.

I do not recall whether Mr. Morgan said anything to me, but I got a good look at his famous nose and tawny eyes. They gave me a feeling of his enormous power.

By that time I had taken up boxing, and the first thought that leaped to my mind was what a figure Mr. Morgan would make in the ring. Then I thought how like Charlemagne he would look astride a horse, with a battle ax in his hand, like the great king of the Franks.

It would make a fine literary effect to be able to say that it was this unforgettable meeting with Mr. Morgan that inspired me to go into Wall Street. Actually, the incident that prefaced my entry into Wall Street was not the kind of episode which would ordinarily be included in an inspirational anthology. It was a visit I made to a gambling house—or "gambling hell," as most good people called it then.

3

About this time my parents were spending their summers at Long Branch, New Jersey, then one of the leading resorts for boating, fishing, bathing, and gambling.

Father was resident physician at the West End Hotel. He had two rooms, an office and a bedroom. I stayed in the city during the week, but on Saturday afternoons Harty and I would go to Long Branch for the week ends. We slept on cots in Father's office.

Occasionally I also put up at a boardinghouse in Little Silver, New Jersey, run by a man known to everyone as

Uncle Dick Borden. Sailing contests on Pleasure Bay were a
lively sport at Uncle Dick's. I remember taking Borden's cat-
boat, *Emma B.*, through the Shrewsbury past Price's Pier. I
was dressed in my usual sailing costume—a pair of duck trousers, no shirt, hat, or shoes.

Handling both the tiller and main sheet, I was showing off
by shaving the pier as closely as I could when I heard a lady's
voice. Looking up, I saw on the pier a dazzlingly beautiful
creature standing beside Freddie Gebhardt, the sportsman.
She was entertaining him with discriminating comments on
my appearance, which modesty prevents me from recording
here.

Nevertheless, I appreciated it at the moment—and still do.
For an instant I relaxed my attention to the boat. A gust of
wind hit the sail. I was brought back to my senses by the
emphatic language of the other boatmen. I had just enough
time to let go my main sheet and ease off. I was good for
little more that day, and went home with my mind still dizzy
with thoughts of the compliments paid me by that beautiful
lady. Later I learned that she was the famous actress Lily
Langtry.

When I was at Borden's I thought nothing of walking the
three miles to Monmouth and back for the races, in order to
have an extra fifty cents to bet. Those were the days of such
famous horses as Tenny the Swayback, Hanover, and Cor-
rection. August Belmont, Freddie Gebhardt, the Lorillards,
Morrises, and Dwyers were the outstanding horse owners of
the time, the Dwyers being probably the biggest plungers in
backing their horses. The jockeys I remember were Murphy,
McLaughlin, and Garrison, from whom the "Garrison finish"
took its name.

A number of gambling houses enlivened things in Long
Branch itself. Near the West End Hotel was Phil Daly's. I
couldn't afford to patronize his establishment since the mini-
mum chips were a dollar, but I would hang around and
watch other people play. It was quite a sight, with bookmakers, touts, sports and sportsmen—there was a distinction

—brokers, merchants, and bankers, but no women. There was a private room for those who didn't wish to be seen gambling in public.

One night I was watching roulette and faro when Pat Sheedy, a well-known gambler, came up and said, "Youngster, I want to speak to you." We walked out onto the porch, where he continued:

"Young fellow, I have been noticing you loafing around here. Take the advice of a man who knows and keep out of places like this. I have seen that sweet-faced mother of yours and that fine-looking father. In fact, your father fixed me up the other night when I had the belly-ache. If you don't keep away from gambling houses you will make them feel sad and will get no good out of it yourself."

But Pat Sheedy's advice made no impression on me. A few evenings later, Dick Bonsal, who was about my age and whose parents were well-to-do and generous with him, suggested that we go over to a place run by another Daly, where chips were only fifty cents. I bought two or three chips, which I used sparingly at the roulette table, betting only on the colors. Soon I was two dollars ahead and feeling pretty good. Suddenly a dead silence, it seemed to me, fell over the room. The man stopped turning the wheel.

I looked up. There in the doorway stood Father. If I could have been granted one wish at that moment, it would have been for the earth to open and swallow me.

Father had given me the money to make the first bet of my life. It was at the races, when I told him I thought that a horse called Pasha would win. Handing me two silver dollars, Father said if I felt that way about Pasha I had better back my judgment. Pasha proved a better looker than performer.

But betting on a horse race was not the same to Father as going into a gambling house. He walked over to the table and in the gentlest, quietest way said, "Son, when you are ready we will go home."

I was ready right then. I walked through the door ahead

of Father. Outside, Harty was waiting. My shame gave way to anger.

"Why in the world," I whispered to Harty, "did you let Father come here?"

Harty explained that he could not help it. The family had been afraid that I might have drowned. Harty said that he had walked up and down the beach calling and whistling for me.

At the hotel Harty and I undressed silently. As we got into our cots, Father's last words were, "To think that at my age I should have to take my son from a gambling house."

It was quite a while before I dozed off, only to be awakened by Mother sitting on the side of my cot. She took me in her arms and whispered a few words of comfort.

I could sleep no more that night, feeling that I had brought shame upon my family. About five in the morning I got up, dressed quietly, and tiptoed out. I went to the railroad station, ate breakfast in a saloon with some coachmen and horse-handlers, and took the first train to New York. As the sun rose, my spirits rose with it. A boy of nineteen in good health doesn't stay down very long.

By the time I reached the city I had forgotten that my departure from Long Branch was a flight from disgrace. Looking up my cousin, Marcus Heyman, who was studying medicine at Bellevue College, I found him and several other young men preparing for an all-day Sunday poker game. I suggested that our house, being unoccupied, would be a good place to play. We were playing cards in the basement when Marcus suddenly jumped up and shouted, "Good Lord, there's Aunt Belle!"

Sure enough, Mother was coming up the front steps. We had started to put on our coats and clear away the evidence of our poker playing when she entered the room. After the escapade of the night before, I thought Mother would surely give me up as an incorrigible gambler. But, apparently without noticing a thing, she ran up and threw her arms around me.

"I am so glad to see you!" she cried. "You have such a sensitive nature that I was afraid something serious might have happened."

I felt thoroughly ashamed of myself but it made me love her all the more. Then she told me that she had a piece of good news. Coming up on the train to New York she was introduced to Julius A. Kohn, a retired clothing merchant who had gone into Wall Street. He told Mother that he had been looking for a young man who would be willing to start at the bottom and be trained for the banking business as such youths were trained in Frankfurt. He wanted someone who was serious-minded, dependable, hard-working, and, he emphasized, "with no bad habits."

Mother told him she knew just the young man he was looking for.

"Who is he?" asked Mr. Kohn.

Without a thought to my gambling, Mother had replied, "My son, Bernard."

The next day I called on Mr. Kohn. He explained that in Europe apprentices worked a long time for nothing, which was all they were worth. He was not prepared to pay me any salary but would try to teach me things I should know if I expected to be a businessman. I gave Whitall, Tatum & Company my notice of departure. Such was my first entry into Wall Street.

4

My new employer was exacting but not unkind. From the first the work fascinated me and provided more of an incentive to learn than I had felt while with Whitall, Tatum.

Among other things Mr. Kohn introduced me to the intricacies of arbitrage. The same security, for instance, might be quoted on the same day at slightly different prices in, let us say, New York, Baltimore, Boston, Amsterdam, and London. By buying in Amsterdam and selling in Boston, or by buying in Baltimore and selling in New York, an arbitrage profit could be made.

Although I was an office boy and runner, I was given the opportunity to figure the arbitrage with foreign countries. This called for a nimble agility at calculating in different national currencies, since even a fraction of a difference in the exchange might mean a profit. By practicing at it, I taught myself almost instantly to turn a given sum from guilders into sterling, from sterling into francs, or francs into dollars, or dollars into marks, as might be required. This proved a decided advantage during both World War One and the Versailles Peace Conference, when I had to handle many international economic problems.

The firm also dealt in new railroad securities which were issued in place of old securities when railroads were reorganized. If the reorganized properties turned out favorably, the new securities eventually would sell for much more than the old ones. By buying old securities and selling the new ones when they were issued in place of the old ones, a profit could be made. Of course, if the reorganization did not go through, you were stuck with the old bonds.

Thus, even as an obscure clerk, I saw arbitrage, foreign exchange, reorganization, and speculation at first hand. The account books in which these operations were entered became my favorite reading. I seem to have had an instinctive aptitude for such transactions. The time was to come when I would have the reputation of being one of the principal persons active in arbitrage operations on this side of the Atlantic.

Shortly after I came to Mr. Kohn, he put me on the payroll at three dollars a week. That summer, though, Father made his first visit to Europe since his departure as an emigrant boy thirty-five years earlier. Uncle Herman, Mother, and we boys went to see him off on the *Columbia* of the Hamburg Line. I had always been a favorite of Uncle Herman's and he asked Father, "Why don't you take Bernie with you?"

Father said he would if I could go home, get my valise and

be back at the boat in time. It was then late at night and the streetcars were not running frequently, but I made the trip home and back in time. I was put in a cabin with three Cubans. The four of us were sick all the way over.

I already have related my impressions of my German grandparents. After visiting their home in Schwersenz, Father took me to Berlin. What I remember most about the city were the Brandenburg Tor and the German officers one saw everywhere on the street.

Father detested the German military spirit and his feelings probably influenced me. The sight of those strutting officers, tricked out in their uniforms, irritated me. By that time I was getting on pretty well with my boxing and felt myself a match for any officer that I saw. I said something to Father about taking a punch at the next officer who brushed me aside on the street. Father advised that would be a pretty foolish thing to do.

Mother had gone to Mr. Kohn and explained my sudden departure for Europe; consequently he kindly took me back on my return. But I did not remain with him long. I was feeling impatient and adventurous. Dick Lydon and I decided we would try to strike it rich—quick—in the gold and silver mines of Colorado. Mother, who might have been a problem, did not object.

After a long ride in the day coaches, we reached Denver and then pushed on by stagecoach to Cripple Creek, a wide open mining town with saloons, dance halls, gambling joints —the whole business. We put up at the best place in town, the Palace Hotel, and were assigned to a large room filled with cots. When we came in late at night, we would have to step over the sleeping forms of other people to get to bed.

All sorts of stories of quick and easy fortunes were going around. As I recall, one of the richest mines was owned by a man who had come to town as a carpenter. We heard, of course, of the rise of Tom Walsh, the father of Evalyn Walsh McLean, who was the owner of the Hope diamond and who was to be a good friend when I went to Washington.

I decided to "invest" my "capital" in shares of what was called "the San Francisco Mine." This was the first stock I ever bought. Lydon and I didn't have enough money left to continue staying at the Palace so we changed to a boarding-house. I also laid aside my New York clothes and went to work as a mucker in a shaft adjoining that of the San Francisco Mine.

A mucker does the heaviest and least-skilled manual labor in a mine. He follows a blasting crew, piling up the rock that is blown loose and putting it into buckets and cars to be taken to the surface. I hadn't been on the job long before one husky miner began hazing me. I decided that sooner or later I would have to prove myself in a fight and, in that case, had better get in the first blow. Without waiting for further annoyances I hit the miner, putting everything I could into the punch, and knocked him down. I had no further trouble.

Lydon worked alongside of me. We were on the day shift, which left our evenings free to patronize the palaces of chance. I favored the one operated in conjunction with the Palace Hotel. It was the toniest establishment in town. Every night small fortunes changed hands over the card and roulette tables.

After a critical survey of how the various layouts operated, I decided that the roulette wheel probably was fixed. At least it always managed to stop in favor of the house when the betting was heavy. I began to place small bets opposite what-ever the big betters were playing. In this way I would win a few dollars every evening.

Just when I thought I had discovered a steady, depend-able source of revenue, the proprietor called me aside and said that he could dispense with my patronage.

Meanwhile I had been promoted to the blasting crew. I held a drill which another man struck with a sledge. This was easier work than being a mucker. My chief interest, how-ever, lay in the adjoining San Francisco Mine.

I held long conversations with the men working that shaft and soon decided that my stock never would match the golden expectations of the fast talker who had sold it to me. I had learned my first lesson in money making—that people who try to get rich from mining often put more into the ground than they take out of it.

New York began to look pretty good. Dick Lydon felt the same way so we quit our mining jobs and returned home. Somewhat chastened, I went back into Wall Street—this time to stay until Woodrow Wilson took me out of it.

Bernard Baruch

7. Learning the Hard Way

THE STRANGE FASCINATION that the stock market exerts upon people has never ceased to be a source of wonder to me.

In my younger days, when I was an active speculator in Wall Street, I quickly learned what extraordinary stratagems people would turn to in hopes of getting a "tip" on the market. They would invite you to dinner, to the theater, to their clubs and country homes, all for the purpose of pumping you. Often they would try to catch you unawares with the most elaborately casual questions, or would seize upon the merest fragment of a conversation to turn you into an involuntary tipster.

Knowing this, I tried to observe in my business affairs a vow of silence that would have done credit to a Trappist monk. Even this reticence, I found, was often interpreted by people as a market tip.

Men and women I had never seen would write me for advice. Such letters still stream in. Even as this was being written the mails brought one plea from a widow, with $15,000 in cash, who asked, "Should I invest now or wait until later so I can build up my capital to live on when I retire?"

Among the other questions put to me most frequently are:

"Can a young man start today with nothing and make a fortune in Wall Street as you did?"

"How did you know the 1929 market was too high?"

"Can you tell me of a safe investment in which to put my savings since I am getting too old to work?"

"I have some extra money I can afford to lose—what would you recommend I do?"

There are, of course, a number of guidelines to investment and speculation which I learned from experience and which

76.

still are applicable today. But from the inquiries pressed on me, it would seem that for many people the lure of the stock market is curiously similar to the medieval alchemist's hunt for some magic means of turning baser metals into gold. If only one has the philosopher's stone—gets the right tip—poverty can be transformed into riches or financial insecurity into ease.

I doubt that anything I write will change this. To many persons Wall Street will always remain a place to bet and gamble. Still, the stock market is far more than an air-conditioned indoor race track.

Actually it could be termed the total barometer for our civilization. The prices of stocks—and commodities and bonds as well—are affected by literally anything and everything that happens in our world, from new inventions and the changing value of the dollar to vagaries of the weather and the threat of war or the prospect of peace. But these happenings do not make themselves felt in Wall Street in an impersonal way, like so many jigglings on a seismograph. What registers in the stock market's fluctuations are not the events themselves but the human reactions to these events, how millions of individual men and women feel these happenings may affect the future.

Above all else, in other words, the stock market is people. It is people trying to read the future. And it is this intensely human quality that makes the stock market so dramatic an arena in which men and women pit their conflicting judgments, their hopes and fears, strengths and weaknesses, greeds and ideals.

Of course, I did not know or even sense any of this when I first went into Wall Street to work as an office boy and runner. I made my full quota of mistakes—being ambitious and energetic, probably more than my share. One could say that my whole career in Wall Street proved one long process of education in human nature.

And as I moved into public life I was to find that what I had learned about people from my speculator days applied

equally to all other human affairs. Human nature remained
human nature whether it stood bent over a stock ticker or
spoke from the White House, whether it sat in on the councils of war or at peace conferences, whether it was concerned
with making money or trying to control atomic energy.

2

My real start in Wall Street came in 1891, when I joined
the brokerage firm of A. A. Housman & Company, at 52 Exchange Place. As with my first job, I got the position largely
through Mother's efforts. In the course of her charity work
she had met A. B. deFreece when he was managing a fair to
raise funds for the Montefiore Home, one of the many chari-
ties fathered by Jacob Schiff. On my return from Colorado
Mother arranged that I meet Mr. deFreece, and he took me
to see Arthur A. Housman.

Housman's younger brother, Clarence, turned out to have
been the good-natured fat boy who had taken me to and from
grammar school when we first moved to New York. Clarence
kept the books of the firm. My job, which paid five dollars a
week, was to act as office boy, runner, comparison clerk, and
general utility man.

I opened the office in the morning and saw that the ink-
wells, pens, and the blotter on Mr. Housman's desk were in
order. Then I took the books out of the safe and put them on
Clarence's desk. I copied the letters, indexing them in the
copybook, and helped get out the monthly statements. I also
had to be on hand, when runners came in, to check on anything that remained to be done.

In those days there was no stock clearing house. Each and
every share sold had to be delivered by 2:15 P.M. the following day. On the northwest corner of Exchange Place and
Broad Street stood a building, several stories high, filled with
brokers' offices. Up and down those stairs we boys would
clatter, making our deliveries. I would shove a bundle of

securities through the cashier's window, crying out, "Hold the check for Housman," and rush off to make the next delivery.

One day, after delivering some stock to Jewett Brothers, I went off to make other deliveries and returned to Jewett's for Housman's check. A number of other runners were standing in front of the cashier's window. I, of course, towered over all of them.

"Where is Housman's check?" I called out over the heads of the boys in front of me.

Receiving no response, I cried out again, "Get a move on there, Mr. Cashier, and give me Housman's check."

The cashier looked out of his cage and, seeing me, merely said, "Get down off that stool."

"I am not on any stool," I replied.

"If you get fresh with me again," he said, "I will come out and box your ears."

"Is that so?" I replied.

He opened the door and came out, followed by two partners of the firm. The cashier looked at all six feet three of me and exclaimed: "Good God!"

They all laughed and went back in again. When I became a member of the Stock Exchange, the Jewett partners used to call to me occasionally, "Get off that stool!"

The first post of advancement I set my eye on was that of bookkeeper. Although I had done some work on Father's accounts, I decided to enroll at night school for courses in bookkeeping and contract law. Even now I can take a fairly complicated set of books and find out what is what without calling any outside help.

While at Kohn's I had learned the importance of being informed about the companies with whose securities we dealt. Now I began reading the *Financial Chronicle* regularly. Every chance I got I would also pull open *Poor's Manual,* cramming into my head all sorts of information about different corporations.

It is too bad that in those days there were no TV quiz programs asking questions worth $64,000 or I might have earned a fortune painlessly. I could rattle off the routes of all the principal railroads in the United States and what commodities and products gave them their main source of revenue. Nor did I have to consult an atlas to know which railroads would be affected by drought in one part of the country or floods in another, by the discovery of some new mine or the opening of some new territory for settlement.

I also kept my good right ear wide open to the talk going on around me. I must have developed into a pretty good listener since I soon had a clearer idea of some of the things going on in the Street than many fairly important persons whom I met.

Soon I got to be known among the runners, clerks, and eventually the junior members of firms as a lad with a ready store of useful information. The fact that I carried this information in my head also brought me to the attention of older men, who often would ask me questions rather than go to a book and look up the answers.

One man I met in this way was Middleton Schoolbred Burrill, almost the only nonprofessional I have known who consistently made money in stock market speculation. The son of John Burrill, whose law clientele included the Vander bilts, young Burrill practiced law in his father's office. He was one of Housman's clients and while in our office would often stop to ask me questions instead of going to the *Financial Chronicle* or *Poor's Manual*.

This was both flattering and helpful. It gave me a better idea of the information a market operator needed, and spurred my zeal to acquire it. Sometimes Mr. Burrill would invite me to lunch. We would sit on stools in front of the luncheon bar in the basement of the old Consolidated Exchange at the corner of Exchange Place and New Street. On such occasions I would get a good meal of roast beef and mashed potatoes. On other days, when I ate alone, a sandwich and a glass of beer were about all I could afford.

At the time, as I recall, it was a source of some envy on my part that I had to lunch on a sandwich while other runners, who were graduates of Harvard and Yale or the sons of well-known financiers, could order themselves a full meal.

It was through Mr. Burrill that I met James R. Keene, easily head and shoulders above any speculator I ever knew. An ardent turfman, Keene owned a horse, later called Domino, which he was racing at Coney Island. He wanted to bet on the horse without ruining the odds by disclosing the source of the wager. Burrill told Keene he thought I would be able to put the money down for him.

Mr. Keene asked me to his office at 30 Broad Street. My answers to a question or two apparently convinced him that I knew enough about race-track betting to turn the trick, and he handed me several thousand dollars in cash. I, who had never bet more than a few dollars on a horse in my life, took a train to Coney Island and got this money down before anyone guessed its source.

Keene's horse won in a canter. I returned to the city on the 34th Street ferry with my pockets literally bulging. I kept worrying that someone might hit me on the head and take all the money away.

When some swelling waves struck the front of the ferryboat, I remember thinking we were about to capsize. Buttoning my coat tightly, I decided that if the ship went down I would strike out to get far away from the crowd so that no one would be able to pull me down. Later I realized how silly these thoughts were, but they reflected my determination to deliver the money safely to Mr. Keene and not come to him with some excuse for having lost any part of his winnings.

3

I had begun to speculate in stocks on my own, maintaining a small margin account with the Broadway firm of Honigman and Prince. Today in buying stocks on the exchange one must put up seventy per cent of the purchase price, but in those earlier years one had only to put up from ten to twenty per cent of the price on "margin," with the broker carrying the balance of the cost. Of course, if the stock went down to where the margin was exhausted, the broker would sell me out unless I could raise additional margin.

Generally I bought and sold ten shares at a time on the Consolidated Stock Exchange. My operations were confined mostly to railroads in receivership and some industrials.

Of course, I made money sometimes. That can happen to any "tyro" and the sad part of it is that it often does, encouraging the amateur to plunge even more deeply. But as soon as I got a few hundred dollars ahead, I would be cleaned out of everything, my original stake included.

I lost not only my own money but some of Father's as well. On one occasion I felt sure that a fortune could be made in an overhead trolley line that ran between the landing and a hotel at Put-in-Bay on a Lake Erie island. The venture had been brought to my attention by a personally charming promoter named John P. Carrothers, whom Father and I had met on the ship returning from Europe in 1890. I was so carried away that I persuaded Father to invest $8000, a considerable part of his savings, in the scheme. Every dollar was lost.

Although Father never reproached me, the loss weighed on my heart. I imagine I took it much harder than Father, who was more concerned with human values than with money.

Not long after the trolley setback, I remarked to Mother that if I had $500 I could make some money in Tennessee Coal & Iron.

"Why don't you ask Father for it?" she urged.

I protested that after the Put-in-Bay disaster, I could not ask him for another penny.

A few days later Father came to me with a check for $500. Memory plays us subtle tricks and I cannot recall whether or not I accepted the money. That detail is obscured by the larger significance of the incident—the profound lift it was to my self-respect to learn that, after I had cost him so much of his earnings, Father still had faith in me.

Unquestionably, Father was psychologist enough to know something of the struggle going on within me. My mind was in a state of balance where the touch of a hand might swerve me in a direction that could determine the whole course of my career.

In such circumstances, some men grow desperate. I grew cautious. I began a habit I was never to forsake—of analyzing my losses to determine where I had made my mistakes. This was a practice I was to develop ever more systematically as my operations grew in size. After each major undertaking— and particularly when things had turned sour—I would shake loose from Wall Street and go off to some quiet place where I could review what I had done and where I had gone wrong. At such times I never sought to excuse myself but was concerned solely with guarding against a repetition of the same error.

Periodic self-examination of this sort is something all of us need, in both private and governmental affairs. It is always wise for individuals and governments to stop and ask whether we should rush on blindly as in the past. Have new conditions arisen which require a change of direction or pace? Have we lost sight of the essential problem and are we simply wasting our energies on distractions? What have we learned that may help us avoid repeating the same old errors? Also, the more we know of our own failings, the easier it becomes to understand other people and why they act as they do.

In those early days it wasn't too difficult to figure out what I was doing that was wrong. There are two principal mistakes that nearly all amateurs in the stock market make.

The first is to have an inexact knowledge of the securities in which one is dealing, to know too little about a company's management, its earnings and prospects for future growth.

The second mistake is to trade beyond one's financial resources, to try to run up a fortune on a shoestring. That was my main error at the outset. I had virtually no "capital" to start with. When I bought stocks I put up so small a margin that a change of a few points would wipe out my equity. What I really was doing was little more than betting whether a stock would go up or down. I might be right sometimes, but any sizable fluctuation would wipe me out.

While I was carrying on these speculations, I had become a bond salesman and customers' man for A. A. Housman & Company. It happened to be a crucial period as far as the country's finances were concerned. The panic of 1893 closed many mills and mines and put into receivership a large part of all the railroads in the country. By 1895, though, one could detect the first promises of better financial weather.

I had never experienced a depression before. But even then I began to grasp dimly that the period of emergence from a depression provides rare opportunities for financial profit.

During a depression people come to feel that better times never will come. They cannot see through their despair to the sunny future that lies behind the fog. At such times a basic confidence in the country's future pays off, if one purchases securities and holds them until prosperity returns.

From what I saw, heard, and read, I knew that was exactly what the giants of finance and industry were doing. They were quietly acquiring interests in properties which had defaulted but which would pay out under competent management once normal economic conditions were restored. I tried to do the same thing with my limited means.

The defaulted securities of railroads interested me particularly—partly I suppose, because the romance of railroading had attracted me from childhood when the brakemen on the freight trains waved to me as they passed Grandfather's house in Winnsboro. Then, this was also the period during which the nation's railroads, many of which had been wastefully overbuilt, were being consolidated into more efficient properties.

The problem was to determine which securities would survive these reorganizations. Those that did would become immensely valuable. Those that did not would be junked as worthless.

At first I made mistakes in picking the right securities. This spurred me to study the railroads involved more closely.

I compiled a list of the railroads being reorganized whose securities seemed to me likely to prove sound investments. To test myself I jotted down in a little black notebook my expectations for these securities.

One entry I made suggested selling New Haven stock and buying Richmond and West Point Terminal, which was later reorganized into what is now the Southern Railway System. Other comments regarding the Atchison, Topeka & Santa Fe and Northern Pacific showed some foresight. Still another successful forecast in my little black book was a prediction that if Union Pacific were bought at the price then prevailing it would pay 100 per cent on the investment when it came out of receivership and was fully developed.

Having studied these railroad securities, my next problem was to interest someone in buying them. That was not easy. I was unknown. A. A. Housman was a small firm. Times were still hard. All the railroads whose securities I was recommending were in default and their owners had suffered heavy losses. The investing public was wary, as it always is when things are cheap.

Since I knew almost no one with money to invest, I combed the business directories for names. I carefully composed dozens of letters, copied them in longhand, and sent them out. The response was virtually 100 per cent negative.

Every afternoon after the Stock Exchange closed, I would walk up Broadway, stopping at office after office, trying to get someone to listen to me. I do not know at how many doors I presented myself or how many miles of pavement I put behind me before I made my first sale.

That first sale—to James Talcott, a leading dry-goods merchant—remains sharp in my memory. Tall and impressive-looking, with a full gray beard, Talcott had the general appearance of a New England merchant. Having been turned away repeatedly by his secretary, I sat down to wait until Talcott left his office. When he appeared in the doorway, I introduced myself and followed him to the sidewalk. A blunt nod was all the acknowledgment I received.

As we walked up the street, I talked as courteously and convincingly as I could, ignoring the plain signs of Talcott's irritation. I put all my persuasive powers into that effort. After repeating several times that he was not interested in anything I had to sell, Talcott finally gave me an order for one lone bond, a six-per-cent Oregon & Trans-Continental, then selling, I think, at about 78.

The commission to A. A. Housman & Company on each bond I sold was $1.25. But more important than the immediate commission was the future to which I was looking. If my recommendations proved profitable I hoped to convert casual purchasers into steady customers.

The issue bought by Mr. Talcott was not affected by the reorganization then in process and mounted in value. That transaction was the beginning of a considerable business our house did for Mr. Talcott.

With other customers as well I would watch the issues I had recommended, and from time to time would suggest changes to safeguard and improve their investments. But if I was the soul of caution with my customers, I still speculated wildly on my own account.

The contradiction in this double financial life that I was leading was brought home to me by an amusing incident. After the Stock Exchange closed for the day I tended to gravitate to the varied pastimes which attracted the other young men about town. Sandy Hatch, a member of the Stock Exchange and a true sportsman, had a string of fighting cocks. The fights, or "mains" as they were called, used to be held at an inn which overlooked the Hudson River at around 175th Street.

One night a main was going full tilt when someone shouted, "The police!"

Out of the windows and every other exit we piled, I not

among the hindmost. The alarm turned out to be a false one. Most of the spectators trooped back to the pit but I went home.

To be haled before a city magistrate for attending a chicken fight, I decided, was hardly the kind of publicity that would help a young broker earn a reputation for sound conservatism among his customers. After that I do not recall ever having attended a main again.

What I was fighting out inside myself, of course, was the age-old conflict that every ambitious youth experiences between the reckless impulse to shoot the works and the cautious desire to mass one's resources for the morrow. In my case, it was the cautious course that tended to win out, but not without many a battle and some setbacks.

8. I Get Married

AFTER FOUR YEARS in Wall Street I had little, if anything, in the way of material assets to show for my efforts. My salary had been gradually increased from $5.00 to $25.00 a week, but this had only increased my ability to speculate at a loss. Despairing of making a killing in the market, I struck Arthur Housman for a raise. And I struck high, asking for fifty dollars a week.

"I cannot give you fifty dollars a week," Mr. Housman told me, "but I will give you an eighth interest in the business."

Actually this amounted to a raise in salary to at least thirty-three dollars a week, since the firm's profits in the previous year had been $14,000. In addition, if business increased, I might net even more than fifty dollars a week.

I leaped at the proposal and became a Wall Street partner at the age of twenty-five.

Being a junior partner in a brokerage house, I decided, called for some expansion of my personal budget. I acquired a Prince Albert coat, a silk hat, and all the accessories that went with them. In those days it was considered the thing to do to stroll on Fifth Avenue on Sunday mornings when the weather was fine. On Sundays I would array myself in all my finery, my shoes polished with more than usual care, take my cane, and sally forth.

I cannot say that these promenades were entirely enjoyable. There were other young men, whom I had known in the Street as apprentices and runners, who were the sons of brokers or bankers and consequently had money to spend on pleasures that were denied me. In their splendid traps, behind spanking teams of horses, they would dash by me as I walked along the Avenue. Often I felt envious.

That was another battle I had to fight out within myself as a young man, to prevent feelings of envy from driving me to rash decisions or to be corroded with jealousy of those who were more successful than I was.

Before offering me the partnership, Mr. Housman had asked why I felt I needed so large an income. I explained that I wanted to get married.

The girl who was waiting for me was Annie Griffen. I had first seen her about the time of my graduation from college. While walking with a boy named Dave Schenck, whose step-father kept a hotel, we passed and he spoke to two most attractive girls. One, Dave said, was a Miss Louise Guindon and the other was her cousin, a Miss Griffen.

One glance sufficed to interest me in the tall, slender Miss Griffen.

I tried to learn all I could about her and her family. Miss Griffen, I discovered, lived with her parents, Mr. and Mrs. Benjamin Griffen, in a brownstone house at 41 West 58th Street, which I passed daily on my way to the Sixth Avenue elevated to go to work. Her father was the grandson of an Episcopalian minister, a graduate and Phi Beta Kappa man of CCNY. He had a son there who was a classmate of my brother Herman.

Mr. Griffen was in the glass-importing business under the name of Van Horne, Griffen & Company. The Van Hornes and Griffens were cousins. Mrs. Griffen was a daughter of W. J. Wilcox, a lard merchant, whose large refinery I had seen burn to the ground some years before. The Griffens kept horses and a carriage.

All this I ferreted out in hope of finding some way of meeting the daughter. Since none of this information, not even our brothers being at the same college, seemed to bring this prospect nearer, my inquiries proved as good as useless.

One day while walking near the Griffen home I saw Miss Griffen approaching. Mustering all my courage, I reached the stoop of her house just as she did. Raising my hat, I asked if I were addressing Miss Annie Griffen.

"No, indeed!" she retorted with a toss of her head and walked up the steps.

That set me back pretty hard, but finally Dave Schenck arranged for us to meet through Miss Guindon, whom Dave knew.

After that I became a regular caller at the Griffen home. Annie's father opposed my courtship, feeling that the difference in our religions would prove an insuperable barrier to our happiness. Fortunately Mrs. Griffen was more favorable to me.

Annie and her mother used to spend their summers at Pittsfield, Massachusetts, while Mr. Griffen stayed in the city. I would go up there on week ends. We would visit Annie's friends and go to dances but mostly we took long bicycle rides together.

In the city I passed the Griffen house daily on my way to work and almost always Annie would be at the window to wave to me. We also had a code of signals. If the shades were up, it meant that her father was out and I could call. If the shades were drawn, I walked on.

At other times Annie and I would meet in Central Park and, sitting on a park bench, I would tell her how we would get married as soon as I had earned enough money to support us. Our hopes would be high one day, when my little speculations would seem to be booming. The next day our hopes would be down, along with the market.

In 1951 Robert Moses showed me a site in Central Park where he wanted to erect a shelter under which people could play chess and checkers. Moses asked if I would finance the building of the shelter. I took one look at the site and agreed. Moses was surprised at how quickly I had decided. I did not tell him that the site he had picked was where Annie and I used to sit.

2

In my first year as a partner, our firm cleared $48,000, of which my share was $6000. That was far more than I had expected to make and might have enabled us to get married had I held on to it. But I still was overtrading. When I struck a line of speculation that my judgment told me was going to turn out well, I would buy stocks or bonds to the limit of my resources. Some market fluctuation would come along and swamp me. Only after this happened again and again did I learn the lesson of not overplaying my hand and of always holding back some part of my capital as a reserve. Had I learned this earlier I would have saved myself many a heartache in going broke again and again.

In the spring of 1897, near the close of my second year as a Housman partner, I managed to scrape together a few hundred dollars with which I bought on margin 100 shares of American Sugar Refining. This transaction marked an important change in my approach to speculation. Before I bought these sugar stocks, I made a thorough study of the sugar company's prospects. One could say I still was gambling, but this time I had formed my own judgment of what would happen after a careful analysis of the facts.

At the time American Sugar Refining controlled three-fourths of U.S. sugar production. It had a $25,000,000 surplus and always had paid excellent dividends. Yet the company's future was clouded in uncertainty.

The company, or "Sugar Trust" as it usually was referred to, had become involved in a commercial war with Arbuckle Brothers, the coffee merchants. Each was invading the other's field.

Another complication was the threat of a congressional investigation. Raw sugar was then imported under an ad valorem tariff. There were rumors that the sugar company's importations had been undervalued. Eventually an investigation was held. The charges were found to have some basis and the sugar company was obliged to pay between $2,000,-000 and $3,000,000 in back duties.

At the time I bought my sugar stock, however, the decisive question was the tariff. Particularly among farmers, considerable antagonism was felt toward the "trusts," and this had been reflected in the agitations of the Populist party. A bill lowering the sugar tariff had passed the House. Since this would have exposed our refineries to foreign competition, the stock of the sugar company dropped sharply.

Following the debate in the Senate, I made up my mind that the Senate would continue the tariff since the agricultural West would feel that a tariff benefited our own sugar-beet growers. That had been the chief argument of the sugar representatives in Washington, and at length it prevailed. When the bill which was passed left tariff rates substantially as they were, the stock of American Sugar Refining rose with a burst, touching 159 early in September.

I had been "parlaying" my profits—that is, as the sugar stock rose, I used my earnings to buy still more stock. When I sold out, my total profit was about $60,000, which made me a Croesus in my own eyes.

The first thing I did was to telephone Annie Griffen to tell her that at last we could get married. At first she couldn't believe it and kept saying, "You'll lose it as quickly as you made it." I assured her, "This time I'll keep it." I told her I was going to speak to her father that very night.

Mr. Griffen received me most courteously but was no less firm in his refusal. He said I was as agreeable a young man as had ever come to his house; but I had my religion and Annie had hers. He insisted that this difference constituted too great a peril for a happy marriage.

I told this to Annie, but it did not change her willingness to marry me. We set our wedding for October 20, 1897.

3

I had hardly cashed in my earnings on the sugar stock than I decided to buy a seat on the Stock Exchange. It cost $19,000. When I told Mother about it I remember how pleased she was and how she told me, "Yes, and you will go further."

That same night Mother and I were playing solitaire. Following an old custom I played the cards while Mother turned the pack. We had just about finished the game when Harty came in. It was past midnight. He and Miss Nethersole had been engaged in a long discussion about the renewal of Harty's contract. The talk had not been a happy one.

As a way out of his difficulty, I offered Harty my seat on the Stock Exchange, to which I had not yet taken title, if he would settle down. He accepted it, ending his career as an actor.

Not until I lay in bed, trying to get to sleep, did I realize what I had done. If I had taken out my heart and laid it quivering on a table, I do not see how I could have felt greater agonies. After tossing restlessly through much of the night, I finally decided there was only one thing to do—get myself another seat.

Annie and I were married in her home by the Reverend Dr. Richard Van Horne, a relative of Mr. Griffen. A little man with a full white beard, Dr. Van Horne had the appearance and manners of a typical minister. Before the ceremony he told me he intended to omit from the Episcopalian ritual certain references to the Father, the Son, and the Holy Ghost. I thanked him for his thoughtfulness in trying to meet the forms of my faith but assured him that as far as I was concerned, he could read the ritual as he had always read it.

For our honeymoon, we made a leisurely trip to Washington and then went by boat to Old Point Comfort on Chesapeake Bay. Never a good sailor, I got seasick. We then went South to my birthplace in Camden.

When we returned to New York we lived for a time with my parents, who by this time owned their own home at 51 West 70th Street. We then rented a small dwelling at 345 West End Avenue, not over fifteen feet wide. Our first child, Belle, was born in August, 1899, at Father's summer cottage in New Jersey. Father delivered her.

The first house we owned was a spacious four-story brownstone at 351 West 86th Street, where Bernard, Junior, was born. Our house was at the very end of the trolley-car line and one of the streetcar drivers, Peter Minnaugh, became a family friend. We always had a warming cup of coffee waiting for him on wintry days. Each March 17, on Bernard's birthday, Peter would dress up and come by to give my son a gold piece.

From there we moved to another spacious brownstone at 6 West 52nd Street, and eventually to Fifth Avenue near the corner of 86th Street.

Remembering the years my wife had waited for me, I always tried to make up for it by surprising her with gifts of various kinds. Once I brought her an expensive ring. "Don't give me anything more," she said, "I have everything I want."

That pleased me.

Mr. Griffen had withheld his consent to the last and had not been at our wedding. In time, however, he became reconciled. I was gratified to hear him admit that he had been wrong in thinking our marriage would not prove successful because of our differences in religion.

Perhaps one reason why our marriage turned out happily was that we respected one another's beliefs. For some years after our marriage my wife would accompany me to the synagogue for Friday evening services. I always observed the Jewish holy days—as I still do. My wife attended her own church.

We agreed that our two daughters, Belle, who was born in 1899, and Renee, who was born in 1905, should be baptized and brought up in the faith of their mother. With my son, we decided to let him make his own choice of religion when he grew up.

There are many aspects of religious belief on which I never have been able to satisfy myself. One rule I always have held to has been never to question anyone's faith or try in any way to influence it. How a man or woman feels about God has always seemed to me an intensely personal matter, something each person should decide for himself or herself—and which others should respect, whatever the decision.

9. My First Big Deal

IN RETROSPECT it now seems clear that my profits in sugar marked the beginning of my education in what makes a successful speculator.

Modern usage has made the term "speculator" a synonym for gambler and plunger. Actually the word comes from the Latin *speculari*, which means to spy out and observe.

I have defined a speculator as a man who observes the future and acts before it occurs. To be able to do this successfully—and it is an ability of priceless value in all human affairs, including the making of peace and war—three things are necessary:

First, one must get the facts of a situation or problem.

Second, one must form a judgment as to what those facts portend.

Third, one must act in time—before it is too late.

I have heard many men talk intelligently, even brilliantly, about something—only to see them proven powerless when it comes to acting on what they believe.

This need to act in time may point to the harshest single dilemma of a democratic society. In a democracy the will of the majority is supposed to govern; but with many crucial problems, if action is delayed until the need is apparent to everyone, it will be too late. To be evident to all, a danger must be on top of us or out of hand.

There are some problems on whose solution we must wait for the workings of time. But with many other problems inaction is the worst possible course.

For example, my experience as chairman of the War Industries Board in World War One taught that if inflation and profiteering were to be prevented in a second war, a ceiling would have to be imposed on all prices, wages, rents, and profits at the very start of the emergency. But when World War Two started, both President Franklin Roosevelt and Congress decided to "wait and see." The necessary over-all ceilings were not imposed for two years, and then only after the inflationary race was on. The same process of wait and err was repeated with the Korean War.

If effective measures to prevent inflation had been taken at the outset of both these conflicts, the burden of our national debt would be hardly half of what it is now. We would not be plagued by many of the problems that afflict us today.

Similarly, in other governmental affairs, things that once were possible became impossible or too costly when action was delayed too long. Whenever I think back to what Woodrow Wilson tried to do, I am struck by how the price of making peace has soared over the years. When Wilson proposed that we join the League of Nations in 1919, this action seemed too drastic for many Americans. But how little it was compared to what we already have been called upon to do for the cause of peace, and how much more we and our children still must do.

All through the cold war we have heard much of policies which were directed toward "buying time." We have not yet asked ourselves: What are we buying time for? Is time working in favor of peace? And, if not, how can we see that it does?

In the stock market one quickly learns how important it is to act swiftly. I recall one unforgettable experience.

I was spending the July Fourth week end with my parents at Long Branch, New Jersey. Late on Sunday night, Arthur Housman telephoned to say that a newspaperman had told him that Admiral Schley had destroyed the Spanish fleet at Santiago. Coming after Dewey's victory at Manila Bay, the news foretold a speedy end to the Spanish-American War.

The next day being the Fourth of July, the American exchanges would be closed. But the London exchanges would be open. Sizable profits could be made by placing orders for American stocks on the London Exchange when it opened. To do that we had to get to New York and be on the cables by daylight.

At that hour on Sunday night, however, no trains were running. Routing out some railroad people, I hired a loco-motive and tender with a coach attached to carry me to the ferry on the Jersey shore of the Hudson. It could not have been much more than two in the morning when Clarence Housman, my brother Sailing, and I were hurtling through the darkness on our way to New York.

That was my first ride on a "special" train. What a thrill it was! As our special roared past sleeping towns and hamlets it seemed to me that I was repeating on a smaller scale the financial feat which legend ascribed to Nathan Rothschild at the Battle of Waterloo.

In honoring Wellington's drafts when the English govern-ment was unable to do so, Rothschild had staked his fortune on the overthrow of Napoleon. Wellington's campaign in Belgium started badly, which depressed English securities. Rothschild, who had crossed the Channel to get first news of events, is said to have been on the field of Waterloo when the tide of battle turned against Napoleon. By getting word of this to London a few hours in advance of the official couriers he enabled the Rothschilds to make large purchases before shares rebounded.

As our train sped through the dark, it seemed that history was repeating itself. Thinking of how American arms had been victorious on land and sea from Cuba to the Philippines, halfway around the world, I felt the surge of empire welling within me. No thought entered my head of the problems and responsibilities that an "American Empire" might bring in years to come.

When we got to our office in lower Manhattan, I found that in my haste I had forgotten the key. Fortunately the transom was open. Sailing weighed only about a hundred and fifty pounds so I boosted him through. Before sunrise I was on the cable.

A few minutes after the London market opened the essentials of the picture were before us. Arthur Housman, who arrived at the office a bit later, cranked the telephone, interrupting the holiday slumbers of our customers. Always an optimist, he was made for the job. Snatches of his excited phrases drifted over to where I was busy with the cables. "Great American victory . . . United States a world power . . . New possessions . . . New markets . . . Empire rivaling England's . . . Biggest stock boom in years . . ."

We got an order from nearly everyone he called. We made large purchases of American stocks in London to fill these orders and to hold for ourselves. The next morning when the Exchange in New York opened, stocks advanced all along the line. Our London purchases showed good profits immediately. We had scored almost a clean beat on the other New York houses. In addition to the quick profits, which were large, the coup gave A. A. Housman & Company the name of being an alert firm which knew when to act.

2

I don't know whether the new fame of our firm was responsible, but a few months later a proposition was brought to Arthur Housman which proved one of the turning points in my career.

It led to the biggest undertaking that had come my way yet, bringing me into stock market operations in a new way. It also marked the beginning of a long and intimate friendship with one of the financial giants of that day, Thomas Fortune Ryan.

Ryan was a striking figure—six feet one inch tall—with the softest, slowest, gentlest Southern voice you ever heard. When he wanted to be particularly impressive, he would whisper. But he was lightning in action and the most resourceful man

I ever knew intimately in Wall Street. Nothing ever seemed to take him by surprise.

The son of a poor Virginia farmer, Ryan had hacked his way to wealth and power. Many people spoke harshly of him as ruthless and not to be trusted. A grand jury investigation of his role in the Metropolitan Street Railway Company, after its collapse, concluded that no crime had been committed but found "many things deserving of severe condemnation." Still, I found him exact in all his transactions with me.

At the time I first met him, Ryan had established himself as a dominating power in Tammany Hall and controlled the New York City Transit System. He was about to invade the tobacco empire of James Duke.

Duke was no light man to tangle with. One story told of him illustrated the force of his character. Once several of his associates used James R. Keene to buy a controlling interest in American Tobacco. Whereupon Duke told them bluntly that while they might own the company they did not own him, Duke, and that he would go out and start a rival tobacco business. Duke's opponents were bested. They were smart enough not to want the American Tobacco Company without his brains.

Duke then had gone on to swallow competitor after competitor until in 1898 only three independents worthy of mention remained outside of his "Trust." One was W. T. Blackwell & Company, whose famed Bull Durham was a favorite of those who rolled their own cigarettes. The other two independents were the National Cigarette Company, whose Admirals ran puff for puff with Duke's Sweet Caporals, and Liggett & Myers, whose Star Brand of chewing tobacco outsold Duke's Battle Axe. Duke was reported then to be spending a million dollars a year promoting the Battle Axe brand.

Today, of course, cigarettes represent the bulk of tobacco sales; but in 1898 we still were primarily a nation of chewers, pipe and cigar smokers, and snuff dippers. Of the three independents, Liggett & Myers, with its chewing tobacco, was the most important property. In those days the only women consumers were country folk, largely in the South, who enjoyed tobacco in a cob pipe or as snuff or a chew. At the time, as well, an energetic campaign was being waged against cigarettes by the churches and Sunday schools. I hope I do not impair anyone's faith in the motives of mankind when I say that much of this high-minded propaganda was secretly financed by the plug tobacco and cigar interests, who used innocent crusaders as catspaws.

I myself had given up trying to learn to chew since it made me sick, and contented myself with rolling my own cigarettes of Bull Durham.

Liggett & Myers, along with Blackwell and National Cigarette, had rebuffed every Duke overture for a friendly merger. They also had successfully beaten off every effort to drive them out of business by the price-cutting and advertising campaigns which Duke waged relentlessly.

Then in the fall of 1898 one of these independents, National Cigarette, was purchased by a syndicate headed by Thomas Fortune Ryan. National then was merged into the newly organized Union Tobacco Company, which, although inconspicuously chartered, actually was controlled by Ryan, William C. Whitney, P. A. B. Widener, Anthony N. Brady, William L. Elkins, and others of that caliber. Its president was William H. Butler, who had been a vice president of the American Tobacco Company but had broken with Duke.

About this time our firm received a valuable lead on the developing tobacco war. It was brought to us by C. W. Hazeltine, or Lieutenant Hazeltine, as we called him. A graduate of Annapolis, Hazeltine had resigned from the Navy for the more remunerative pursuit of business. Returning to the service for our brief war with Spain, he was now out of uniform again.

One day he came into our office to see Arthur Housman. After a brief talk together, he and Mr. Housman drew up their chairs at my desk. Hazeltine explained that he had learned that Union Tobacco was planning on buying Liggett & Myers, which would make it a worthy rival of Duke's company. Hazeltine stressed that he knew the Liggett & Myers people well and that he thought he could bring us into contact with them.

My first move was to call on George Butler, a brother of William H. Butler, the one-time American Tobacco executive who was now president of the Union, and then on Mr. Ryan, neither of whom I had ever met before.

Their conversation was guarded at first, but I gathered that Hazeltine was correct about their wanting to purchase Liggett & Myers. Moreover, with the information Hazeltine had given me, I was able to convince these gentlemen that I might be useful to them in the matter.

As far as Butler and his brother were concerned, I learned that this was to be a real war against Duke. Butler's object was to unite the three big independents under the Union standard in a combination that could make it hot for Duke.

Not long afterward—early in December of 1898—Union Tobacco announced that it had acquired Blackwell with its famous Bull Durham brand. This left Liggett & Myers as the one large independent not under the control of either Duke or Ryan.

Whatever he may have thought of Butler's insurgency before this, Duke now realized that he had a fight on his hands. The Liggett & Myers shares happened to be held mostly by St. Louis people. Duke's agents hastened to St. Louis and began dangling attractive offers before the Liggett & Myers stockholders.

Ryan summoned me to his office, where he introduced me to William H. Page, a lawyer. Ryan told us to go to St. Louis and try to beat the Duke people to the punch. Page and I went out on the train together.

As in my case, this was Page's first undertaking of importance for Mr. Ryan. In St. Louis we established ourselves at the Southern Hotel. George Butler was already there. We started by looking up Colonel Moses Wetmore, the president of Liggett & Myers.

Colonel Moses was a colorful figure—affable and astute. He owned the Planters Hotel and maintained an apartment there in which we spent some delightful evenings.

Another person much in evidence was William J. Stone, nicknamed "Gumshoe Bill," who was either an attorney for Liggett & Myers or for Colonel Wetmore, I forget which. "Gumshoe Bill" had been governor of Missouri. Later, as a U.S. Senator, he was one of the eleven "willful men" who filibustered against President Wilson's effort to arm our merchant ships just before our entrance into World War One.

Curiously, I remember little of the pourparlers, which extended over several weeks. Our tactics, insofar as we had any tactics, consisted first of all of being agreeable socially.

St. Louis, then at least, was semi-Southern and no place for high-pressure methods. Butler, an old friend of Colonel Moses, was an excellent card player and a fine storyteller. So was Page. Nearly every evening they met the Colonel in his apartment at the Planters for a friendly glass and a game of cards. The mission assigned to Lieutenant Hazeltine and myself was to keep in touch with some of the Liggett heirs who were large holders of stock. I can best describe the whole campaign in the words of Page, who said, "we wore Colonel Moses down with amiability."

Many newspaper stories were run about the negotiations, and for the first time in my life I found myself in the spotlight. Naturally this was not unpleasant to a twenty-eight-year-old, undertaking his first important business mission. One day, the papers would report that representatives of the Trust had been victorious. Next day, the situation would be "in doubt." The day after, the story would be that Colonel Wetmore had sold out to us.

Local feeling was much excited. St. Louis was proud of Liggett & Myers and wished the company to maintain its independence. There was a special prejudice against the Trust. On one occasion about a hundred members of the local grocers' association marched in a body to the Liggett &

Myers plant bearing badges and signs reading, "Opposed to Trusts." Colonel Moses met them personally and without promising anything sent them back happy.

The upshot of the business was that the Liggett heirs and other stockholders gave the Colonel an option on their shares. This option, together with his large personal holdings, put the Colonel in a position to decide the course of events. He chose to come with us. An agreement was formulated giving us an option on more than one half of the capital stock of Liggett & Myers. The price was a little more than $6,600,000.

When the papers were being drawn up the question arose as to who should pay the legal fees, an item of some $200,000. Page and Governor Stone decided to toss a coin. We lost but I believe it was worth it because of the friendship that was created among the St. Louis tobacco people.

3

By this time the battle between Ryan's crowd and Duke had spread over a wider front. As part of the struggle, Duke had set up a new subsidiary, the Continental Tobacco Company, whose shares were traded on the Curb Exchange.

The Curb Exchange in those days was situated in the open street in front of the Stock Exchange. The brokers would gather on Broad Street and transact their business in the open air, rain or shine, blizzard or heat wave. Often they got orders to buy and sell through signals from clerks in the windows of the offices nearby. The brokers would signal back the orders as they were entered.

To harass Duke and to impress him with Union's strength and resources, Ryan decided on an operation against Continental's stock. I was recalled from St. Louis and placed in charge of the operation. In St. Louis I had been one of a crowd. Here I was to be in command, taking orders only from Ryan.

I would see him every morning. He resided on West 72nd Street, only a few blocks from where we lived, and I would stop in on my way downtown. Usually this was before Mr. Ryan was up. Generally I was ushered into his bedroom and sometimes he talked to me while he shaved.

Some years later there was much talk of an estrangement between Ryan and his wife, but at that time they seemed a devoted couple. Ryan, it was true, appeared to have no thoughts except for matters of business. His wife, in contrast, was wrapped up in her home and her growing family. Her children, all boys, fairly overran the house. That winter she knitted a little woolen jacket for our baby girl, Belle.

The trading in Continental Tobacco shares was my first large operation on the Curb Exchange, and one of the few I ever conducted there. I was not then a first-rate floor trader and, indeed, never became one. Somehow I lacked that talent. Fortunately I found this out early enough. Many men will save a few dollars in commissions by acting as their own brokers, only to lose thousands.

For this operation I engaged two brokers. Mr. Ryan allowed me $200,000 in the matter of losses. I started my operation shortly after New Year's of 1899.

Continental was selling at 45. I drove the stock down to 30 in six weeks. Never could the stock have been driven down that far but for the fear that a tobacco war was at hand which would mean losses to the Continental Company.

Usually a broker speculating on the short side of the market will continue to sell a stock when it is dropping in an effort to drive it down still further. I adopted the tactic of buying when the market was weak, reselling the stock when it rallied. This enabled me to make a net profit even while pushing down the price of the Continental stock.

One day when I had been more than usually successful, Mr. Ryan rushed down to our office and told me to let up. He asked me how much money I had lost for him. I told him that I had lost nothing but had made a good deal for his account.

"I want you to annoy them but I don't want you to ruin them," he admonished me, but I knew he was pleased.

Through the raid on Continental, Ryan had demonstrated his power to shake the Trust. No sooner was I told to stop my operations than rumors of an understanding between Duke and the Ryan forces were heard on the Street.

At their March 1, 1899, meeting, the directors of American Tobacco authorized the purchase of Union Tobacco. Union was to bring with it Blackwell's Bull Durham, National Cigarette, and the Liggett & Myers option. Ryan, Widener, and Brady were elected directors of American Tobacco. The net result of the whole transaction was that Ryan and his people virtually perfected American Tobacco's monopoly at a handsome profit to themselves even while they broke into Mr. Duke's inner circle as well.

The Butlers had started Union Tobacco to build a combination that would humble Duke's Trust, but Ryan saw another solution and Ryan had his way. The charge was made that from the beginning Ryan was acting in secret collusion with Duke. I do not know the truth of the matter, but that hypothesis is difficult to sustain in the light of the operations Ryan directed me to make in Continental shares.

With the end of the warfare in tobacco shares, the stock of American Tobacco and its subsidiaries soared to such an extent that the whole operation by both Duke and Ryan was more than paid for, covering all their previous temporary losses.

One further point might be noted. In time the government forced the breakup of the Tobacco Trust despite Duke's bitter opposition. I happened to meet Duke some years later. "As hard as I fought the dissolution of the Tobacco Trust," he told me, "I'd fight even harder any effort to put it back together again. We made more money after we were broken up and had competition."

That is often the way of monopoly. Its disadvantages are not known even by those who operate the monopoly.

4

This tobacco venture was the beginning of my business association with Thomas Ryan, who remained my friend until his death in 1928. Ryan was not an easy man to know. Toward some people he exhibited a curious inconsistency— sometimes being generous, at other times relentless.

I annoyed him several times by declining to be tied to him except on a specific venture, and by insisting on playing the game according to the rules as I saw them and not as he or anyone else saw them.

This attitude of independence came to test early in our relationship when Ryan and William C. Whitney tried to put James R. Keene behind prison bars. They sought to indict him on charges of undermining a bank they were interested in. When they asked me to testify, I refused.

Those old wars were bloody and implacable ones in which the antagonists neither gave nor asked for quarter.

I thought that my refusal to testify against Keene would mean an end to my association with Ryan, but after that he seemed to give me more of his confidence than ever. It was a source of some pride to me that I was able to hold the confidence of both Ryan and Keene even when they were such bitter enemies.

Once in those early days Mr. Ryan asked me to come to his office in the newly formed Morton Trust Company. His desk was in an inside room. I asked how he felt about the attacks— which were justifiable—being made upon him because of the Metropolitan Street Railway Company. In his usual calm, slow, low voice, he replied, "Well, you don't see any brickbats coming through that window."

Then he rose and went to a large safe, saying, "Here are a lot of things I wish you would take down and sell."

The safe was filled with Georgia Pacific First, Second, and Third Incomes. The bonds had been tossed carelessly into the safe as if they were worthless. At the time, as I recall, their average price was about 9.

I got a horse-drawn cab. The bonds filled the bottom of the cab, leaving no place to put my legs when I sat on the seat. Thus I drove to our office. I began to study the Georgia road and to try to interest people in the bonds.

One day when the bonds were priced around 30, Mr. Ryan telephoned and wanted to know why I had not sold them. I told him I was following his instructions to sell when I deemed it best and I felt the bonds would go still higher. He kept after me so I sold them at around 50. Eventually they advanced to nearly par.

Not long after the Liggett & Myers deal, Mr. Ryan gave me an order to buy control of the Norfolk & Western. I managed to buy a large block of stock for Ryan without advancing the price materially, but not enough for control.

Another time Mr. Ryan asked me to acquire control of the Wabash Railroad. By then I was a big trader in my own right and could execute orders for others without arousing the suspicion that I might not be buying for myself. Sometimes, in fact, the very people who had given me purchase orders would try to throw dust into the eyes of the curious by saying, "I wonder whom Baruch is buying all that stock for."

One aspect of this Wabash purchase may be worth noting to illustrate how brokers worked together. As I walked to the Wabash trading post, I saw Dave Barnes sitting there. Dave was a good friend whom I had come to know at Long Branch. He and some friends liked to swim out into the ocean with small flasks of whiskey strung around their necks, taking nips from the flasks to keep from getting cold.

On this day Dave was offering Wabash common, which was around 3 or 4 a share, and preferred around 17. If I bought Dave's stock, I knew he would turn around and start buying Wabash shares to sell back to me at a higher price.

I went over and, sitting down next to him, said, "Dave,

take my advice and don't sell this stock, but call it a day and leave the crowd."

"All right, Barrie," he replied and got up and left. For some reason unknown to me Barnes always called me Barrie.

So I went on buying Wabash—common and preferred—but Barnes never interfered with me. Had I tried to outsmart him it might have cost my client many thousands of dollars. I simply asked Dave to lay off and let me execute my order. He knew that some day I would do the same thing for him. That is how the brokers of that day got along when they knew and trusted each other.

The commission to our firm for my part of the Liggett & Myers transaction was $150,000, not a very large commission considering the size and importance of the deal, but I did not know as much about commissions then as I did later on. Nevertheless, that $150,000 was a big thing for A. A. Housman & Company. It contributed considerably to our profit that year, which was $501,000. One third of this profit went to me, my share having been generously raised from one eighth by Arthur Housman. We were now in large offices at 20 Broad Street and on our way to becoming one of the big brokerage houses of the financial district.

10. I Make a Mistake

WITH MY SHARE of that good year's profit in hand, I bought another seat on the Stock Exchange for $39,000. This was a bit more than twice the $19,000 I had paid two years earlier for the seat I turned over to Harty, but I didn't mind the increase in the cost.

Seeing my name listed among the members of the Exchange acted as a wonderful cordial to my spirits. Aglow with pride and self-assurance, I began looking about for new financial adventures. But I was soon to learn that it is one thing to make money and another thing to keep it. In fact, making money is often easier than keeping it.

The blunder I now committed would not be excusable even for the rankest amateur in the stock market. I heard that American Spirits Manufacturing was a good thing to buy. Thomas Fortune Ryan had expressed this opinion, or so I was told by a man much closer to Mr. Ryan than I was. Having faith in Mr. Ryan's sagacity, I bought.

American Spirits Manufacturing Company was a remnant —hangover might be a more accurate word—of the old Distilling & Cattle Feeding Association, or "Whiskey Trust," which went to smash in the panic of 1893. At the time I bought its stock, American Spirits was still the largest manufacturer and distributor of liquor in America. Hearing that a move was brewing to combine American with three other large liquor concerns, which would have just about bottled up the whiskey business in the United States, I put everything I had into American Spirits stock.

News of the forthcoming consolidation was made public— but, contrary to expectations, the fizz went out of American Spirits stock. Since I had left myself without cash reserves, I was forced to sell other holdings to cover my margins. It proved a case of sending good money after bad.

Within a few weeks after the successful conclusion of the Liggett & Myers operation, which had left me thinking rather highly of myself, I was scraping bottom.

It was one of the quickest losses I ever have suffered, and the largest loss in proportion to my total fortune. I had bought my wife a shiny black cabriolet, with plate glass lamps, manned by two liveried footmen. I had to tell her we would have to give up our "two on the box" and defer our other dreams.

Rather sheepishly I admitted to Mr. Ryan the cause of my comedown in the world.

"Did I tell you to buy that whiskey stock?" he asked.

No, I said, I had never asked him about it, but I had heard a man close to him who liked me say that Ryan thought well of it.

"Never pay any attention to what I am reported to have said to anybody else," Ryan replied in his quiet voice. "A lot of people who ask me questions have no right to answers. But you have the right."

I learned a good deal from this misadventure in whiskey. It taught me one thing about tips, namely, that people sometimes drop remarks calculated to bring the little minnows into the net to be served up for the big fish. I had been a little minnow.

The longer I operated in Wall Street the more distrustful I became of tips and "inside" information of every kind. Given time, I believe that inside information can break the Bank of England or the United States Treasury.

It is not simply that inside information often is manufactured to mislead the gullible. Even when insiders know what their companies are doing, they are likely to make serious blunders just because they are in the know.

There is something about inside information which seems to paralyze a man's reasoning powers. For one thing, people place a great store on knowing something other people do not know, even if it is not true. A man with no special pipelines of information will study the economic facts of a situation and will act coldly on that basis. Give the same man inside information and he feels himself so much smarter than other people that he will disregard the most evident facts. I have seen insiders hold on to their stocks when it was obvious to nearly everyone else that they should be sold.

Over the long run, I have found it better to rely on one's own cold detached judgment of the economic facts. Otto Kahn, of the famous banking house of Kuhn, Loeb & Co., liked to relate how he met me one day when there was considerable market activity in Union Pacific. He started to tell me something when I stopped him by saying, "Please don't tell me anything that is happening to Union Pacific. I don't want my judgment affected by anything you might say."

The whole chronicle of the American Spirits enterprise was strewn with the wreckage of fortunes. James Keene remarked to me afterward that some of the men connected with it were so crooked they could meet themselves coming around a corner. This observation is not offered to excuse myself or to explain my losses. Nothing but my own bad judgment was responsible.

My course violated every sound rule of speculation. I acted on unverified information after superficial investigation and, like thousands of others before and since, got just what my conduct deserved.

2

After the Whiskey Trust debacle, it took some months to get back my courage, but this came in time. Looking about for an opening, I began to take note of the doings of ex-Governor Roswell P. Flower.

Henry Clews once said that Flower reminded him of a well-fed farmer in Sunday clothes. The description was a good one. Flower had, indeed, begun life on a farm in up-state New York and, fatherless at an early age, was left not only to shift for himself but to play a man's role in the family. He had been a congressman and governor of New York.

Mr. Flower was an executive of proven experience. Both in Chicago Gas and the Chicago, Rock Island and Pacific, he had shown he could take a rundown corporation and lift its earnings by introducing competent administrative methods. So high was Governor Flower's prestige that it was said he could run up any stock on the board by repeating to friends in the Street that it was due for a rise.

At the time of which I write, Governor Flower had taken charge of the Brooklyn Rapid Transit Company. Its stock was selling at around 20. The Governor announced that B.R.T. had been mismanaged and under competent direction was capable of earnings which would justify a value of 75 for its stock. He began to straighten things out in the company. Its revenues increased. Up went the stock.

In the spring of 1899, B.R.T. was a leader in the market. I had made some moves on the rise but was beginning to become apprehensive. The company's statements were not as clear as such statements should be. I had a hunch that something was not quite right.

Still, every prediction Governor Flower had made to date had been fulfilled. When the stock was at 20 he had declared it would go to 75: when it was at 50 he had predicted it would go to 125. Each of these forecasts had come true.

In April the stock touched 137 and then began to sag. There was some talk whether the stock had been pushed up too fast and too high for any sound prospect of earnings. I shared the belief that it had.

The morning papers of May 12, 1899, carried a statement over Governor Flower's name that the Transit Company's earnings were increasing steadily and that its prospects were rosy. This had a stimulating effect.

But in the afternoon the stock broke when the story

reached the Exchange, coming from I know not where, that Governor Flower was dangerously ill. That evening, after the Exchange closed, the *Wall Street Journal* published a reassuring leader under the headline, "Ex-Governor Flower All Right." The article said he had suffered an attack of indigestion. But by the time the newspaper reached the street, Governor Flower's condition had changed and he was dying.

Fatigued, he had gone to a Long Island country club for a day's fishing. The weather was warm, and after a substantial luncheon such as the Governor always ate—only he called it dinner, not luncheon—he drank a pitcher of ice water. Almost immediately he was stricken. At ten-thirty that night his death was announced.

The next morning a virtual panic reigned on the Stock Exchange. Disastrous consequences might have ensued but for the strong pools which were organized to cushion the shock in the market. Participating in these pools were J. P. Morgan, the Vanderbilts, Darius Mills, John D. Rockefeller, Henry H. Rogers, and James Keene.

After dropping to 100, the stock rallied and crept up to 115 as the story of the big fellows' support spread. Then the big fellows, having averted a serious panic, quietly began to step out of B.R.T. While the rest of the market advanced, B.R.T. sank toward par. One September day it struck par. To hold the price there Allie Wormser, the sportsman son of one of the partners of I. & S. Wormser, bid par for two or three thousand shares. In a flash, I sold them to him.

They never sold at that price again. Before the year was out, B.R.T. was down in the 60's. In the whole B.R.T. transaction, my profit was about $60,000. My confidence began to return.

3

A critical test of this newly returned self-confidence was soon to come. In the spring of 1901—I was thirty-one at the time—the organizers of the Amalgamated Copper Company got together to put up the market value of their stock. The Amalgamated had been formed in 1899 as a combine which proposed to do for copper what Rockefeller had done with Standard Oil. In his sensational *Frenzied Finance,* published in 1905, Thomas Lawson told the strange way in which this outfit was put together.

The Amalgamated organizers began by purchasing Anaconda Copper and other properties from Marcus Daly for $39,000,000. According to Lawson, Daly and his friends received a check on the National City Bank for this sum with the understanding that they were to cash it later.

Then the subscription books for shares in Amalgamated, which was capitalized at $75,000,000, were opened. Lawson was put in charge of arousing public interest. Some of the most luminous names in American finance—Henry H. Rogers, William Rockefeller, and James Stillman of the National City Bank—were advertised as sponsors of the company. As a result the issue was oversubscribed at $100 a share. Lawson went on to say that with this $75,000,000 in hand, the organizers told Mr. Daly that he could cash his check.

He did, leaving a balance of $36,000,000 to the credit of the company, whose organizers had not risked a penny of their own money.

None of these details was known, however, in the spring of 1901, when the Amalgamated organizers set out to control the world's copper supply. By June they had boosted the stock from around par to 130. Wall Street buzzed with talk of it going to 150 or 200.

At about this time, though, I happened to have a long talk with Herman Sielcken, a noted coffee merchant, whose judgment was sought after in all business matters. At the time he was in his vigor, just beyond middle age, sturdily built and over six feet tall, with black, piercing eyes. He enjoyed speculating in the stock market but his operations were confined to comparatively small amounts, more to test his judgment than to make money, since his coffee business was highly successful.

On this afternoon, at the Waldorf, where he lived, Mr. Sielcken drifted into an exposition of copper conditions. The high price then prevailing, he thought, was curtailing the use of the metal throughout the world. The market was becoming glutted. Our copper exports were declining. Moreover, the memory of an attempted copper corner in France a few years earlier was having its effect. Mr. Sielcken predicted that the Amalgamated's efforts to jack up copper prices would fail even as had the French corner.

I thought over Mr. Sielcken's remarks and made an investigation of my own. My findings justified his fears. During July and August the Amalgamated Copper stock began to drop. On September 6, 1901, President William McKinley was shot while attending the Pan-American Exposition at Buffalo. Only the power and prestige of J. P. Morgan averted a panic on the Stock Exchange. Stocks broke but rallied. About this time I decided to sell Amalgamated Copper short.

In selling Amalgamated short, I was, of course, backing my judgment that the stock would go down regardless of what the company's organizers might do to try to lift the stock. If the stock continued to rise, I would have to pay dearly for every share.

I had scarcely begun my operations when Thomas Ryan approached me and said, "Bernie, I hear you are short of Amalgamated Copper. I just want to let you know that the big fellows in it are going to twist your tail."

Among the "big fellows" who were working with Amalgamated was James Keene. Ryan's word and Keene's position naturally made me stop and think. But after thinking it over anew, I still felt convinced that the Amalgamated organizers were trying to defy the law of supply and demand. Recalling the teaching of Professor Newcomb at City College, I decided that, with the supply of copper likely to exceed demand, the price would have to drop, and so I continued to sell short.

At first I made money, for shortly after the Morgan rally the stock sagged back to around 106. Presently, however, Amalgamated rose again.

On September 14, President McKinley died, after assurances of his recovery had been spread from the most authoritative sources. This had a bad effect on the market. Moreover, there were whisperings in the Street that some of the insiders in Amalgamated Copper were trying to sell their stock. I increased my short position, but cautiously.

My confidence in the basic strength of my position grew as I heard squawks from the big insiders. I was told that if I continued to sell the stock I would only antagonize the big fellows, to which, in youthful cockiness, I replied in the words Bob Fitzsimmons once used, "The bigger they are, the harder they fall." I was also being told of how wicked it was to be short of the market and to tear down a constructive enterprise.

All this was nonsense, of course. If the Amalgamated organizers had not overcapitalized and then blown the stock up, it never would have risen to such heights or descended to the depths it afterward did. What was dropping the copper shares was the irresistible force of economic gravitation seeking its proper level.

I am not imputing evil motives. Many times, men engaged in enterprises of this kind have a vision of empire which, if proven sound, justifies the high prices they may have paid for properties. But I felt the whole course of the Amalgamated Copper people was unjustified by sound economics. I did not think them wise in jacking up copper prices artificially. That opinion I backed with my money and the money of no one else.

In the face of these attacks, I sat silent, knowing that if I was right, I would win. If I was wrong, I would lose.

This attitude of silence may have been a mistake. Perhaps I should have fought my critics with their own weapons, exposing their errors of judgment as I saw them, and even dealing in personalities. But I have followed this policy of silence throughout my Wall Street career. Possibly I overdid it, but I wished to go my speculative way alone and not have others following me as a result of anything I might say.

All eyes were centered on the approaching meeting of the board of directors of Amalgamated. Would they continue their eight-per-cent dividend? Cut it? Or omit it?

If they continued it, we "shorts" might be in a bad way. It was a week of excitement and uncertainty. On Thursday, September 19, the Exchange closed for McKinley's funeral. The consensus of New York's financial writers was that the dividend would remain unchanged.

The directors' meeting was held on Friday, September 20, 1901. After the market closed, came the momentous news that the dividend had been reduced from $8 to $6. In the short Saturday session Amalgamated lost about 7 points, closing just above 100. I expected that on Monday the crisis in my operations would come.

Then a strange thing happened, one that put me on the road to making an immediate fortune through no wisdom or forethought of my own. My mother telephoned saying, "Son, you know Yom Kippur is coming?" It fell on Monday, the next business day.

My heart sank. I knew Mother would expect me to keep that holiest of Jewish holy days, the Day of Atonement, which meant utter seclusion from all mundane matters.

I made my decision and set about doing what I could to anticipate what might happen. I told Eddie Norton, the broker whom I had been using to hammer down the stock, to continue his operations. Then, to protect myself against a possible rise in the stock, I told Harry Content, another broker, to start buying Amalgamated stock if it rose to a certain price. Although I was almost certain the stock would go down, one never could tell what these powerful interests might have up their sleeves. Thus I sought to protect myself against every contingency.

Then I left word that on Monday I would be inaccessible to everyone on all business matters, regardless of their nature.

Nevertheless, on Monday my telephone started ringing. We were still in our summer house at South Elberon, New Jersey. When New York could not reach me, the Long Branch brokers were asked to reach me. But I would take no message. In the afternoon my wife and I visited Mother at her house about a mile away. The telephone calls followed me there.

Only after sundown, which ends the holy day, did I learn what had happened. Amalgamated had opened at 100. Within an hour it dropped two points. A further decline was followed by a rally which held the stock above 97 until noon. If I had been on the floor at the time, I probably would have closed out then, taking a comparatively small profit and that would have been the end of the story. But, in the afternoon, the stock declined steadily, closing at 93¾, which left me a handsome profit and a fine margin of safety against a rally.

Thus fortified and confirmed in the belief that Amalgamated was destined to drop still further, I let my profits run. In December the stock touched 60.

I do not recall at just what figure I closed my transaction but my profits were around $700,000. It was the largest sum of money I had made up to that time in any single operation. It was made possible by two things—my acquiescence in my mother's request to observe a religious holiday and by the errors of the Amalgamated people in trying to defy the law of supply and demand.

Both my failure in whiskey and my success in copper emphasized one thing—the importance of getting the facts of a situation free from tips, inside dope, or wishful thinking. In the search for facts I learned that one had to be as unimpassioned as a surgeon. And if one had the facts right, one could stand with confidence against the will or whims of those who were supposed to know best.

Later in public life I found this rule equally valid and applicable. In every government assignment that was given me I would begin with a relentless search for the facts of the situation. President Wilson took to calling me "Dr. Facts."

I strove to let the facts shape my recommendations. Many times, as in my long fight against inflation during World War Two and afterward, friends would come up to me and argue, "Bernie, why aren't you more reasonable? What you propose isn't politically possible."

But even in such situations I held my ground, feeling that if the facts called for certain measures nothing less would suffice. I still believe that no President or Congress can make two and two equal anything but four.

11. *When Panic Strikes*

RATHER OFTEN I am asked why it is that we do not have any present-day equivalents to the financial giants who dominated Wall Street at the turn of the century. Is it that Americans have really become a new and softer breed?

Part of the answer, of course, is that today's stock market is drastically different from what it was in the days of Morgan, Rockefeller, Edward H. Harriman, and others. Government regulation has made illegal many of the practices engaged in even as late as 1929. The kind of trading that I did for Thomas Ryan in his tobacco war with James Duke would not be possible today; nor what I had done with Amalgamated Copper.

And, of course, the level of present-day taxes means that no matter how huge one's profits may be, a considerable part of them goes to the government.

Still, I believe, the main reason why Wall Street has lost that quality of dramatic personal adventure which was so marked in my youth will be found in the astonishing extension of the range and area of economic interests covered by the market's activities.

This change, in turn, reflects the equally astonishing transformation of America from a frontier-pushing people, concerned mainly with subduing a continent, to the prime stabilizing force for the whole of western civilization.

One might label this change as a shift from an era of almost unrestrained individualism to one of global responsibility. The meaning of this shift is something I would like to come back to later in this narrative, because it covers so much of our national history and remains one of the keys of understanding which may help us unlock the future.

My own career seems almost to have been a span between these two eras, not because I foresaw what was coming but primarily because I was thrust into the picture in such a way that I could hardly help but contribute to this transition. I came into the world of business and finance just in time to see the titans of finance at the zenith of their power. From the atmosphere generated by their example—and struggle—I was thrust abruptly into all the problems of global responsibility by my appointment as chairman of the War Industries Board in World War One.

After that war was over, when others sought a return to "normalcy," I continued to grapple with these problems in successive posts, from being an adviser to Woodrow Wilson at the Paris Peace Conference to representing the United States on the United Nations Commission on Atomic Energy.

For forty-odd years, in fact, I have found myself in the position of trying to reconcile what I learned about business in my earlier years with the newer national and global needs that a shrinking world has forced on us.

The extent to which the Wall Street of fifty years ago was subject to the influence, if not domination, of a few individuals may be difficult to realize, since it differs so markedly from today. The glamour figures of those days were largely financiers, with the newspapers and Sunday supplements generating much mystery and intrigue over what "they" were doing—the "they" being the Morgans and Harrimans, the Ryans, Rockefellers, and other financial "big shots."

As an amusing example of how the market could seem to be dominated by some bold figure, I recall a story about Dan Reid, who was a director of U. S. Steel but who still liked to play the role of the great big bear from time to time.

During one heavy stock decline, Reid raided stock after stock until he seemed to be in full control of the whole market. Actually his "raids" were made possible by an unsound market condition which gave a man with abounding courage an advantage that could be only temporary. None knew this better than Reid. Just the same, even the most powerful bankers were afraid of what Reid might do.

Reid happened to be quite fond of Henry P. Davison, then rightfully the most important junior partner of J. P. Morgan's. One day Reid telephoned Davison and asked:

"Harry, do *you* know what I am going to do?"

"No," said Mr. Davison.

"Do you *want* to know what I am going to do?"

"Yes," said Davison eagerly.

"You *really* want to know?"

"Yes," said Davison, ready to expect anything.

"Well," replied Reid, "I'm not going to do a damn thing."

Almost at once the market righted itself. Today, of course, no one man could run the market ragged for even a few days or stabilize it by a telephone call.

Perhaps an even more revealing illustration of the compact intimacy of the old stock market could be seen in the old Waldorf-Astoria, then located where the Empire State Building now stands. In those days, after the closing gong had sounded on the Exchange, most of the traders would gather at the Waldorf. To belong to the "Waldorf crowd" meant that a man had arrived. I had won admittance to this circle on the strength of the reputation I made in the purchase of the Liggett & Myers Tobacco Company.

On an afternoon or two at the Waldorf one might brush elbows with Richard Harding Davis, Mark Twain, Lillian Russell, Gentleman Jim Corbett, Admiral Dewey, Mark Hanna, Chauncey Depew, Diamond Jim Brady, Edwin Hawley, and countless presidents of banks and railroads. Judge Elbert Gary, the head of U. S. Steel, lived there, as did Charley Schwab and James Keene. It was at a private dinner party in the Waldorf that I saw John W. Gates place a $1,000,000 bet in a game of baccarat.

The fact that nearly everyone of importance in Wall Street could be found at the Waldorf made it a highly revealing laboratory for the study of human nature. Once, as will be related later, I used this fact to conduct an experiment in human psychology, by which a company was financed through the mere showing of a certified check. The various "rooms" of the Waldorf-Astoria—the Empire Room or Peacock Alley, the billiard room, or the Men's Café with its famous four-sided mahogany bar—were really like so many exhibition galleries in which every human trait was on display.

Sitting in these rooms, it was always an intriguing exercise to try to detect the doers from the braggarts, the genuine human article from the spurious. Nor will I ever forget how panic struck the Waldorf one night and transformed it from the preening ground of all that was fashionable to a lair of frightened animals.

It was the first time that I had witnessed a panic, and it lasted for only one night. Other panics I later experienced, such as those of 1907 and 1929, had far more devastating effects on the economy. Still, this particular panic of May 8, 1901, seemed all the more revealing, perhaps because it came and went so swiftly or because through chance I was able to watch it as if I were a spectator and not one of its hapless victims.

2

As with most financial panics the stage had been set in advance by extravagant hopes and talk of a "New Era." Varied factors contributed to this surge of optimism. Our victory over Spain had stirred fantastic dreams of imperialism and dazzling predictions of new foreign markets. The public was in the stock market as never before.

It was at this time, I believe, that women came into the market for the first time in any numbers. Over their teacups in the Waldorf's glass-enclosed Palm Room they talked knowingly of what U. S. Steel or Union Pacific or Amalgamated Copper was bound to do. Bellhops, waiters, barbers—everyone—had a "tip" to pass on. Since the market was rising, every bullish tip came true and every tipster seemed a prophet.

Several times it seemed that the market had run its course and that a healthy reaction was on the way. Then a new stock would be brought forward and there would be another balloon ascension. On the last day of April, 1901, the market had the biggest day in its history to that time—3,270,884 shares were traded. This represented an average of a million dollars a minute changing hands during the five hours the Exchange was open. The commissions to brokerage houses alone aggregated $800,000.

On May 3 the market broke from seven to ten points. Many persons, including myself, thought this was a sign that the long-anticipated decline had come. But then on Monday, May 6, a strange new factor entered the market—a spectacular rise in Northern Pacific.

In my entire career on the Stock Exchange, I do not recall another opening similar to this one. The first sale of Northern Pacific was at 114, or four points above its Saturday closing. On the second sale it jumped to 117. Thereafter the day was marked by spasmodic up-rushes as Eddie Norton, the floor member of Street & Norton, bought every share in sight at the market.

No one seemed able to fathom the cause of this rise. Directors of the Northern Pacific could not explain it. Bankers could not explain it. Eddie Norton, who was doing the buying, was not talking.

By a rare piece of good fortune I was one of the few persons in the world who knew, on that fateful Monday morning, the central fact behind the Northern Pacific's puzzling performance—that it represented not some mere market manipulation but a mighty battle for control of the road between E. H. Harriman and James Hill, represented by their respective bankers, Kuhn, Loeb & Company and J. P. Morgan.

Before disclosing the curiously informal manner in which I learned this information, let me sketch what was at issue between the contending giants.

The rise of Edward H. Harriman, who had come to Wall Street as an office boy, had long been a thorn in Mr. Morgan's side. Early in Harriman's climb he had met and bested Morgan not once but two or three times. A violent personal enmity grew up, which Mr. Morgan did not temper by his habit of referring to Harriman as "that two-dollar broker."

In the late nineties the Union Pacific seemed one of the most hopeless roads in the country. After Morgan refused to reorganize it, Harriman bought control, rehabilitated, and extended the road. He not only made it pay handsomely but he turned it into a worthy rival of the Great Northern and the Northern Pacific, which were under Hill-Morgan control.

Then Harriman bought the Southern Pacific, moving, as always, so quickly and silently that his object was accomplished before his adversaries knew what was in the wind. Thus did "that two-dollar broker" become one of the foremost railroad men of the world.

Incidentally, our firm did a large business for Mr. Harriman which was handled first by Arthur Housman and then by Clarence Housman. In 1906 Harriman had the Housmans place heavy bets on Charles Evans Hughes in his race for Governor of New York against William Randolph Hearst. After several hundred thousand dollars had been wagered, the Housmans stopped. Hearing of this, Harriman called them up.

"Didn't I tell you to bet?" he demanded. "Now go on."

Clarence Housman told me that when he was admitted into Harriman's office to report how much had been bet, he saw "Fingy" Conners, the Democratic boss of Buffalo. Conners may have been there to talk about contracts for handling Buffalo's wharf freight, but we were more cynical in explaining his presence there.

Harriman's purchase of the Southern Pacific was also handled largely through A. A. Housman & Company. Edwin C. Hawley conducted most of the operation. However, I had no part in the transaction and at the time did not know Mr. Harriman.

I do remember one day seeing on the floor of the Exchange a slightly bow-legged, nervous little man, with large round spectacles. Turning to one trader, I asked, "Who is that little fellow buying all that U.P. preferred?"

I was told he was Edward Harriman. I have no idea why he happened to be on the floor of the Exchange that day. I never saw him there again.

With Harriman controlling Union Pacific and Southern Pacific, the Hill-Morgan interests needed an entrance into Chicago. So they bought the Burlington, on which Harriman also had his eye. Harriman asked for a third interest in the purchase. Morgan refused. Harriman's response was one of the most audacious strokes in Wall Street's history—a secret move to purchase in the open market a majority of the $155,-000,000 common and preferred stock of the Northern Pacific Railroad.

Early in April, after refusing Harriman an interest in the Burlington, Morgan sailed for Europe. Harriman and Jacob H. Schiff, the senior partner of Kuhn, Loeb & Company, began purchasing the stock of the Northern Pacific.

Under the spur of this buying, N.P. rose about twenty-five points. But with the whole market surging forward, little was thought of it. Ironically, the general view was that N.P. was being bought by the public in anticipation of the strong position it would attain because of the Burlington deal. Even some Morgan and Northern Pacific insiders, tempted by the high prices, sold their Northern Pacific stock.

Late in April, James Hill, the veteran president of the Great Northern, in far-off Seattle, smelled a mouse. Ordering a special train and a clear track, Mr. Hill broke the existing record on a run to New York. He arrived on a Friday, May 3, and put up, as was his custom, at the Netherlands Hotel. That night Mr. Schiff informed him that Harriman controlled the Northern Pacific.

The shaggy-haired Westerner refused to believe it. Mr. Schiff, always the suavest of men, assured him that it was true.

Schiff, though, it turned out, was not entirely right. Harriman held a clear majority of the preferred stock and a clear

majority of the aggregate capital stock, common and preferred, but not a majority of common alone. On the next day,
a Saturday, Harriman telephoned Kuhn, Loeb to buy 40,000
shares of N.P. common, which would have given him a majority. The partner who took the message waited to consult
Mr. Schiff, who was at a synagogue. Schiff said not to make
the purchase that day.

By Monday it was too late. After his talk with Schiff, Hill
had sought out Robert Bacon of J. P. Morgan & Company. A
cable was sent to Morgan in Europe. On Sunday, May 5, Mr.
Morgan replied, authorizing the purchase of 150,000 shares
of Northern Pacific common at the market. What Schiff had
overlooked was that the Northern Pacific directors had the
power to retire the preferred stock and thus, through control
of the common stock, still could retain control of the railroad.

It was at this point that I got my line on what was going on.
This is how it happened.

3

As an office boy at Kohn's I had acquired the habit of getting downtown an hour or two before the Exchange opened
to see whether the London quotations offered opportunities
for making an arbitrage profit. On Mondays in particular I
did that to take advantage of possible developments over the
week end.

On the Monday morning that was the beginning of the
puzzling day in Northern Pacific, I was standing at the arbitrage desk where London cables were sent and received. Beside me stood Talbot Taylor, one of the better brokers and
the son-in-law of James Keene, who was the man the Morgans usually turned to for difficult market operations.

I drew Taylor's attention to the fact that Northern Pacific
could be bought in London several points below the New
York price.

Taylor's brown eyes regarded me intently. His face was expressionless.

"Bernie," he said, tapping his lips with the butt end of his pencil, "are you doing anything in Northern Pacific?"

"Yes," I replied, "and I'll tell you how to make some money out of it. Buy in London, sell here, and take an arbitrage profit."

Taylor went on tapping his lips, then his forehead, with the pencil. At length he said, "I would not arbitrage if I were you."

I did not ask why. If Taylor wanted me to know he would tell me. I offered to let him have some of my previous London purchases if they would help him any.

"All right," he agreed, "you can buy N.P. in London, but if I need the stock I want you to sell it to me at a price and a profit that I will fix."

To this I agreed. Taylor stood there for an instant. Then, taking my arm, he led me out of earshot of anyone else.

"Bernie," he said in almost a whisper, "I know you will do nothing to interfere with the execution of the order. There is a terrific contest for control and Mr. Keene is acting for J. P. Morgan.

"Be careful," concluded Taylor, "and don't be short of this stock. What I buy must be delivered now. Stock bought in London will not do."

With this priceless information, Eddie Norton's buying later that day was no mystery to me, of course. I could have told others what was going on and, if I had, much of what later happened may never have taken place. But that would have meant breaking Taylor's confidence. Once the word got around, Taylor would have found it more difficult to execute the purchase orders that had been given his firm.

Brokers often have told me in confidence of their orders, knowing that I would keep their secret and not upset their operations. Usually I tried to avoid such confidences since they could prove embarrassing. Several times I have been forced to abandon actions I had already decided upon so it would not appear as if I were using confidential information against the people who had given it to me. Still, this was one occasion when a fellow broker's confidence did mean a great deal.

As I walked away from the arbitrage desk I pondered what Keene's son-in-law had told me. With Morgan and Harriman eager to acquire every possible share, the available supply of Northern Pacific stock was likely to be "cornered" rather quickly. Traders who had sold the stock short, anticipating its decline, would be unable to cover themselves. They would be forced to bid fantastic prices for Northern Pacific. To cover these losses they would have to dump other securities. A corner in Northern Pacific, in other words, would produce a general collapse in the market.

And so I decided to go short in several other leading stocks in the market, to profit when these securities were dumped. I resolved not to do any trading at all in Northern Pacific. As it turned out, being on the sidelines proved the best place from which to observe the wildest situation the Stock Exchange had ever known.

On the following day, Tuesday, May 7, it was clear that the stock had been cornered. There was virtually no Northern Pacific stock that anyone wanted to sell. During the trading it touched 149 and closed at 143. But the really wild scramble came after the three o'clock gong.

Under the Stock Exchange's rules of that day, all stock bought or sold had to be delivered by the next day. If someone sold a stock short, the practice was to borrow the stock certificate from some broker, if necessary, paying a premium for its use. If a trader couldn't borrow the stock certificates he needed, the man to whom the stock had been sold could go into the market and pay any price for it. The trader who had been caught short would have to make good this price.

But in the case of Northern Pacific there simply weren't enough stock certificates to cover the needs of all the traders who had sold short. When the closing gong sounded the frantic traders surged around the Northern Pacific trading post bidding premium rates for any stock that might be available.

I have used the files of the New York *Herald* to stimulate my recollection of the scenes that took place. The picture this newspaper gives of the wild scramble on that day is not over-drawn if my memory is any criterion.

When one broker walked into the crowd, other traders, thinking he might have some Northern Pacific stock, charged him, banging him against the railing.

"Let me go, will you?" he roared. "I haven't a share of the d——d stock. Do you think I carry it in my clothes?"

Then, through the desperate crowd strode Al Stern, of Herzfeld & Stern, a young and vigorous broker. He had come as an emissary of Kuhn, Loeb & Company, which was han-dling Harriman's purchases of Northern Pacific. Stern blithely inquired: "Who wants to borrow Northern Pacific? I have a block to lend."

The first response was a deafening shout. There was an infinitesimal pause and then the desperate brokers rushed at Stern. Struggling to get near enough to him to shout their bids, they kicked over stock tickers. Strong brokers thrust aside the weak ones. Hands were waving and trembling in the air.

Almost doubled over on a chair, his face close to a pad, Stern began to note his transactions. He would mumble to one man, "All right, you get it," and then complain to another, "For heaven's sake, don't stick your finger in my eye."

One broker leaned over and snatched Stern's hat, with which he beat a tattoo on Stern's head to gain attention.

"Put back my hat!" shrieked Stern. "Don't make such a confounded excitement and maybe I can do better by you."

But the traders continued to push and fight and nearly climb over one another's backs to get to Stern. They were like thirst-crazed men battling for water, with the biggest, strong-est, and loudest faring best.

Soon Stern had loaned the last of his stock. His face white, and his clothes disheveled, he managed to break away.

The next day, May 8, the corner in Northern Pacific was acknowledged and the panic spread. The shorts, knowing that they would have to acquire stock to cover themselves before the day's trading was over, bid wildly. The stock opened at 155, twelve points above the last quotation of the previous day. Soon it advanced to 180.

During the day Mr. Schiff made the public announcement that Harriman controlled the Northern Pacific. But the Hill-Morgan forces refused to strike their flag. They were banking on the judgment of their field marshal, James Keene, the greatest market operator of his time.

Keene never appeared on the floor during this or any other of his operations. He was not, indeed, a member of the Exchange. Throughout the Northern Pacific contest he remained inaccessible in the office of Talbot Taylor's firm. To send reports to Keene, Eddie Norton would pass the word to Harry Content, who in turn would wander around the room a bit and then come up to Taylor and give him the information for Mr. Keene.

On the Exchange floor fear had completely taken the place of reason. Stocks were being dumped wildly, dropping from ten to twenty points. There were rumors of corners in other stocks.

In a panic it is not easy to avoid being swept along with the mad tide. In this case, however, having made my plans in advance, I was able to step aside and keep my wits. When stocks were dumped I bought—my net profit that day was more than I made on any other one day before or after.

I also decided that there would be no corner in any other stock. I reasoned the railroad bankers had had just about enough and soon would be trying to bring the panic to an end. The whole situation, as I saw it, was in the hands of two titanic forces who would have to compromise sooner or later —I felt sooner.

Still, the scenes of that afternoon and evening, after the gong put an end to the trading, showed no surface indications of peace between the warring factions.

Pandemonium reigned in the loan crowd from three until four-thirty. When Al Stern appeared again, he was shoved against a pillar as the traders surged upon him to renew the loans of the day before. Stern climbed on a chair and cried to the traders to keep off and listen to what he had to say.

When the crowd finally quieted, Stern broke the crushing news—those who had borrowed his stock would have to turn it in as he could renew no loans.

This action, I might explain, was not taken to squeeze the shorts to make them pay to the last dollar of ability as Jay Gould did in his Chicago & Northwestern corner of 1872. The reason for the action was that the Harriman and Morgan forces were at the showdown point in their struggle for control of the Northern Pacific. Neither could tell how much of the stock each side would be able to vote until the actual stock certificates were in hand.

That night the public rooms and corridors of the Waldorf were jammed, but by a far different kind of crowd than had peopled this palace of leisure and gaiety only a few days before. The ladies were gone. Men neglected the amenity of formal clothes.

Have you ever noticed how animals behave on a sunny day when no danger threatens? They lick their coats, preen themselves, strut and sing, each trying to put on a better show than the other fellow. So with human beings. And like animals, when fear strikes their hearts, they forget their elegances and sometimes even the common courtesies.

One look inside the Waldorf that night was enough to bring home this truth of how little we differ from animals after all. From a palace the Waldorf had been transformed into the den of frightened men at bay. Men milled about from one throng to another, eager to catch the news of any change in the situation. Some men were too frightened to take a drink; others were so terrified they could only drink. It was, in short, a mob, swayed by all the unreasonable fears, impulses, and passions that play on mobs.

Only the stoutest could maintain outward signs of composure. I saw Arthur Housman in the company of John W. Gates of "Bet a Million" fame. The bluff, breezy Chicagoan kept up his old bravado. He denied all rumors connecting him with a short interest in Northern Pacific, saying that he had not lost a cent and that if he had, he wouldn't squeal.

The latter part of this statement was true, if the first part was not. As a matter of fact, all the millions Gates had made were in jeopardy. He and other big fellows were asking one question—would compromise be reached in the course of the night?

4

The next morning a tense, white-faced, almost silent band of men surrounded the Northern Pacific trading post. No word of compromise, no hope for truce had emanated from behind the guarded doors where sat the rival generals and their chiefs of operation.

A babble of voices drowned the echo of the gavel. Within an hour Northern Pacific was selling at $400 a share. Before noon, it was $700. Shortly after two o'clock 300 shares were sold for $300,000 cash—$1000 a share.

I happen to know that Eddie Norton personally sold that stock short. As he told me later, he was gambling that the price could not stay that high and that if it did, there would be general ruin in the market.

With Northern Pacific soaring, the rest of the list collapsed, losing up to 60 points as stocks were thrown over at any price. Call money loaned by banks to brokers opened at 40 per cent and touched 60. All sense of value and sanity was gone.

Eddie Norton stood with tears in his eyes at the thought of the imminent ruin of many of his friends. The wildest rumors sped to and fro. One report, which I later learned was cabled to London, was that Arthur Housman had dropped dead in our office. To contradict this he had to show himself on the floor of the Exchange.

Scenes in the brokerage offices were as heartrending as those on the floor. My friend Fred Edey, of H. B. Hollins & Company, rushed to the offices of J. P. Morgan to warn that there would be twenty failures by nightfall if loans were not forthcoming. From banker to banker Edey went, pleading and persuading. His efforts brought millions of dollars into the Exchange and helped parry disaster.

Two-fifteen was the deadline when the shorts had to put up the stock certificates to cover their sales of the previous day. A few minutes before, Al Stern, the Kuhn, Loeb emissary, came onto the floor. Mounting a chair and shouting to make himself heard, he announced that his firm would not enforce delivery of Northern Pacific purchased yesterday.

Stern was followed by Eddie Norton, who announced that his firm as well would not demand delivery of 80,000 shares due them.

The crisis was over. Northern Pacific sold off to 300. The general list steadied.

At five that evening the crowds at the Waldorf were relieved by a bulletin over the ticker that said Morgan and Kuhn, Loeb would provide stock for those short of it at 150. These were much more generous terms than most of the shorts had expected to get. The panic was ended.

No man was more relieved than the picturesque Gates, who no longer had been able to conceal the truth of his position. He held court that night in the Men's Café of the Waldorf, flanked by Max Pam, his attorney, and Arthur Housman, while people fought to get near him. He was chipper but it required a good deal of effort.

"What do you think of the flurry, Mr. Gates?" he was asked.

"Flurry?" he retorted. "If you call that a flurry, I never want to be in a cyclone."

"Are you broke?" someone asked impertinently.

"Just badly bent," retorted the game old warhorse. "You

know, I feel like a dog I used to own out in Illinois. That dog got kicked around so much he walked sort of sideways. Finally he got accustomed to the kicks and did not mind them and walked straight. A while ago I was walking sideways. I was kicked all out of shape but along about sunset this evening I managed to right myself. Now I am able to walk as straight as the next fellow and look forty ways for Sunday."

A day or so later Mr. Gates sailed for Europe with the whole affair dismissed from his mind, or at least so far as anyone could judge from outward appearances.

When the smoke blew away there was some question as to who, after all, controlled the Northern Pacific. Harriman was a lion. He was ready to fight on. But Morgan and Hill had had enough. They were willing to compromise to avoid future hostilities. An agreement was reached whereby Harriman obtained representation on the boards of both the Burlington and the Northern Pacific, which was more than he had asked for in the first place.

12. Some Waldorf Characters

HISTORIANS HAVE WRITTEN of the Northern Pacific corner as the climax of the era of the titans of finance. In the years that followed there were other contests for power between so-called "giants," but none ever approached the intensity of the Harriman-Morgan struggle.

One aspect of this struggle is particularly worth noting. Although on the surface it seemed like a clash of two powerful personalities, in a larger sense it was merely a struggle over two different ways of achieving the same thing—the more efficient consolidation of the nation's railroad system.

Both Morgan and Harriman were instruments of our national growth. They may have affected the form which that growth took, but if they had not been on the scene the growth would have continued anyway.

This, as I look back at it, may well have been the essential significance of the scenes at the Waldorf-Astoria that I witnessed. The Waldorf was thronged by characters who considered themselves the main show. But weren't they really only so many bold outward—and passing—figures in a larger drama, which was the development of the United States itself?

There was always a good deal of strutting and bragging at the Waldorf, but I wonder how many people really were fooled. One broker, Eddie Wasserman, for example, was known as a good man with one failing—he liked to exaggerate the size of his operations. One day he walked up to Jacob Field, one of the shrewdest traders in Wall Street, and asked:

"Jake, how much business do you think I did today?"

"One half," Jake replied instantly.

A little fellow with a German accent, Jake was not an educated man. His brokers would follow him around the floor since he did not always write down his trades correctly.

Once Jake was given a dinner by a number of appreciative friends. As guest of honor he sat between two charming ladies. They hardly knew what to talk to him about. Finally one asked if he liked Balzac. Pulling his mustaches as he always did when he was at a loss what to say, Jake replied, "I never deal in dem outside stocks."

But if Jake did not know his French authors, he knew Wall Street. At this dinner he gave each lady who was there 100 half-shares of Reading. Each half-share was worth about $4.50 at the market. He told the ladies to keep the stock because before long it would be selling for 100. He was wrong. It went to 200.

The parade of characters at the Waldorf was endless, but three men in particular intrigued me—Diamond Jim Brady, James R. Keene, and John Gates. Each posed the same riddle of human nature in a different way—what was the real character of the man that lay beneath the exterior he showed the public?

2

I never see a flashy dresser today without thinking how pallid his appearance would be beside Diamond Jim Brady. Jim loved to startle people and to be talked about. He never would use old money. If crumpled or dirty money came his way he sent it to the bank for crisp new bills. Whenever he appeared in public he always wore formal clothes, and generally he had a beautiful woman on his arm.

But for all his penchant for show, Jim was a kindly man and a wonderful friend. There was not a particle of malice in his make-up.

It was commonly thought that Brady was deeply in love with Lillian Russell. Actually for years he danced attendance on Edna McCauley, while big, handsome Jesse Lewisohn, who was the heir apparent to the Lewisohn copper fortune, squired Lillian Russell. The four went around together so much that they seemed inseparable friends. One day Brady came to me and said, "Bernie, it's terrible but Jesse has run off and married Edna." Some years later, Lillian Russell married Alexander P. Moore, who became ambassador to Spain.

Brady was a salesman of railroad equipment and a good one. He accumulated a large fortune through prodigious effort. I will leave it to a better student of psychology than I to reconcile James B. Brady, the sound and conservative businessman, with Diamond Jim, the Broadway showman.

Jim had a way of talking, breathing in his words, and laughing at himself. He once told me, "A fellow wanted to bet me he could eat more ham than I. Before I bet I asked him how many hams he could eat."

Jim touched neither tea, coffee, nor alcohol. He did not smoke. But I have never known any three men to eat as much as he did. He consumed ice cream by the quart or oranges by the dozen at a single sitting. When he traveled he carried crates of oranges with him. I have seen him eat three or four dozen oysters as a before-dinner appetizer.

A pound of candy was just a tidbit for Brady. He was, in fact, Page and Shaw's largest customer. They put up a special assortment for him containing ten or twelve varieties, about a quarter of a pound of each.

Jim was an enormously fat fellow about six feet one, but he loved to dance. He and my youngest brother, Sailing, were particularly close friends and they liked to go to dancing contests, which Sailing often won. At one dancing party at Brady's bachelor home on West 86th Street I received the prize for being the most graceful dancer. It was a watch which, except for its size, would have been more suitable for a lady than a man. The case was encrusted with pearls.

Jim did most of his entertaining in public, but once I told him my wife and I would like to have some of our friends see his jewelry. He said to fix the time and he would have dinner ready for them. We invited about twelve persons. Never have I sat down to a more elaborate repast or one that was better served. With every course, each lady at the table received some novelty or gift of jewelry.

On an occasion of this kind Jim ate no more than his guests. He had had his real dinner before the guests arrived. He did the same thing when he dined at the home of a friend.

That evening Jim had his personal jewelry brought from the vault and shown to us. There were twenty-five or thirty sets of jewelry, each consisting of collar buttons, studs, cuff buttons, waistcoat buttons, scarf pins, watch chain and fob, a spectacle and card case, suspender clasps, a belt buckle, ring, lead pencil, and a removable head for his cane. These articles were set with diamonds, emeralds, rubies, sapphires, pearls, moonstones, and several other combinations of stones. One complete set of gunmetal, Jim explained, he reserved for funerals.

Then Jim showed us his wardrobe. An entire rack was devoted to dress suits and dinner coats made up in pearl gray, navy blue, and plum colors, as well as in black. I have never seen so many suits and pairs of shoes outside of a store. The closets were lined with Paisley shawls. The bathroom to the guest suite had a solid silver tub; in the dressing room was a gold toilet set.

Jim owned a horse called Gold Heels which he entered in the Suburban or Brooklyn Handicap. "Nothing to it," Jim assured his friends, "Gold Heels will win by a city block." This seemed the general opinion for Gold Heels was the favorite, sixteen to five. In his box that day, surrounded by admiring friends, Jim was in his glory. He kept repeating that Gold Heels would win by a city block.

The race turned out to be one of the closest I have ever witnessed. As the horses turned into the stretch, two or three of them nose and nose, Jim waved his arms and opened his mouth but no sound came forth. Jesse Lewisohn, who had bet heavily on Gold Heels, stood there mopping his brow.

Gold Heels won by a nose, and Jim's friends gathered around to offer congratulations. Lewisohn, still pale, complained, "I thought you said the horse would win by a city block."

Jim's face went red. Pointing to the board where the winners were posted, he sputtered and stuttered and finally blurted, "Whose number is up?"

I have often felt like giving the same answer to persons who are led to success through great difficulties only to complain because the going was hard.

3

If ever there was a true "wizard of Wall Street" he was James R. Keene. No one I ever knew approached him in his skill at operating in the market. His masterpiece of market making was in U.S. Steel, which he handled at Morgan's behest.

When the steel trust was formed a market had to be established for half a billion dollars of common stock and another half billion of preferred stock. Few believed that a billion dollars of securities could be put out for sale to the public without depressing either the steel stock or the general market. But Keene had an uncanny ability to mix orders to buy and sell so that the market would respond to his control. He handled the marketing so well that all that the Morgan firm had to put up was $25,000,000. The public supplied the rest of the funds.

I might add that under the SEC's regulations, Keene's methods in making a market are no longer permitted.

Keene was self-educated and one could call him self-made, except that all men are self-made. Born in England and reared on the Pacific Coast, he had been a cowboy, mule-skinner, miner, and newspaper editor before buying a seat on the San Francisco Mining Exchange, where he found his métier.

Of medium stature, he was always immaculately dressed,

though not overdressed. His short gray beard, which led to his being nicknamed "the Silver Fox," always appeared freshly trimmed. About the only external evidence he gave of his rough-and-ready beginnings was the robust California profanity he could use when excited. At such times his thin, high-pitched voice imparted a peculiarly penetrating effect to the profanity.

Keene came to New York in the seventies, when Jay Gould was at the height of his operations. By the time I came to know Keene, he had made and lost several fortunes. He took losses without turning a hair. Once he had to sell his household goods, but even then he sought the sympathy of no one and declined all offers of assistance.

Keene took more care in preparing a financial campaign, and was quicker and surer in its execution, than any man I know. As long as he thought he was right he was patient, very patient. But when he believed himself wrong, he could turn in an instant.

One of his operations taught me a great deal about men. Keene was marketing the stock for the U.S. Cordage Company when he learned that the company's earnings did not measure up to what they should have been to justify the price of the stock. Keene quickly stopped buying and started selling the Cordage stock he had bought for the pool of operators he represented. What impressed me was not only how quickly he decided to sell but that he sold the stock of the other traders in the pool first before protecting himself.

Another time a rather heavy speculation was going on in the stock of the American Sugar Refining Company. A report reached the Exchange that there was yellow fever aboard a ship which had come into the harbor with a cargo of raw sugar. The sugar company's stock began to drop. But Keene, who believed in the stock, didn't run away from it. He went to its support with buying orders.

At the time Middleton Burrill—it was he, the reader will recall, who introduced me to Keene—asked Keene what the effect of the report of the yellow fever would be on the market. "Well," replied Keene in his English way, "I would not say it was exactly a bull argument."

Keene usually operated on the bullish or optimistic side of the market. It was he who first made the remark, "You don't see any Fifth Avenue mansions built by bears," which some writers have attributed to me.

Once Keene was asked why, since he had made his fortune, he continued speculating in Wall Street. He replied, "Why does a dog chase his thousandth rabbit? All life is a speculation. The spirit of speculation is born with men."

Keene liked to gamble. He was the owner of a number of famous race horses. Foxhall, named after Keene's only son, won the Grand Prix in Paris in 1881. Keene's favorite horse was Sysonby.

After its death, Keene gave Sysonby's skeleton to the Museum of Natural History, where the famous horse was mounted and placed on exhibition. Once while at a horse show, Keene suddenly felt a surge of nostalgia to see Sysonby. With some friends he left the show and went to the Museum, where he spent several hours reminiscing about Sysonby's exploits.

I have seen Keene at the end of a bad day, after a drink or two, perhaps, but still spruce in appearance and as poised as ever. Once when I reported to him on how bad a day it had been in the market, he remarked, "I get awful tired sometimes, but I come again."

That remark became a famous saying in Wall Street which men would repeat when things went against them. I know I often thought of it during troubled hours and, like Keene, decided to "come again."

4

Keene's quiet, reserved manner contrasted completely not only with Diamond Jim Brady but with John Gates. Flashy, noisy, and bumptious, Gates was unquestionably the greatest gambler I ever knew, in the market or out.

He had everything a successful gambler needs, which is like saying he was one man in a million. Successful gamblers are that rare. Gates was all nerve—and no nerves. Beneath his roughness lay a cool, bold, penetrating intelligence.

Gates started out as a salesman—and a typical Midwestern drummer he must have been—with loud vest, imposing watch chain, and a derby cocked on one side of his head. A salesman Gates remained to the end. If Gates was not always meticulously correct in the claims he made for his goods, the same can be said of other salesmen, great and small. He had an abounding faith in the future of the United States. He believed it would grow to exceed anyone's expectations. He could spread his optimism as if it were a contagion.

I liked Gates and enjoyed our associations, in business and otherwise, but I learned early that when he threw his arm around your shoulder and said, "Bernie, I want to do you a favor," it was a good time to put your watch in your shoe. If Gates was aware of the prudent steps I took to vaccinate myself against his virulent optimism—and I am sure a man of his intuition must have been aware of this—it made no difference in our relations.

Gates' favorite haunts at the Waldorf were the mahogany bar and the billiard room. Usually he had a glass in his hand, but the impression that Gates drank a great deal is a mistaken one. He ate all he wanted but drank sparingly.

Once Gates administered stern punishment to a famous chain of bucket shops. Whether he was actuated by motives based on ethics, a drive to make money, or the itch to have some excitement, I would not attempt to state.

In those days a bucket shop was strictly a gambling organization where patrons could bet on the rise or fall of prices on the Big Board. No transfer of ownership of securities took place. Some of the larger bucket-shop operators, when they found the "orders" heavy on a particular issue, would go into the Exchange and force the stock up or down to wipe out their patrons.

Gates and a few others decided to give the bucket-shop operators a dose of their own medicine. They placed heavy "orders" with one particularly large bucket shop on stocks which had remained virtually stationary for some time. Then they suddenly bid up the price. When they sent their man around to close their accounts and take their winnings, he found a new firm's name on the glass door of the bucket shop's office. Only by threats of a suit and an exposé did Gates force the bucket-shop operators to pay part of their losses.

Gambling was a relaxation for Gates, who burned up energy at a terrific rate. He would play poker or whist during a whole train trip between Chicago and New York, winning or losing large sums of money, and still arrive in town as fresh as a daisy.

I remember running into Gates and Colonel Ike Ellwood in London. The three of us met at the Ascot races on a smotheringly hot day, all dressed up in tall hats and Prince Alberts, as we had to be to get into the royal enclosure. I strolled outside the enclosure to where the bookmakers were. There was Gates, his tall hat pushed to the back of his head, his Prince Albert and waistcoat unbuttoned.

"Have you anything good on this race, John?" I asked.

"No, I haven't, Bernie," he said, "and I'm making only a little light bet."

His light bet turned out to be £7000.

Talkative gamblers usually talk themselves out of money. It was different with Gates. He could talk the other fellow out of money—even in a clay pigeon shooting match. While John was a pretty good shot at pigeons, he was not so good that many men could not beat him. Yet John would bet on himself and win from fellows who were better marksmen than he. He did it by talking all the time, pushing the bet up and up until his opponent grew nervous. Later John would throw his head back and laugh as he told how he had won a shooting match by changing it into a talking match.

Bernard Baruch

Many stories have been told of the remarkable race in which Royal Flush won the Goodwood Cup in 1900. This is my recollection of the story as I heard it from Gates.

It seems that John A. Drake, the sportsman son of a famous governor of Iowa and—barring Gates himself—the biggest plunger I ever saw, was taking a string of horses to England. Gates, wanting to have a little fun, bought a half interest.

In England they hired a crack trainer and won several races. At some track their fancy was taken by a horse named Royal Flush. Although it had never won a race, they bought the horse. Royal Flush was turned over to the trainer.

Presently Gates learned that the unknown was showing marvelous speed. Gates took a famous trainer, John Huggins, to one of the secret trials. Huggins walked with a limp which Gates imitated as he told the story. With a profusion of gestures, Gates would re-enact the scene of that trial—how Royal Flush, with his head swinging, came over the top of the hill and Huggins threw up his hands and cried:

"My God, no horse can run that fast!"

But all this was kept quiet. When Royal Flush was entered in the Goodwood Cup, the bookmakers first posted him at 50 to 1. The favorite was Americus, which was owned by Richard Croker, the boss of Tammany Hall.

Then Gates and Drake began their betting campaign, laying money on Royal Flush all over the world, from England to South Africa, from Amsterdam to Australia. Even so, the sporting fraternity got wind of the betting. No logical explanation could be offered for this phenomenal support of an unknown horse, but the odds came down.

On the day of the race, the excitement was intense. Gates told me how, just before the race, he asked a bookmaker if he would take a "little light" place bet at 4 to 5 on Royal Flush. Whenever Gates mentioned a "little light bet" it was time to look out. The bookmaker said "yes," and Gates said, "Put down 50,000 pounds." That was equivalent to nearly $250,000.

No one knows how much Gates and Drake won on that race. The suspicion that there was more than met the eye in the winning of the Goodwood Cup would not down. If memory serves me correctly, an investigation followed which resulted in ruling the horse—and some of his human connections—off the English tracks.

Still, all his foolishness aside, John W. Gates earned his place among the architects of America's industrial structure as it exists today. He had an inspiring vision of the future of this country and was, I believe, the first man to conceive of a billion-dollar corporation. Characteristically he announced it one evening while shooting pool at the Waldorf. I might add that this was when billions were not tossed about with the abandon that became common in later days.

Some men called Gates' idea a delusion of grandeur, but one no more prone to pursuing rainbows than the elder J. P. Morgan saw it as a practicable thing. The result was the formation of the United States Steel Corporation.

Gates had been the star salesman for Colonel Ike Ellwood, who was the first manufacturer of barbed wire. Presently Gates started a rival barbed-wire works and forced Ellwood to buy him out. A series of mergers followed that resulted in the American Steel & Wire Company, which Gates disposed of to Morgan as a part of the Steel Corporation.

For president of the new corporation Morgan took thirty-seven-year-old Charles M. Schwab from the Carnegie Steel Company. A few years later Elbert H. Gary, an Illinois lawyer and steel man whom Gates had first introduced to Morgan, took over as head of the company. In Gary, Morgan surely found a personage as different from Schwab or Gates as day is from night. And as different from Morgan, too, for that matter. If Elbert Gary ever had any fun in his life, I don't know how he did it.

There has been much discussion as to how Morgan came to form the United States Steel Corporation. As I recall, the immediate thing that moved him was the threat of a price war in the industry. But whether the machinery of consolidation actually was set in motion by the persuasion of Frick, Schwab, Gates, or someone else remains a bit of a riddle. Each story has its own supporters.

At any rate Gates thought himself entitled to a place on the board of directors. His exclusion by Morgan started a feud between them that lasted as long as Gates lived. Into at least one of their financial battles I found myself drawn in an important role.

Father and Mother were a handsome couple. A line
in the family Bible recording Mother's birth reads,
"God grant her a blessing." I like to think that this
line prophesied Mother's marriage to Father, since
the name "Baruch" is the Hebrew word for "blessed."

149.

As a child I was shy and sensitive, something of a mama's boy. I was freckle-faced and relatively short—and I had a temper that I found hard to control.

At twenty-two I was a boxing enthusiast. The self-control that I learned in the ring has helped me all through life.

At thirty-five I was a seasoned speculator and a millionaire, but I often wished that I had not given up my earlier intention to study medicine.

One glance sufficed to interest me in the tall, slender Annie Griffen, but it took seven years before we were finally wed.

152.

Mother and Father were proud of their four sons and took
Annie to their hearts at once.

My business activities brought me many friends. One of them was Clarence Mackay, who played an important role in the development of the communications industry.

Early automobiles were expensive and unreliable, but I was an enthusiastic motorist and often took my car abroad.

155.

Thomas Fortune Ryan had the softest, gentlest Southern voice you ever heard. But he was lightning in action, and one of the most resourceful men I ever knew.

Daniel became the leader of the remarkable Guggenheim family, whose cohesion was a prime source of strength. They created wealth and used their fortune wisely to support scholarship, art, music, and science.

I never see a flashy dresser today without thinking of Diamond Jim Brady. But for all his penchant for show, he was a kindly man and a wonderful friend.

Courtesy of Brown Brothers

William Crocker was the kind of banker who did not desert his clients when things went bad. Always meticulous, he was one of the most engaging personalities I have known.

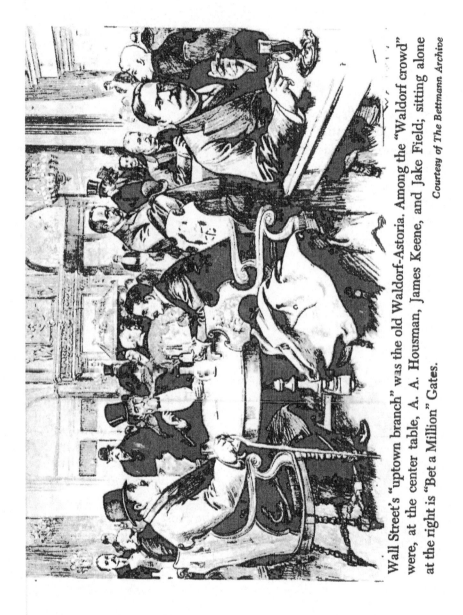

Wall Street's "uptown branch" was the old Waldorf-Astoria. Among the "Waldorf crowd" were, at the center table, A. A. Housman, James Keene, and Jake Field; sitting alone at the right is "Bet a Million" Gates.

Courtesy of The Bettmann Archive

Edward Harriman had a frail frame but a giant's energy and imagination. He was the man I did my best to emulate when I first entered Wall Street.

Courtesy of The Bettmann Archive

The unfortunate choice of a word denied me the chance of being associated with the elder J. P. Morgan, easily the dominant financial figure of his time.

Courtesy of
The Bettmann Archive

World War One took me out of Wall Street and into
public affairs. After having served as chairman of
the War Industries Board, I was called to Paris by
Woodrow Wilson to help draft the treaty of peace.
There I came to know Louis Loucheur of France,
Winston Churchill, and David Lloyd George.

In 1917 my parents celebrated their golden wedding anniversary at a party given at Sherry's in New York City.

The rambling white frame house at Hobcaw burned
to the ground in 1929 and I replaced it with a red
brick porticoed dwelling.

In my Hobcaw album are snapshots of three of the Cains brothers with Charlie, our chef; Jim Powell, my superintendent; and myself, in the act of shooting quail.

Photo at left
courtesy of David Goodnow

163.

My father's pioneering in physical medicine and rehabilitation led me to help establish the Institute of
Physical Medicine and Rehabilitation at Bellevue
Hospital. This center has become a model for the
whole world.

13. My Big Disappointment in Life

ALTHOUGH I HAVE HAD relatively little to complain of in my life, one disappointment I have felt quite keenly—that I never got to own or run a railroad.

This had been my ambition since childhood, when I waved to the brakemen on the freight cars of the Charlotte, Columbia and Augusta line as they rolled past my grandfather's garden in Winnsboro.

The closest I came to realizing this dream was after World War One. In a long talk with James Duke and Tom Ryan, I pointed out to them the marvelous opportunities for economic development that lay in the South and how that development could be spurred by the Atlantic Coast Line railroad, which stretched from New York to Florida.

Ryan remarked to Duke, "Why don't we buy the railroad for Bernie and let him run it?"

Not long after that my wife and I were guests at Duke's house on 78th Street and Fifth Avenue. After dinner some bridge tables were set up and I found myself at the same table with Henry Walters, the head of the Atlantic Coast Line. During one hand Duke, who did not play bridge, came up to Walters and said, "I'd like to buy the Atlantic Coast Line for Bernie, here. How much do you want for it?"

"Yes?" Walters asked in surprise. "One sixty-five a share."

"I'll take it," said Duke without a second's hesitation.

The next morning, however, Walters went to J. P. Morgan, who vetoed the deal. Later I was told the Morgans felt that I might transfer the railroad's financing to Kuhn, Loeb. This

I would not have done. The business would have gone to the bankers who gave the road the best deal.

Oddly, this was not the first time the House of Morgan frustrated my dream of running a railroad. The first occasion occurred in 1902, when I tried to gain control of the Louisville and Nashville Railroad. This was the same operation in which John Gates is reputed to have bluffed Morgan into paying him a profit of $7,500,000 for control of the railroad. Perhaps it is not too late for me to fill out the story of what happened with some hitherto unpublished details.

During the summer of 1901, while Wall Street was still recovering from the Northern Pacific panic, I made a study which convinced me that L. and N. had the makings of a great railroad and represented perhaps the best buy on the Stock Exchange. I began purchasing the stock, then under 100, with the thought of committing to it most of my free capital—something no one should do without very careful thought.

Realizing that my resources would be insufficient to acquire control, I asked a few friends to join me. One man I approached was Edwin C. Hawley, whose experience and skill in railroad matters I valued highly. He was president of both the Minneapolis and St. Paul and the Iowa Central railroads; he also had bought the Huntington holdings in the Southern Pacific for E. H. Harriman.

First, I showed Hawley how cheap L. and N. was in comparison with nearly every property listed on the Exchange. Then I sketched the possibilities of expansion as I saw them: a hook-up with the Chicago & Eastern Illinois to get into Chicago, and a hook-up with either the Atlantic Coast Line, the Southern, or Seaboard to be able to tap potentialities of the South.

The L. and N.'s stock, I pointed out to Hawley, was held largely abroad by the Rothschilds, whose American representative was August Belmont. Absentee ownership and loose operation had retarded the road's development. With American ownership a new and aggressive management could be substituted.

Hawley was one of the few men I knew who had a natural poker face. It was pale and cameolike, and when he talked he hardly opened his lips. On this occasion he gave me no direct answer and I thought I had made no headway with him.

Jake Field and a number of others came in with me. Jake, who had made a good deal of money in the Northern Pacific corner, took 10,000 shares. One day Jake noticed me buying the stock on a scale down and said, "Dat's foolish. I always like to buy de second bundle higher dan de first, and de third higher dan de second."

In other words, Jake was willing to back his judgment, but that judgment had to prove itself right almost immediately. Generally speaking, Jake's theory is sound.

As my friends began to buy, their activity brought in other buyers, which pushed L. and N. up. Soon, most of the people who had bought at my suggestion decided to sell and take their profits. Jake Field sold, although I tried hard to dissuade him. This left me one of the largest stockholders aside from the Rothschilds. Again I began to look around for financial allies, meantime continuing to buy.

2

Through January of 1902 into February the market activity in L. and N. just simmered along. Then, suddenly, trading in the stock began to boil.

My first inkling of the upsurge of interest came one day as I was sitting at the L. and N. trading post. I was surprised to see another buyer place some orders. I decided this purchaser was after a large block of stock. Each time he started to buy, I bid higher. Eventually the source of this buying was revealed as the Chicago & Eastern Illinois crowd.

Then John Gates came into the picture. He bought heavily, first through a Washington broker, W. B. Hibbs, and later through his son's newly-created firm, Harris, Gates & Company, in New York. These purchases by Gates created a suspicion that the rise of L. and N. was merely a speculative manipulation.

In the midst of all this activity, Ed Hawley appeared at my office one March afternoon just after three o'clock. In his poker-face manner of talking, he said:

"Bernie, you can buy control of the L. and N. for me."

I pointed out that the purchase would require a large amount of money, and asked who his associates were. He named George Crocker, H. E. Huntington, Mrs. Collis P. Huntington, L. C. Weir, president of Adams Express Company, General Thomas Hamlin Hubbard, the railroad attorney, and my partner, Arthur A. Housman. All these names with their holdings were later recorded publicly, along with my own.

My initial talk with Hawley on the possibilities of the L. and N. had made a deeper impression than I had realized.

Before consenting to act for Hawley and his group, I disclosed to him how much L. and N. stock I had. I offered to pool my holdings with the stock I would be buying for him at the average price paid for his stock and mine. He said this would not be fair to me since it would reduce the profit I already could make on the stock I had bought. However, Hawley asked me to hold my stock in case he needed it for control. I agreed.

That night I slept little, planning my campaign. The aid of Hawley and his associates might help me realize my dream of running a railroad. At the same time I could see how—with Gates, Hawley, and others in the picture—things might take a quite different turn. In any case the first step was to buy as much L. and N. stock as we could. The best opening move, I decided, would be to acquire options on large blocks of the stock in London. At dawn I was in my office, in cable contact with London, where I bought an option on 20,000 shares, paying about $70,000.

When Hawley came to my office that forenoon I was on the

floor of the Exchange. Over the board telephone I explained what I had done. He did not like the option I had bought in London.

I could understand his reluctance. The option for which we were paying $70,000 simply gave us the right to buy the stock within ninety days by paying the market price that prevailed the day the option was agreed to plus interest. This meant that by the time the option was exercised, the stock would have to rise sufficiently to more than cover the cost of the option and interest. If, for example, the market price was 107, the stock would have to go to about 111 for us to break even in exercising the option.

I told Hawley I figured the stock would rise to 130 or thereabouts—which proved correct. The big advantage of the option was that it enabled us to accumulate a good deal of stock quietly and without bidding the price up as rapidly as if we bought it outright.

Urging Hawley to take the option for the full 20,000 shares, I told him if he did not wish to, I would take half of the option and get someone else to take the other 10,000 shares. Hawley finally took 10,000 shares—primarily, I think, because he did not want to show a lack of confidence in my judgment. At his suggestion I took the option for the other 10,000 shares.

Under the spur of all this buying, the trading in L. and N. rose in volume from only a few thousand shares on April 1 to an average of more than 60,000 shares on April 4 and 5. Then, between April 7 and April 10, came four climactic days, with more than 600,000 shares traded, which threatened to produce a "corner" in L. and N. similar to that which had prevailed with Northern Pacific.

The Northern Pacific corner was precipitated largely by the mistake of Jacob Schiff in not buying the common stock that Harriman had ordered on Saturday, only to find that by Monday it was too late. Curiously, the near-corner in Louisville and Nashville was also caused by a blunder—this time by August Belmont, who represented the Rothschilds as chairman of the L. and N.

The L. and N. happened to have in its treasury 50,000 unlisted shares of its own stock. Watching the price of L. and N. climb in the market, Belmont saw an opportunity to sell these shares at a good price and get a tidy bit of extra capital for the railroad. On April 7 he had the L. and N. board of directors authorize the issuance of these 50,000 shares. It does not seem to have dawned on Mr. Belmont that a campaign was under way to buy control of the L. and N. under his very nose.

My advice, which Hawley approved, was to snap up the Belmont stock as fast as it was offered. The Gates crowd pursued the same tactics.

Under the Stock Exchange's rules thirty days had to pass before these new shares could be listed. This meant that the Belmonts could not deliver these new shares and were technically "caught short" unless they could borrow the stock certificates to make deliveries.

Gates at first wanted to squeeze the Belmonts. I did not. Hawley and I met each afternoon to discuss the strategy for the coming day. If we made it hard for Belmont, I told him, there would be a corner and I, for one, could not consent to be a party to a repetition of the scenes of the Northern Pacific panic of eleven months before. Hawley and I agreed to lend the Belmonts stock at fair rates with which to make deliveries. Gates later announced that he had no intention of permitting a corner.

Up to this point, the Gates people and ourselves had been two separate camps, opposing each other all along the line. We had felt that Gates was preventing us from getting the road at a fair price. But by this time it had become clear that we would have to reach some kind of understanding with Gates.

3

While Hawley and I were in the Men's Café at the Waldorf, we noticed Gates at a nearby table. I suggested that Hawley go over to Gates and see if by pooling our resources we could not control the property. Hawley talked with Gates and found that between them they pretty nearly held control. Then and there an agreement was reached whereby the Gates crowd and ours were to act together to get control, after which operation of the railroad was to be left to us. This was just what I wanted.

The next morning we asked "Corney" Provost, a broker, to acquire the 40,000 shares we still needed for control.

Meanwhile, the threatened corner and the activity in L. and N. had disturbed J. P. Morgan & Company, which had its own railroad interests in the South. Mr. Morgan was then in France, but George W. Perkins, a Morgan partner, approached Gates and asked what price we would take to yield control of L. and N.

While these negotiations were still going on, early one morning Talbot Taylor told me that Perkins, acting on word from Mr. Morgan, had consulted James Keene during the previous night. Keene had advised Perkins to pay what he had to, even if the price was pretty high. This news sent me flying up to Hawley. His office was on the thirteenth floor and I remember thinking how slow the elevator was.

I found Hawley putting on his hat and coat to start for Morgan's, where he and Gates were to meet Mr. Perkins. My own desire, I stressed, was not to sell at all; but if Hawley and the others wanted to sell, they should stand pat and get a good price.

Hawley returned from Morgan's in high spirits. By the time Hawley had arrived Gates had made the trade, and all Hawley had done was to agree with it. The Morgans were to take one third of our holdings at 130, and we were to give them a six months' option on the balance at 150. Alas for my dream of owning a railroad.

Hawley was surprised when I told him I did not like the deal. True, 130 for one third of our stock meant a good profit, since we had bought the first third of our holdings at prices which averaged out to less than 110. But what if economic conditions turned bad and Mr. Morgan decided not to exercise his option, as was his right? If that happened, the stock would be left in the hands of speculators who would want to sell. They might dump the stock with disastrous results. But Hawley pooh-poohed these fears.

"If you don't think it is such a good trade," he told me, "you can sell your stock in the open market."

"Do you mean that?" I asked in surprise.

"I certainly do," replied Hawley. "If you don't think we made a good trade, and since you were not consulted, I'm willing to let you out. I wish you would leave in ten thousand shares as proof of good faith and a compliment to me. I don't want Gates and the other fellows wondering why you don't want to go along with them."

I agreed to do that. I sold everything except 10,000 shares —and soon after a third of these were taken by Morgan, leaving me with only 6666 shares.

4

Although keenly disappointed at losing the chance to run this great southern railroad, I was in fine financial shape. My firm, however, still was involved through the personal holdings of Arthur Housman and because we were carrying large amounts of the stock for some of Hawley's associates.

I tried to explain to Housman how precarious a position he and the others would be in if Mr. Morgan decided not to take up the option. An optimist, Mr. Housman would not agree with me about the dangers of the Morgan agreement.

Pretty soon Gates' son, Charley, learned that I had sold

nearly all of my L. and N. stock. I did not tell him why I had done this. The only two men I explained my position to were Hawley and Arthur Housman, whom I felt bound to tell. But Gates figured things out for himself, and I cannot imagine that it gave him much comfort.

Toward the end of May, which was before the option expired, J. P. Morgan & Company announced the purchase of the Monon Route—the Chicago, Indianapolis and Louisville Railroad—for the L. and N. and Southern railroads.

At this action, I suggested that Hawley write Morgan & Company that inasmuch as the credit of the L. and N. had been pledged to buy the Monon without consulting us, we took the action as prima facie notice that Morgan intended to exercise the option on the remaining two thirds of our stock.

When this letter was sent I had the first good sleep I had enjoyed since I set out on the L. and N. venture. All of us were happy. The Monon announcement changed Morgan's option to a contract to buy.

Mr. Morgan returned from Europe during the latter part of August, 1902. He sent for Hawley, who went over with Charley Gates. I had a talk with them beforehand. The general financial situation was looking increasingly cloudy.

"If he makes any proposition other than taking up these shares under the option," I said, "you should decline it. Stand on a firm sale because of the Monon transaction."

Sure enough, Mr. Morgan asked for six months' extension of the option. Several conferences followed between Mr. Morgan and our people. At one meeting Mr. Morgan told Gates that we would get more for our holdings by waiting. If the courts sustained the Northern Securities Company, against which President Theodore Roosevelt had brought his famous suit, Morgan said he might form a Southern Securities Company which would increase the value of southern railroad stocks.

Hawley, I believe, would have agreed to extend the option or to a delay of some kind. But Gates stood firm. In all, the option covered 306,000 shares, a third of which Morgan had paid for earlier. He now took up the remaining 204,000 shares at 150. Before another six months passed, stormy financial weather had engulfed the country. There is no telling what would have happened if all that L. and N. stock had been dumped on the market.

My personal profit in this final part of the operation was comparatively small, since I had only 6666 shares left in the option lot to Morgan. But the transaction as a whole, from beginning to end, netted me about $1,000,000. This probably was as much as—if not more than—any other single individual made from the operation. Since I had bought earlier than anyone else, my shares had cost me an average of fifteen points less.

It was widely advertised at the time, and has been frequently repeated since, that Gates and his associates cleared $7,500,000 on the deal. The deal has also been pointed to as a typical Gates coup—an example of how, by threatening to control a railroad, he bluffed Morgan into buying it to keep it in reputable hands. It tickled Gates to have people think he had thrown the harpoon into Morgan, and Morgan himself must have believed it, since his people helped spread the tale.

Still, that Gates went into this operation to embarrass Morgan does not fit the facts. Actually I had far more to do with the start of the activity of L. and N. than Gates, who moved into the situation only after it was ripe. My first motive had been to get to own or operate an important railroad. When that hope faded and the struggle developed along lines I had not foreseen in the beginning, my object became to extricate our crowd. We held a third of the 306,000 shares which were taken by Morgan, while Gates and his associates held the rest.

When the L. and N. business was settled I was a rich man. I had also come off well enough to attract the attention of a few thoughtful people in financial circles. In particular I was pleased by an offer from Anthony N. Brady to become a member of the executive committee of the Central Trust Company.

Acceptance would have meant associating with men like Frederic P. Olcott, Adrian Iselin, Jr., James Speyer, C. N. Bliss, Augustus P. Juilliard, and James N. Wallace. It was quite a temptation and a most unusual offer to be made to an unattached operator as I was.

A little later I was offered a directorship in the Phoenix Life Insurance Company. I declined both the Phoenix and Central Trust offers. As I explained to Mr. Brady, it was my intention to continue to speculate in the market, and I did not believe a man should speculate who was a director of a bank or insurance company.

What I did not tell Brady was that I had begun to entertain strong doubts over whether I wanted to remain in Wall Street.

14. A Turning Point

I SHALL NEVER FORGET the day I went to Father and told him I was worth a million dollars. His kindly face assumed a quizzical expression, as if he experienced some difficulty in grasping the fact of a million dollars. Thinking that he might be questioning the accuracy of my accounting, I offered to show him the actual securities.

"No," he said, "I will take your word for it," and began to talk of something else.

Perhaps I should not have expected any other reaction. Father always had regarded making money as of secondary importance compared to moral values and one's usefulness to the community. This had been his attitude in South Carolina when Mother complained of the time he took from his practice for his experimental "farm." It had been his attitude when I lost his savings in the Put-in-Bay railroad speculation and he thought it so important to demonstrate his confidence in me that he allowed me to risk more of his savings.

Still, Father's reaction set me to reflecting along lines that had disturbed me more than once before. Of what use to a man are a million dollars unless he does something worth while with them?

Able to buy anything I wanted that was for sale, I realized how much there was that could not be bought for money. I found myself contrasting my own career with that of Father's —my money making against his accomplishments in medicine and hygiene and in helping his fellow man.

I found myself wishing that I had not given up my original intention to study medicine. I envied my brother Herman, who by this time was a doctor.

I decided at least to identify myself in a way with my

father's work. At that time the first of the public baths Father had fought for were being erected on Rivington Street in New York and two of Father's books on hydrotherapy had been translated into German and French. But Father still underwent the drudgery of the general practitioner, making his calls with his own horse and buggy and hardly knowing what an unbroken night's rest was. When Mother and he dined with friends he was always liable to interruption. They did not go to the theater without leaving his name at the box office.

Although I never heard him complain, these things were plainly beginning to wear on him. On his sixtieth birthday, in July, 1900, I asked him to give up his practice and accept an income that would enable him to further his work on the experimental and laboratory side of medicine. The idea of this new freedom appealed to him. He was also happy that his son was able to make the offer. Up to that moment he had taken little interest in the fact that I was a wealthy man.

Still, Father hesitated. He had a few patients he could not desert. He understood them so well he felt that he could not turn them over to another doctor. He kept those patients and remained at their call day or night.

I like to think that the time I was able to buy for Father helped him spread his pioneering work in hydrotherapy. By 1906 he was recognized as the foremost American authority in this field. He held the chair of Hydrotherapy at the College of Physicians and Surgeons of Columbia University from 1907 until 1913.

In those years many doctors tended to dismiss hydrotherapy as a form of quackery. I did not appreciate the obstacles Father had to overcome until the late 1940's when I gave sizable sums to a number of universities and medical institutions to advance the study of physical medicine. I also helped establish as part of Bellevue Hospital in New York an Institute for Physical Medicine and Rehabilitation which has become a model for the whole world.

In pressing these advances I found that I had to fight one

part of the American Medical Association before physical medicine would be recognized as reputable. In the spring of 1957 I was particularly gratified to learn that the American Medical Association was awarding its Citation for Distinguished Service to Henry Viscardi, Jr., for his work in physical rehabilitation. Viscardi, who was born without legs, has helped rehabilitate many handicapped persons to where they are able to hold productive jobs. It has been a long fight that my father began, but the medical profession seems finally to have been won over.

To get back to the summer of 1900, helping Father enlarge his usefulness brought me much satisfaction. But helping other people do things does not really fill an emptiness within oneself. A man is made whole only by his own acts. I still felt dissatisfied with merely making money. I also realized that while giving money to a worthy cause was a step in the right direction, it could not prove as gratifying as the personal efforts I might make in behalf of some cause.

2

Still, I really did nothing about these stirrings of discontent until they were reawakened more than a year later by a dinner party at the Waldorf. It was given for "Hi" Barber, president of the Diamond Match Company.

After a cold buffet, the table was made ready for baccarat. John Drake, who had been a partner with Gates in backing Royal Flush for the Goodwood Cup, and Loyal Smith, a real estate operator, were co-bankers. We took our places and bought chips. White chips represented the smallest denomination. They were $1000 apiece.

Gates was playing the tableau opposite mine. After a few rounds of two-, three-, and five-thousand-dollar bets he began to call us pikers and to raise his stake. Harry Black and "Huddie" Hudson followed him up to $25,000; then Hudson refused to go any higher. I saw Gates was fixing to plunge, and placed a limit of $5000 on my bets. My precaution was emulated by at least two of the other guests, Hugh Wallace, later ambassador to France, and Willis McCormick.

This annoyed Loyal Smith, who was taking in the winnings and paying out the losses of the bank. "I can't bother with you pikers," he said. "You'll have to pay in and take out for yourselves."

Up went the betting—fifty, seventy-five thousand dollars on a play.

What is it that turns ordinary betting into a reckless gamble? Desperation on the part of a heavy loser is one factor. Again, I have seen a run of luck go to a fellow's head and make him think how much more he might win if the stakes were raised. But in this game there were no heavy losers or heavy winners. All through the evening the game ran strangely even for both the large and small betters. It was lose and win, then win and lose, with no one getting far either way.

Perhaps it was the inconclusive nature of the play that bothered Gates. Anyhow he tossed out two yellow chips, worth $50,000 apiece. The bank accepted the bet. Other players raised their bets as well, but I stuck to my limit of not more than five $1000 chips.

It was the first time in my life I ever had seen $100,000 risked by one man on the turn of a card. For a moment I wondered if it was real money. When I saw the look on the faces of Drake and Smith, I knew it was.

Gates wasn't satisfied. He tossed four yellow chips onto the table. The bankers consulted each other and accepted the dare. No one attempted to duplicate that bet. At $200,000 a play, all of us were pikers now. Gates made several more such bets only to find that he stood even.

Then he picked up his chips, chinked them together for a moment, and with a dexterous movement of his stubby fingers laid out two equal stacks before him. He placed one stack on his own tableau and the second stack on the tableau I was playing. Each stack stood ten yellow chips high— $1,000,000 in all!

"Just a little light bet," Gates said, looking up expectantly into the faces of the bankers. If he breathed a bit heavily, as he sometimes did under the stress of excitement, or if there was an unnatural note in his voice, I could not detect it.

The rest of us looked at the bankers, too. Smith demurred. He said that was too much for him to risk.

"Come on," urged Drake, "let's give him a run for his money."

After some persuading Smith consented to accept the bet. Drake picked up the cards to deal. His face was pale but his hands were steady. Behind him stood Smith, white as a ghost, with perspiration trickling from his forehead.

I looked at my two cards. They showed a natural nine, which I exposed quickly. Gates, who was wagering on my cards as well as on his, had won the first bet of $500,000.

Then Gates turned his cards up on the other side of the table. They did not suit him. He drew to improve and lost. Gates and the bank were even.

Even Drake, one of the nerviest men I have known, was satisfied with this outcome. But Gates was not. When he bet, he bet to win.

The rest of the evening was anticlimactic, the bank having announced it would cover no more $500,000 bets. We played for quite a time, though, with the stakes high enough to suit me. Too high, in fact, so I just trailed along with my white chips, and never more than five of them on the line at a time.

Strangely, the balanced run of the cards continued. The large betters broke about even. The heaviest loser was the one man who of all those present could least afford to lose. I myself quit $10,000 behind.

3

The next morning I stopped, as I often did, at the bachelor apartment of Ed Hawley at 57th Street and Broadway and rode downtown with him. He told me what had brought

Gates and Drake to New York. They were participating in a pool with Keene, Dan Reid, Hawley, and several others to put up the market. I said nothing.

Hawley went on to explain how they intended to buy 300,000 shares of varied stocks. All the way downtown Hawley regaled me with details of the proposed pool, which he invited me to join.

I made no comment. To myself I was thinking that the formation of a pool by a speculative crowd is a sign of weakness.

When we arrived at the foot of the stairway at 20 Broad Street, where my firm had its offices, Hawley asked, "Well, Bernie, what interest will you take?"

"Perhaps twenty-five per cent," I replied.

Hawley raised his eyebrows. "I don't think we can let you buy that much," he replied.

"I don't want to buy anything, Ed," I said. "I want to sell."

Then I went on to explain that during his talk my mind had been on the game at the Waldorf the night before. I had found that game both disturbing and instructive. It had shown me what happened when money came into the hands of people too easily. Such money did not seem real.

When men tossed around such huge sums in bets, at cards, and at the races, it meant that they had lost all sense of value and of economics. No market in the hands of such people, I told Hawley, could be a stable or genuine one.

The market already was high enough, I went on. If anything, it was too high.

My words may have made some impression on Hawley, who at bottom was a sound man. Still, at the moment he would not agree with me. His parting remark was not to be bearish unless I wanted to get singed.

I climbed the stairs and put in orders commencing to sell. My partner Arthur Housman, ever the optimist, did not agree with me. That afternoon the bull crowd at the Waldorf rode me considerably. Still, behind their bantering I thought

I sensed a feeling of insecurity, as if they were talking strong to cover up their own weaknesses.

Turning to Hawley I remarked, "A man would certainly be a fool to go to sleep with his finger in that crowd's mouth."

"Well," he conceded, "maybe you're right."

Under the spur of heavy buying by the pool, the market went up at first. But soon it sagged.

"That's just the bears," said the wise ones. "The decline won't last."

But the market continued downward. After a particularly bad drop I was sitting at a table in the Waldorf bar listening to some of the traders comfort themselves. Jake Field, who was also on the bear side of the market, was doing the talking for both of us. I never would argue about what was going to take place but tried to let the results speak for themselves. Pretty soon James Keene came up.

"Gentlemen, what do you think of the great firm of A. A. Housman & Company?" he asked in his high-pitched voice. "At the head of it you have a roaring bull, and at the other end a snarling, scratching bear!"

Perhaps it salved their wounded egos to be able to blame their losses on the bears. But what had crumbled the market, of course, was not my selling but the fact that stock prices had been pushed far too high—beyond any economic justification at the time. If anything, the criticism and operation of the bears saved the plungers and the public from heavier losses by preventing further advances which could not have been sustained and which would have made for an even more disastrous drop when the reckoning came.

Even veteran market operators find it difficult to realize that manipulations have only a limited and temporary effect on the market. In the end it is always the economic facts—the value—which is the determining force. Bears can make money only if the bulls push up stocks to where they are overpriced and unsound.

Bulls always have been more popular than bears in this

country because optimism is so strong a part of our heritage. Still, overoptimism is capable of doing more damage than pessimism since caution tends to be thrown aside.

To enjoy the advantages of a free market one must have both buyers and sellers, both bulls and bears. A market without bears would be like a nation without a free press. There would be no one to criticize and restrain the false optimism that always leads to disaster.

4

At about this time I also came to dislike the fact that as a broker I was handling speculative accounts for other people. As I had explained to Anthony Brady in refusing to join the executive committee of the Central Trust, I did not believe that a speculator should be a director of companies. I had come to feel—and later experiences fortified this belief—that a speculator should travel his road alone.

The simple truth is that there are no "sure things" in the market. And I did not want to be responsible for others who might be following my judgment. Even the best of speculators must be prepared to be wrong in a certain percentage of his operations. In such cases he must be able to strike his tent on the instant and conduct a swift, skillful, and silent retreat.

This he will be unable to do if he has made the mistake of inducing a whole host of camp followers to go along with him. If he has taken that responsibility, common decency demands that he give them a chance to escape equal to his own. In the few times when I found myself in this predicament, I either have acted for all or notified the others immediately of what I intended to do. But this is a fearful responsibility.

As I have remarked, I had not yet come to so strong a feeling of why the speculator should go his way alone, but I was beginning to feel that something was wrong in my continuing to service the accounts of others while engaged in speculations of my own.

To cut myself off from these other accounts, however, would mean retiring from the firm of A. A. Housman & Company, which was a difficult step to take.

And once I left the firm, what then? That was not an easy question to answer.

At thirty-two I had all the money I imagined I should ever need or want. I had, in fact, $100,000 for every year of my age, and I had it in cash. This fortune had been made in five years' time.

No one else in my family, certainly no one since the Revolution, had been rich except for Grandfather Wolfe, who had died a poor man. Still, most of Father's people and Mother's had lived useful and contented lives. I found myself wondering whether I shouldn't leave Wall Street to study law and become a kind of defender of poor or unfortunate people.

I decided to go to Europe that summer—this was 1902—and think things through.

Feeling that the market generally was rather high, I had turned most of my holdings into cash. Just before my departure, to redistribute my capital somewhat, I took some money out of our firm and walked over to the National City Bank to deposit it. Going in without an introduction, I asked to see James Stillman, the president. In those days banks did not have as many vice presidents as they do now, and I was turned over to the cashier, Horace M. Kilborn.

When Mr. Kilborn asked what he could do for me, I replied that I wished to open an account. He asked who I was. This was a blow to my youthful ego, since I had thought my name must be known to the bank because of my activities in Amalgamated Copper and other fields in which Mr. Stillman was interested.

A bit abashed, I offered as a reference Herman Sielcken, the coffee merchant. This, I could see, made some difference. Then Mr. Kilborn asked the size of the account I expected to open. I produced a certified check for $1,000,000. The effect was one that any prima donna might have envied.

Sailing with me to Europe were my wife, my father, and Henry C. Davis. He had been brought into A. A. Housman & Company because Arthur Housman felt we needed someone who could tell us what was going on in the United States west of Hoboken. Davis, who knew more about the United States than almost anyone I ever met, had done a fine job of educating us in the Housman company. On this trip, I was trying to reciprocate by acquainting Davis with Europe. But the effort didn't work.

Davis went to London with us but would go no farther. He didn't care for places where, as he put it, "I can't speak the lingo." Davis didn't like Europe, didn't know it, and didn't want to know it.

He had been a rod boy in the engineering corps that laid out the Northern Pacific Railroad. He knew and cared little about stock market operation. When he wanted to know whether stocks would go up or down he would look out over the heads of us ticker-watchers to the broad country and find the answer there. I remember riding with Davis past a vast field of waving grain.

"Just shave the whiskers off the earth that grow every year," he said. "That's the way for all of us to prosper."

From London my wife, Father, and I set out on a leisurely journey across Europe which carried us as far as Constantinople. Father then went off on a tour of professional circles in Vienna, Berlin, and Paris, where he was becoming increasingly well known. My wife and I drifted back to Paris.

As far as my future was concerned, I was no further in my thinking than when I had started. I had abandoned the idea of becoming a legal defender of the poor when I figured how long it would take to go back to school and start in a new profession. But what I wanted to do, I could not say.

We were staying at the Ritz Hotel in Paris. One night I was awakened from a sound sleep by a cable from my youngest brother saying that my partner, Arthur Housman, was in danger of being wiped out. This meant, of course, that our firm was in jeopardy as well. I almost sank to my knees from shock.

I arranged to have some money transferred immediately from my account to the firm and took the first available steamer back. At the dock I was met by Arthur Housman. He told me there had been a sharp drop in the value of two railroads, the Minneapolis and St. Louis and the Colorado & Southern, in which he and Ed Hawley had invested. I took over my partner's account, putting up enough money to be able to hold the securities in which his fortune was tied up. These securities stayed in my box until some time later, when the affairs of these two railroads improved and Mr. Housman was able to sell the securities at a profit.

Nothing ever gave me greater pleasure than to use my credit and funds to tide Mr. Housman over this critical period and to help him keep the fortune he had built up over a lifetime. He had given me my start in Wall Street and had done as much and perhaps more for me during my early struggles.

My mental tossings and reflections over what turn my career should take did lead to one important decision—my gradual retirement from A. A. Housman & Company. This was a difficult step to take, since my sentimental attachment for the Housmans was strong; but I felt much better after my decision was made. No man can serve two masters at the same time. I would now be able to establish and maintain absolute financial independence.

I mentioned how I felt to Thomas Ryan. He told me I was doing the right thing. Afterward he tried several times to get me associated with him, but I repeated his earlier advice and told him I wanted to go my way alone.

By August, 1903, my retirement from the firm became complete. I moved to quarters at 111 Broadway, which I was to occupy as long as I was a member of the New York Stock Exchange. Although I was thirty-three years old, the thrill of moving into my own office ranks with those which came when I hit a home run with several men on base; when Fitzsimmons told me I had the stuff champions were made of; when I landed my first job, sold my first bond, and cut the first coupon from a bond of my own—a Georgia Pacific First Mortgage five per cent Consolidated Bond.

The day I opened my new office Mother sent me a telegram which I framed and hung on the wall. She also gave me a green china cat, spotted with red, which still stands on my desk. Father gave me a photograph of himself inscribed with these words: "Let unswerving integrity always be your watchword."

The first rule I set for myself was "No accounts for anyone." I stuck to this rule with but few exceptions. One such exception was Senator Nelson Aldrich of Rhode Island, with whom I had become associated in a rubber exploration and development company. After one rubber-company meeting, Senator Aldrich asked me how a man could invest some money advantageously. I told him that I thought United States Steel underpriced because I felt the country was in for a business revival that would call for huge steel orders. When he asked me to buy some stock for him, I said that I never carried accounts for others.

Senator Aldrich was about the age of my father—he had been a soldier in the Union Army. He looked at me tolerantly and said:

"Now, son, you buy that Steel and put it in my name. I mean to tell the first person who is entitled to the information that I am buying Steel and that I gave you the order."

I bought the stock and delivered it to him. Presently he told some of his friends close to the Steel Corporation what he had done. They said they feared he had made a mistake. The Senator replied that he was following the advice of his young friend Baruch.

"Oh," the Steel people said. That, as it was reported to me, was all they said.

Although I did not always agree with Senator Aldrich in his political views, we remained good friends until his death.

I was pleased to notice that the shares I had bought for him were part of the estate he left.

But except for a few such personal favors, I would handle no accounts. My whole object in opening my own firm was to be able to pursue my own speculative way alone, so that if my judgment was faulty no one else would suffer.

But having taken all these steps to put myself in the position where I would be able to speculate more freely, a peculiar thing happened. Instead of speculating more than I had done previously, I speculated less. After the autumn of 1903 less and less of my time was given over to the ups and downs of the market. I found that I had turned toward new horizons, in which constructive enterprise and investment took more and more of my time.

15. With the Guggenheims

IN 1889 WHEN MOTHER stopped me from going to Mexico to learn ore-buying for the Guggenheims, she undoubtedly changed the course of my life. Sixteen years were to elapse before another offer came from the Guggenheims. In those sixteen years the Guggenheims had risen from the owners of a half interest in two Colorado mines to become the most powerful single force in the whole mining industry.

Those sixteen years had also brought a considerable transformation in the embarrassed, gangling youth who sought his first job from Daniel Guggenheim. My financial judgment had been tested repeatedly—often against the market trend— and the offers of directorships that were made to me reflected the growing respect that others entertained for my skills both as a negotiator and a market operator.

I also had acquired capital of my own. After the panic of 1893 I sensed that fortunes could be made by purchasing securities at low depression prices and profiting from the recovery that was bound to come. But since I had no money to invest, I could not take advantage of the opportunities I saw.

When the panic of 1903 struck I was in a far different position. Feeling the market was being pushed too high I had sold much of my holdings in 1902, so that when the market dropped I would have the cash to buy securities and wait on the future growth of the country. I was able, in fact, not only to expand the range of my economic interests but even to take the initiative in launching new enterprises.

Perhaps the main financial achievement that followed the 1893 panic was the consolidation of the nation's railroads. The years that followed the 1903 panic were marked primarily by a tremendous expansion of the base of raw materials that was needed by America's rapidly growing industries. In the decade before World War One, I invested in companies which sought to develop new sources of supply for such varied materials as copper, rubber, iron ore, gold, and sulfur. Always restless by nature, as soon as one of these enterprises reached the dividend-paying stage, I usually got out and searched about for another. One thing that pleased me particularly about these ventures was that they were a means of wresting new resources from the earth and putting them at the disposal of mankind. These enterprises, in short, were creators of true wealth, not of money but of things that were useful.

The knowledge I acquired through these investments was also to prove of enormous value when Woodrow Wilson named me to the Advisory Commission of the Council of National Defense after the outbreak of World War One. The first job entrusted to me was responsibility for assuring adequate supplies of raw materials for our preparedness program. This, in turn, led to my being named as chairman of the War Industries Board.

I first entered the world of raw materials as an agent of the Guggenheims. They were a remarkable family. Old Meyer Guggenheim, who headed the clan, was one of my father's patients. Although I never spoke with him, I did see him from time to time and remember him as always smoking a cigar, indifferent to the ashes which spilled down over his coat.

A story one of his sons liked to tell revealed a good deal about old Meyer. Someone had come to Meyer Guggenheim with a scheme for making money, exclaiming, "See, Mr. Guggenheim, what wealth, what power that would give you!"

Stroking his side whiskers, the old man remarked: *"Und denn?"*

This was characteristic of all the Guggenheims. They believed a project had to do more than just make money. They showed the same breadth of interests in their philanthropies, using the bulk of the family fortune for the support of art, music, aeronautics, and scholarship.

Old Meyer was well over fifty years old when he became interested in mining. The family fortune had been made largely in lace and embroidery, but Meyer felt that this field did not have too much of a future. On the urging of a storekeeper who was one of his customers, Meyer Guggenheim had bought a half interest in a lead and silver mine—the A.Y. and Minnie—in Leadville, Colorado.

In 1881 he decided to have a look at this mine. He found it flooded with water. Old Meyer put up the money for the equipment to "unwater" the mine. It turned out to be a virtual bonanza.

Meyer Guggenheim set about to learn the mining business and ordered his seven sons to do likewise. The cohesion of the family was a prime source of strength. The mining and smelting of gold, silver, lead, copper, and zinc are closely related. These and other metals often are found mixed in the same ore. In fact, ore is easier to smelt if it contains the proper mixture of metals. Each of the Guggenheims set himself to learn a different phase of the industry, the whole family operating like a perfectly disciplined army under the direction of the commander-in-chief, old Meyer.

Simon, the sixth son, for example, spent two years in Europe, where he learned Spanish and French to be able to better serve the family interests in Mexico. Then he was packed off to Colorado to work as a timekeeper in a refinery at Pueblo.

Daniel, who speedily showed himself even more capable than his father, became the leader of the band. Many stories are told of his reign over the mining industry, a reign which lasted until his death in 1930. One story, which I think showed his true character, was of how he set an example of patriotism to other industrialists during World War One.

We had not yet entered the war but had begun to strengthen our defenses. The Armed Services estimated that they would need immediately 45 million pounds of copper.

As commissioner for Raw Materials in the Council of National Defense, I had to see that copper was forthcoming. One problem I faced was to determine what would be a fair price for the government to pay.

I sought out Eugene Meyer, Jr., who knew the copper business, and who was a man of the highest integrity, with a keen desire to be of public service. Meyer suggested that we take the average price over the ten years before the war. This worked out to sixteen and two-thirds cents a pound. At the time copper was selling for thirty-six cents a pound.

Would the industry make such a price reduction? In those days Daniel Guggenheim used to hold open house at five o'clock every Sunday at the St. Regis Hotel, where he lived. Any friend who wished to drop by could call at that hour knowing Daniel would be home. Meyer and I went up to the St. Regis. We asked if we could talk to Mr. Dan alone.

I told Mr. Dan that in buying the materials for the preparedness program we wanted to set an example that would inspire the rest of the country. It looked increasingly as though we might be drawn into the war. Many American families might soon be sending their sons to the colors. These families should not feel that the war was being fought so that rich men or big corporations could make large profits. I wanted the price of copper to be cut low enough so it would be clear that industry was ready to bear its burden.

Mr. Dan listened quietly. When Meyer and I finished, he said, "I'll have to speak to the brothers. Then I'll talk to the other copper producers." Asked how long it would be before we could expect an answer, he said, "Pick me up on the way downtown tomorrow."

We did. As Mr. Dan got into the car he said, "I think I can get you your copper."

I relate that story to illustrate the Guggenheim family character. It was this same character, I believe, which explained their success in mining.

They had been in the business about a year when they learned that mining was most profitable when combined with smelting and so they built a $1,250,000 refinery at Pueblo, Colorado. Much of the ore smelted in this refinery came from Mexico. When Congress put an embargo on the Mexican ore, the Guggenheims built a smelter in Mexico.

During the 1890's the silver and lead business had a hard time of it and in 1899 eighteen concerns were merged into the American Smelting and Refining Company, in which H. H. Rogers, the Rockefellers, and the Lewisohns had a large, if not a controlling interest. The Guggenheims were invited to join the "trust" but declined unless they could have control. The others would not agree to that.

A life and death economic struggle followed between the Guggenheims and the Trust, in which the Guggenheims won almost every engagement. By 1901, the Trust surrendered to the Guggenheims practically on their terms. Daniel became chairman of the executive committee of American Smelting, four of his brothers were made directors, and the family held a majority of the stock.

2

It was some time after this consolidation that I became interested in American Smelting & Refining shares. With the assistance of Solomon Guggenheim, I had made a study of the company. I began to buy its stock and recommended it to friends as an investment. One result was a marked activity which pushed Smelters, as the common stock of American Smelting & Refining was usually referred to, from about 36 to around 80 in eighteen months. This rise took place before all stocks were lifted by the general speculative wave which originated in 1905.

Still, the competition between the Guggenheims and the Rockefellers had not been quieted completely. In 1904 the Rockefellers acquired the Federal Mining & Smelting & Lead Company of California. There were two other large smelting companies on the Pacific Coast, the Tacoma of Washington

193.

and Selby Smelting & Lead of California. Acquisition of either of these properties would have made the Standard Oil group serious competitors of the Guggenheims on both the Pacific Coast and in Alaska, which was just being opened up. At the time people entertained vast notions of Alaska's potentialities—greater than events even to the present have justified.

The Guggenheims had made several unsuccessful attempts to purchase the Selby and Tacoma properties. I suggested to Daniel Guggenheim that I try to swing the deal myself.

My friend Henry C. Davis was well acquainted with William R. Rust, the president and operating head of Tacoma Smelting. Davis told me that Rust, personally, had no prejudice against the Guggenheims. If I laid my cards on the table, Davis thought Rust would do what he could to help me.

This was good news, but the first person I had to win over was right in New York, not five minutes' walk from my office. He was the fabulously wealthy Darius Ogden Mills, a veteran of the 1849 California gold rush, who in his eightieth year still retained active charge of his widespread business affairs. One example of his business efficiency was the Mills Hotels, which he built to help needy people. These institutions were set up to provide rooms for twenty cents a night and meals for fifteen cents. Yet they were managed so well that they returned a small profit.

Darius Mills was the largest stockholder in Tacoma and a heavy stockholder in Selby. He received me with dignified, old-fashioned courtesy at his office in the Mills Building on Broad Street. He had side whiskers but his upper lip and chin were clean shaven. In appearance and manner he reminded me of my planter grandfather in South Carolina, Saling Wolfe.

We had a long talk during which Mr. Mills reminisced of how, during the gold rush, he had often slept under a wagon. When we got down to business I asked for an option on his Selby and Tacoma stock. He refused the option but did tell me to go ahead and negotiate, and that he would not deal with the Rockefellers in the meantime.

Early in January, 1905, Henry Davis and I took a train to the West Coast. With us went A. C. Jopling, an attorney from the office of William H. Page, who, the reader may recall, was my associate on my first mission of this kind—the purchase of the Liggett & Myers Tobacco Company for Ryan. We met Rust at the Tacoma offices in Everett, Washington. My offer of $800 a share for the common stock was so attractive that within a few days a forty-five-day option was signed and in our hands. This option called for the delivery of 90 per cent of the common stock, four existing contracts with gold mines, three of which were situated in Alaska, and the resignation of all the Tacoma directors.

Then we moved down to San Francisco and began to work on the Selby people. They presented more difficulties. The Selby's stockholders were scattered and some of them did not care to relinquish their voice in the business. Besides, the fact that I might not be acting for myself alone began to leak out. The San Francisco newspapers drew attention to my affiliations with the Guggenheims. The inferences drawn from this gossip were largely true, of course, but they made our negotiations more difficult.

Meanwhile the Rockefellers had gotten on the scent. One day I received a wire from New York to close the Selby option without delay. As if that wasn't exactly what I had been trying to do all along!

In purchasing the Tacoma Smelting Company I had been impressed by Billy Rust and I asked him to help me with the Selby people. Darius Mills also promised to use his telling influence. After yielding a few points I managed to get everything settled except the formality of signing. Then, in the first week of March, I caught the Overland for New York. Jopling stayed on to wind up things.

A few days after my return to New York the Selby option went through. Then Fred Bradley, a San Francisco mining engineer, became obstreperous and threatened to knock the

Tacoma negotiations into a cocked hat just when I was about to take up the option. Bradley and his associates gave me an uncomfortable three weeks during which the telegraph wires were kept hot. But thanks to Billy Rust and Henry Davis he finally was won over.

Through these options the Guggenheims were able to checkmate the Rockefellers on the Pacific Coast and in Alaska. It had been stipulated in advance that if I succeeded I would be rewarded handsomely. Originally Daniel Guggenheim had planned to unite the two Pacific Coast smelting companies into a new corporation, and I was to receive a block of shares as my fee. But Daniel changed his mind and absorbed the Selby and Tacoma into the American Smelting & Refining Company.

This new arrangement required a different settlement of my claim. I was asked to discuss the matter with Samuel Untermeyer, one of the shrewdest lawyers of that day. I believe this was my first business meeting with him. Mr. Untermeyer set out to drive the best bargain he could for his client, and I reacted like a cat whose fur has been brushed the wrong way.

If a new corporation had been set up as originally planned I would have made about $1,000,000 for my work. I told Mr. Untermeyer that was what I was asking for and declined to debate the matter. Mr. Untermeyer inquired if I intended to "hold up" the American Smelting & Refining Company.

Leaning across the table that stood between us, I replied, "No, Mr. Untermeyer, I had not thought of that until now."

Then I said good day and left the room.

The question was referred to Daniel Guggenheim, who settled it characteristically. "If Bernie says he ought to get $1,000,000, that is what he will get."

When I received my check, I paid off the legal and incidental expenses, amounting to about $100,000. Then I wrote out two checks for $300,000 each, one to Henry C. Davis and one to William R. Rust.

There were not two more surprised men in America than

Davis and Rust when they got those checks. Both protested against receiving them. I told them they had to take the money because they had earned it. This was true. Without their help I never could have closed the deal.

3

One thing that had brought me back from California in a hurry was the continued rise of American Smelting shares. During my two months' absence—from early January to early March—the stock had gone from somewhere in the 80's to over 100. Then, while I was terminating the Selby and Tacoma options, Smelters crossed 120. This seemed like an unhealthy rise to me. I had recommended the stock to friends and, if the rise continued much longer, feared that many of them would get hurt. I went to the Guggenheims, told them of my fears, and informed them that I had to advise my friends to sell.

The Guggenheims did not like this. They did not agree with me that their stock had been marked up too high. Their reaction is another example of how difficult it is for "insiders" to hold an objective judgment about their own properties and of how little highly successful businessmen may know about the stock market. The Guggenheims knew mining better than anyone else in the world, but they did not know the stock market as I knew it.

Great builders seldom acquire the technique of the stock market. E. H. Harriman was a notable exception. But James J. Hill, who built the Great Northern Railway, was like a child when it came to market operations. I distrust supposedly versatile people, for I have learned that few men can do more than one thing well.

I sold as I told the Guggenheims I would. Some of my friends also sold their Smelters shares. My advice was ignored by others, particularly by those close to the Guggenheims.

The bull market of 1905 and 1906 was booming along and

my quiet warnings were without effect. After a momentary decline, Smelters began to climb, slowly at first, but gaining speed as it went. In August, 1905, it crossed 130, early in November, 140, and before the month was out it stood at 157½.

Definitely, I did not like the looks of this.

Although displeased by my attitude toward their stock, the Guggenheims derived some satisfaction from the fact that my pessimistic predictions seemed confounded. Solomon Guggenheim showed his faith in me by confiding his desire to acquire the National Lead Company to complete American Smelting's mastery of the lead industry.

The strongest of the independent producers, National Lead had a small capitalization—150,000 shares, I think. Normally there was little trading in this stock, but good earnings statements and the general advance of the whole market had carried National Lead upward during October and early November of 1905.

Nevertheless, I told Solomon Guggenheim that the best way to acquire National Lead was to buy a majority of its stock in the open market. He gave me an order to do so. I asked him to disclose this to none of his friends and to as few members of the firm as possible.

The next morning I directed that prince of brokers, Harry Content, to buy control of National Lead at the market. I told him to bid up the stock fast in the beginning to discourage competition. The longer we waited, I felt, the less chance we would have to buy enough shares for control.

When the Exchange opened at ten o'clock I sat down before the ticker in my office. A telephone with direct connection to the Stock Exchange floor was at hand. National Lead opened at around 57. As Content bought, the stock rose about three points. Then Content reported some persistent opposition buying.

Immediately I told him to stop buying. Presently Content informed me that whoever was buying had become fearful and stopped. Then the competitive buyer began to sell.

Whereupon I renewed Content's order to bid the stock up so fast that opposition buyers would be afraid to pay the price. This I knew would encourage selling and deter other buyers.

When the gong rang at three o'clock, the Guggenheims had control. It had been acquired in a single day's trading. So adroitly had Content done his work that the stock closed at 64 and a fraction, a rise of less than 8 points over the opening price.

Has there ever been another broker who could do that?

The acquisition of National Lead jumped American Smelting to new highs. In January, 1906, it touched 174. Jubilant interests close to the management were talking 200 for the stock.

Then came a general break in the market. Smelters dropped to 161, rallied, then broke again. Guggenheim brokers fought to stem the decline—without avail.

When misfortune overtakes us, all of us are prone to blame someone else if we can, and usually we think we can. This instinct for the preservation of self-esteem is one of the more deep-seated traits of human nature. The story went out that the break in Smelters was due not to the stock having been overpriced but to the "bear" operations of B. M. Baruch. Some of the very people I had warned when the stock was at 120, and had repeatedly warned after that, were sufficiently blinded by disappointment to repeat this story.

It was a falsehood out of whole cloth. To sell short stocks with which I had been so closely identified was contrary to the code which I have never broken. I never would "raid" the stock of a corporation owned by people who had given me the opportunities I had been given by the Guggenheims.

This unpleasant gossip reached the Guggenheims and caused several of the brothers to avoid me. I was heartsick. Still, I resolved to make no denial of the charge until one of the Guggenheims should repeat it. I waited. Eventually, I learned that Solomon Guggenheim had said that I had sold their stock short.

I went to see him and, with a calmness that required some effort, recapitulated the whole story of the rise and decline of the Smelters shares, showing how false was the accusation he had voiced against me. When I left him he was still angry but more, I think, because he had ignored my advice than because of any belief that I had been "raiding" his stock.

The day after this painful interview, a broker who was a relative of the Guggenheims told Solomon that he and others had been wrong about my alleged short position in the market. Solomon Guggenheim immediately came to me with an apology.

The flurry was not over yet. A cruel rumor questioning the financial stability of the Guggenheims began to be whispered around Wall Street. Such a rumor at such a time can do much harm, besides being a torture to one's peace of mind. One afternoon I went to the Guggenheim offices at 71 Broadway. Three or four of the brothers were there. I asked if they would accept a deposit of $500,000 as a mark of my confidence. With tears in his eyes, Mr. Dan thanked me on behalf of himself and his family. When I asked what else I could do, he said, "Nothing, except assure the people that the company is all right."

The best way I could do that was to buy American Smelting stock, which I did.

Another incident strengthened my relations with the Guggenheims. The Guggenheim Exploration Company owned a large amount of Utah Copper Company stock which it wanted to dispose of. Someone had suggested that the Exploration Company sell this stock, which promised to be profitable, to a syndicate in which the Guggenheims were interested. After outlining the situation to me, Daniel Guggenheim remarked, "You know, we are going to take you in here just like one of the brothers."

"If you are putting me on the basis of one of the brothers," I replied, "as one of the brothers I shall speak."

I then told him it would be a serious mistake for the Guggenheims to sell themselves stock owned by another company they controlled. It would look as if the Guggenheims were taking advantage of other stockholders of the Exploration Company. Mr. Dan raised his hand. "You don't have to go any further," he said, "you are right."

Deeply affected, he shook hands with me and thanked me for having brought his attention to what might have been a serious blunder. On several occasions he referred to this incident.

16. *Searching for Rubber*

THE FIRST automobile I owned was an eight- or twelve-horsepower Panhard which had run second in a race from Paris to Bordeaux. I bought it in 1901 at the suggestion of A. C. Bostwick, who was the heir to a large fortune made in Standard Oil.

That Panhard was a speedy monster for its day and I was a proud man to own it, and prouder yet when I learned to drive it myself. Along with the car I had acquired a chauffeur named Heinrich Hilgenbach, who was thoroughly versed in the art and mystery of operating an automobile. Heinrich was a good man when sober. But his delinquencies added too much to an already zestful sport.

The Panhard ignition system consisted of hot tubes which exploded the gas with a report like a young cannon. This made some persons afraid to ride in it. Everyone along the North Jersey shore, where we summered, knew when our Panhard was coming. People would jump out of their buggies to grasp the bridles of their horses.

At least one neighbor—the father of Eugene Meyer, Jr.—considered my Panhard "a public nuisance." But this I did not learn until many years later.

The possession of this Panhard raised me to such rank as a personage that the New York *Herald* printed my picture at the wheel. This was the first time I ever had done anything that entitled me to so much space in the estimation of a New York newspaper editor.

My second automobile was a forty-horsepower Mercedes with a yellow body. It cost $22,000. W. K. Vanderbilt had one like it. Or rather I had one like Vanderbilt's, for his was the first car of that kind in America.

The Mercedes also was equipped with hot tubes. The first day I went out in it we got as far as Grant's Tomb when the Mercedes broke down. Later I ran it in an exhibition race on the Long Branch track against Bostwick, who was in an American car, and did a little more than a mile a minute. Everyone thought it wonderful, none more so than I.

One traffic rule in those early auto days was that when a person in a buggy raised his hand the auto driver had to stop and wait for the buggy owner to get out and hold his horse. The speed limit in New York was ten miles an hour. Automobiles were prohibited in Central Park. Because of this I did most of my motoring in New Jersey. European roads were so superior to ours in those days that I took my car abroad during the summer just to get a chance to run it to my heart's content.

Those early automobiles were expensive and uncertain playthings. A tire that held up for a few hundred miles without a blowout had rendered good service.

I cannot pose as one of those farsighted persons who foresaw the astonishing development of the motor car. I did, however, think that the increasing popularity of the automobile "fad" would be strongly favorable to the rubber industry.

Among the industrial shares I had bought during the panic of 1903 were those of the Rubber Goods Manufacturing Company, then one of the few large American concerns making rubber products. My ownership of these shares led me into a study of rubber consumption which, in turn, inspired the vision of a gigantic combine which might do for rubber what the Rockefellers had done for petroleum.

With my own financial resources I could not manage this myself and so, even before the first shock of the 1903 panic had passed off, I began looking about for some creative industrialist, with adequate capital, who could exercise such leadership. The Guggenheims filled the bill in every way, and it was to Daniel Guggenheim that I first went with my dreams of a rubber empire.

I asked Mr. Dan to join me in buying control of the Rubber Goods Manufacturing Company. Since its shares had risen somewhat from the panic lows at which I had bought, I offered to average what I had paid for my stock with the higher prices that would have to be paid for the additional shares needed to gain control. I was willing to pay that premium to be associated with the Guggenheims.

Mr. Dan said he would think over the matter and consult his brothers. Time passed and I heard nothing more.

When my Rubber Goods stock rose to where it offered a handsome profit, I sold out, relegating my visions of a rubber combine to the limbo of unrealized expectations.

Some months later Mr. Dan inquired about those rubber holdings of mine. When I told him I had wearied of waiting and closed them out, he said he was sorry I had. He then asked me to look into another rubber proposition.

Its aim was to find a large and truly dependable source of rubber. If that could be done the industrial uses of rubber could be expanded enormously. At the time, plantation rubber was only beginning to be cultivated. Nearly all the available rubber grew wild, most of it coming from the Para district of Brazil on the lower Amazon. The quality of this rubber was not uniform. It was collected by natives, who could not be relied upon for a sure supply.

In those days, 100,000 tons was a lot of rubber for the whole world. During World War Two, when I was chairman of the Rubber Committee, we needed 672,000 tons a year for the U. S. alone.

An inventor named William A. Lawrence had developed a process for taking rubber from guayule, a silvery-leafed shrub which belonged to the aster family and was indigenous to northern Mexico. Lawrence had interested Thomas Ryan and Senator Nelson E. Aldrich. They, in turn, sought to enlist the Guggenheims, even as I had earlier. It was this proposition of Ryan and Aldrich that brought Dan Guggenheim to me.

I went to Mexico to investigate firsthand guayule's prospects. I found that this shrub, which grew wild over millions of semidesert acres, could be cultivated by simple methods and would mature in about three years. The more I explored the matter the greater became my interest. Here at our very door, and in a healthful climate, it seemed, lay a possible source of rubber that could compete with the product of the fever-ridden jungles of South America and Africa.

My investigation contributed to the formation in November, 1904, of the Continental Rubber Company, which subsequently became the Intercontinental Rubber Company. Senator Aldrich, Mr. Ryan, Daniel Guggenheim, and I held equal amounts of stock. Additional shares were taken by young John D. Rockefeller, H. P. Whitney, Levi P. Norton, C. K. G. Billings, and some of their relatives and friends.

2

Mexico was not the only country where we looked for rubber. At one time, in fact, our company had expeditions searching over much of the earth. Our men penetrated the upper reaches of the Amazon, crossed the Andes, and worked down their western slopes. In Africa they ascended the Congo and its tributaries. Other parties explored Borneo and the Straits Settlements.

We lost two men in Africa and one off a ship in the Caribbean in a storm. William Stayton, later known for his fight to repeal the Prohibition Amendment, got stranded in the jungles of Venezuela. After many adventures he reached the coast. Sighting a small schooner, he hailed it and then swam out to it. The meeting proved fortunate for the ship's company as well as for Stayton. The schooner's crew had come down with yellow fever. Stayton, who had been educated at the U.S. Naval Academy, took command of the vessel and brought it into port.

Our entry into Africa came at the invitation of King Leopold II. Leopold was a remarkable man. While still young he found that the revenues of his small kingdom were inadequate to satisfy his extravagant tastes or the grandiose ambitions he entertained for his country. Leopold set out to remedy both deficiencies by making Belgium a colonial power.

Through a series of adroit maneuvers he organized the rich Congo basin into the ostensibly independent Congo Free State and then brought it under the sovereignty of Belgium. As a financial coup, this operation, carried on under the very noses of England and the other powers, would have done credit to a Morgan, Harriman, Rockefeller, or Ryan.

The richest of the Congo concessions were reserved for the Belgian crown. Their exploitation, particularly in the early years, was carried on brutally. Congo rubber became known as "red rubber" in part because of its color but mainly because of the blood of the natives who were said to have been sacrificed to its production. Some of these atrocity stories were circulated by other powers that had been chagrined by Leopold's statecraft. Still, despite the Belgian counterpropaganda which attributed everything to the jealousy of rival nations, I always believed the "red rubber" appellation deserved.

By the summer of 1906, Leopold, who was seventy-one years old, felt that it was time to reorganize the Congo's administration. Moreover, he no longer was in a position to disregard the opinions of the world outraged by his treatment of the natives. Leopold inquired as to who was the ablest Catholic capitalist in the United States. He was given the name of Thomas Fortune Ryan, who in those days had a private chapel in his home.

At the moment of Leopold's inquiry, Ryan happened to be in Switzerland. He was devoting much of his time and money to acquiring an art collection. Summoned to Brussels, Ryan was presented to Leopold, who made his proposals. The result was the formation of the American Congo Company and the Société Internationale Forestière et Minière du Congo, commonly known as the Forminière. American Congo held a concession to search for and develop new sources of rubber, the Forminière was to be a more general enterprise for the development of mineral and forest products.

Leopold was a sharp businessman. He received one half of the capital stock in each enterprise for the concessions. With the Forminière an additional quarter of the stock was reserved for Belgian capitalists, leaving Ryan with only a twenty-five-per-cent interest. I can't imagine anyone except a king, and a smart king at that, inducing Thomas Fortune Ryan to take so short an end of any deal.

Flattered by the royal patronage, Ryan came home filled with ardor for his new projects. He succeeded in getting the Guggenheims, H. P. Whitney, Senator Aldrich, myself, and one or two others to go in with him. At first Daniel Guggenheim was not interested. As a man who prided himself on his relations with labor, he did not like Leopold's reputation as an employer. He made the fair treatment of native workmen a *sine qua non* condition to his participation.

I was also slow in joining the venture because I suspected that Leopold's move was aimed at disarming American criticism of his policies. But Ryan was so enthusiastic, so certain that these concessions comprised a great humanitarian opportunity as well as a chance for each of us to become something of a Cecil Rhodes, that when Guggenheim went in I decided to follow. As it turned out, Ryan's predictions of a reformation of labor conditions in the Congo were borne out.

Two years of hazardous exploration proved the American Congo Company concession to be barren. However, diamonds were found on the Forminière property, making its stock a good investment. Ryan never lost his enthusiasm for his Congo companies. One reason, I suppose, was because a king had called him in to start them. When the diamonds first were discovered, Ryan used to carry a number of them around in his pocket and exhibit them with the delight of a boy showing off a prize collection of marbles.

3

But our main rubber searching effort was concentrated on Mexico. On my visit there early in 1904 I had arranged for the purchase of several million acres of land to grow guayule and for the construction of a factory to extract the rubber from the guayule plant by the new flotation process under the Lawrence patent.

We traveled in our private railroad car. With me were my wife; my brother Sailing; Eddie Norton, the broker who had figured so prominently in the Northern Pacific corner; and several other persons whose names I no longer recall.

We crossed into Mexico at Laredo. At Agua Caliente, which is the highest point on the railroad, I suddenly felt pains in my stomach and chest. The pains passed away when the train descended from the extremely high altitude.

In Mexico City we stayed at the Iturbide Hotel—the "Ity Bitty." We saw our first bullfight. I am fond of most sports. Horse racing in particular has always thrilled me, and even today I still hunt for quail in South Carolina. But this first bullfight was all I ever wanted to see. Several of the horses were gored by the bulls, which sickened me.

My wife and Sailing spent most of their time shopping for various things, including semiprecious stones and Mexican jewelry. While they were acting as tourists, I plunged into negotiations with the Mexican officials. I soon found myself deep in legal, technical, agricultural, and even social problems, all of which gave me more than a superficial understanding of the republic to the south of us.

The Mexico I came to know during my sojourn there presented a picture of striking contrasts. Porfirio Diaz had gathered about him a coterie of exceedingly able and polished men who moved in a society as elegant as that of any European capital. But beyond their garden gates were millions of peons with little chance to better their lot.

Such a state of affairs could not last forever, as we were to discover, although I did not foresee it at the time. Questions of this sort did not concern me as deeply as they should have at that period of my life.

Before going to Mexico I had heard much of the peculiar methods said to be in vogue in dealing with officialdom there. In my own dealings, I can only say that I did not find Mexicans any different from other people with whom I have done business. I found some Mexicans who were honest and some who were not, some selfish, some patriotic—in short, what one would expect of any country.

The man who impressed me most among the Mexicans I met was Pablo Martinez Del Rio. He spoke English, French, German, and Italian. With the figure of a grandee, a good education, and wide cultural background, he would have attracted notice in any company in the world.

Señor Del Rio was fearful of letting Americans have too much economic influence in Mexico. As he explained to me, he was afraid that the concessions granted Americans might some day be used as an excuse to seize northern Mexico.

Some years later I recalled his words when some of our oil people proposed doing just what Del Rio feared—and, but for Woodrow Wilson, they might have had their way.

It was shortly after we entered World War One. President Wilson had invited me to a White House discussion of an oil shortage which threatened to disrupt our military plans. One official proposed that we seize the Mexican oil fields in Tampico. Squadrons of marines had already been alerted. The President had only to give the word for them to push off.

President Wilson hardly waited for the finish of the argument. When aroused, he would speak in firm, measured tones, which left no doubt what was in his mind.

"What you are asking me to do is exactly what we protested against when committed by Germany," he reprimanded. "You say this oil in Mexico is necessary for us. That is what the Germans said when they invaded Belgium; 'it was necessary' to get to France. Gentlemen," he concluded, "you will have to fight the war with what oil you have."

For our rubber project in Mexico, we bought more than three million acres of land. We purchased all this land through regular channels, paying a fair price and nothing more. I heard of short-cuts but never found occasion to try one. We represented ourselves as anxious to bring an industry to Mexico that would put to use millions of acres of its idle lands, and give work to its people. It seemed to me that this is what Diaz honestly wanted to do. We made many contracts with Mexicans which were lived up to in about the same degree that contracts are followed elsewhere.

In fact our big contract trouble arose not in Mexico but in the United States. We had erected a factory at Torreon to extract the rubber from the guayule plant. Even before this factory was in operation, we signed an agreement under which the Rubber Goods Company of America would take practically the entire output of the Torreon plant for two years. No sooner did the Torreon plant begin to produce crude rubber than the Rubber Goods Company repudiated the contract. It was alleged that our product fell below specifications. This was not true.

Although usually I can find a way to compose differences outside of court, I wanted to sue the United States Rubber Company, which had bought control of the Rubber Goods Company. But Morgan and George F. Baker of the First National Bank pulled us off the suit. Then I recommended that we buy the United States Rubber Company as a manufacturing outlet for our raw material. Failing in this I endeavored to make a trade with the Diamond Rubber Company. By trying to get overly favorable terms my associates spoiled this.

Angered because I was not permitted to fight the United States Rubber Company, I stepped out of the Intercontinental, disposing of my holdings. The Intercontinental found other buyers for its product, however, and was paying dividends when in 1910 the Madero revolution overthrew Diaz Opposing armies overran our plantations and eventually the

Torreon plant closed down. The soundness of the undertaking had been established, however.

Although I believe that old Diaz did much for his country, the Mexico that emerged from the chaos which followed Diaz' overthrow has been a better Mexico. At the time I was there I felt that Americans were neglecting their best opportunities in Mexico. Although the situation has changed for the better, I still think much more progress can be made.

4

Part of the trouble in Mexico—and this is even more true of underdeveloped countries elsewhere—has been the heritage of suspicions left over from the imperialism of the past. Having been born in the Reconstruction South, I know how bitter and strong the memory of past wrongs can be. Yet if the economic problems of these underdeveloped countries are to be made manageable, the past must be buried and not remain a ghost to frustrate the present.

In many parts of Asia, Africa, and South America, the thinking of the government leaders is so steeped in memories of old grievances that they cannot see clearly their own interests.

One particular blindness in these countries is the failure to understand the profit motive. Society can progress only if men's labors show a profit—if they yield more than is put in. To produce at a loss must leave less for all to share. A profitable enterprise contributes more to national independence than an unprofitable one.

True, profits may often be unjustly shared. But such abuses can be corrected without destroying profits.

The profit motive is also an invaluable tool of individual freedom. What causes men to work? There are three general inducements: the love of one's labor or the desire to be of service to others; the desire for profit and gain; and the fact that people are forced to work by some higher authority.

Where the appeal to man's desire to better his own lot is active in a society, less force is needed than where this incentive is lacking.

Much of this misconception of the profit motive among underdeveloped countries reflects the false notion spread by Karl Marx that imperialism is something peculiar to capitalist economies. In many of these underdeveloped lands the capitalist nations did act as the agents of imperialism. But the history of ancient Rome, Greece, and Persia shows that imperialism existed long before capitalism came to flourish.

The actions of the Soviet Union are further proof that imperialistic tendencies can exist without the profit-making motive. In fact, at a time when the capitalistic countries have been abandoning their old empires, the Soviets have been pressing every means at their disposal to build a new empire. As is shown by the chronicle of events since the end of World War Two, the Soviet Union has become the most imperialistic of all nations.

Instead of trying to judge a nation by some ideological label like "capitalism," "socialism," or some other "ism," I would suggest a different measure—namely, the progress a nation is making in bettering the living conditions of its own people.

I urge that as a yardstick because rarely do the waters of foreign policy rise above their own domestic level. No nation will operate very differently abroad than it does at home. A country which devotes its resources to improving the living of its own people usually will guide its foreign policy to help other nations lift their living standards. A government which deliberately depresses the living of its own people is likely to be driven to push down the living standards of every nation it deals with.

The introduction of outside capital really means bringing into a country resources which that country does not already have. Along with that capital also come management skills which underdeveloped nations often lack.

As long as too much is not paid for these resources and

management skills, the underdeveloped country will profit by such investment. In this connection the underdeveloped nations must recognize that if they increase the risks that a foreign investor must run, they increase the cost that they must pay for any investment.

In short, what both the underdeveloped and developed nations should be striving for is agreement on the terms that would make private investment mutually profitable. It should not be too difficult for an understanding to be reached on a set of fair investment practices between countries. Certainly foreign investments should always improve living standards. They should also contribute to the training of skills of every kind in the underdeveloped countries, steadily expanding the number of trained workers and managers. Where local capital is available it should be given as large an interest as possible.

For their part, the underdeveloped countries must learn the importance of orderly government. They should beware of the blandishments of any ideology which promises everything but ends only in enslavement. It takes time to learn the arts and disciplines of self-government. In our own foreign policy we should not strive to outpromise others but should help these newly independent nations gain the time they need to learn how to govern themselves.

We and these newly independent countries have at least one interest in common on which we both can build—that these countries remain free.

17. *Copper for America*

BY THE TURN OF THE CENTURY I had come to realize that anything that happened in the world could affect the markets for securities or commodities.

My arbitrage operations in London and episodes such as the coup we pulled off after the battle of Santiago had helped give me a sense of geographic continuity, of how quickly events in the furthermost corner of the world would be felt in Wall Street. From my dealings in copper, sugar, rubber, and other raw materials I also had learned that supply and demand in any commodity worked itself out on a world-wide basis.

Not until World War One, though, did I really come to appreciate how truly total had become the continuity of happenings and forces in our world. With the demand for everything in excess of available supplies, I was forced to weigh the relative importance of the many competing uses for the same things. Often it was a matter of balancing one urgency against a higher urgency. To get mules which General Pershing needed to haul guns to the front, for example, we had to trade to Spain part of our own short supply of ammonia sulfate. Similarly, I often had to decide where the same tonnage of steel would make its greatest contribution—if used to build a destroyer or a merchant ship, if kept at home or sent to a French artillery factory.

All this, of course, I was forced to learn while the war was raging. However, even before the war, as a result of my financial experiences, I had acquired some awareness of the intertwining ties that bound together economics and national defense.

In particular, two developments of the early 1900's fore-shadowed the shape of things to come. There was the emergence of Germany and the United States as new naval powers. Then there was the dawning of a new "electrical age."

This new technology spurred a world-wide hunt for raw materials of every sort. Marxists have pictured this search for new supplies of raw materials as reflecting a profit-making drive which was supposed to be one of the weaknesses of the capitalistic system. This belief still is held by some people.

But this Marxist dogma never was an adequate explanation of what was happening. The urge for profit was there, of course. But actually the drive to tap nature's resources all over the world was spurred by the total march of our industrial civilization. The new technological advances which were to make possible so spectacular an increase in the living standards of the masses of people required additional physical resources. This same technology also transformed the needs of security and national defense. As old weapons were rendered obsolete, for example, whole naval fleets had to be rebuilt.

Nor was this hunt for new materials directed solely abroad. Between 1880 and 1890, for example, the world output of copper increased tenfold and the whole surface of the globe was combed in the search for new ore bodies. It was this surging demand which drew the Guggenheims into the copper business. But this same demand also opened the way for the use of lower-grade ores in our Western states, which eventually made this country virtually self-sufficient in copper supplies.

I have always advocated a more intensive development of our own domestic ores and am pleased to have helped finance our first major experiment in this regard. Nine years of effort and as many millions of dollars went into this project before it proved itself.

2

Near Bingham, Utah, there happened to be a cavernous gulch of mineralized porphyry rock. Tests showed that this porphyry was impregnated with copper, but the ore was so low in grade that no one seemed to feel that it could be mined profitably. One old-timer in the Bingham district, Colonel Enos A. Wall, did buy 200 acres of this copper canyon and spent $20,000 trying to develop it—without success.

Just when it looked as if Wall's money were lost, along came a young mining engineer from Missouri named Daniel C. Jackling. A big, bluff, strapping, red-faced fellow, Jackling looked like a miner, although he had started out as a college professor. Jackling, who had been operating a zinc plant in Canon City, Colorado, believed he could devise a way of profitably working that low-grade ore.

A foreign-born capitalist named Delamar held an option on the Bingham property but let it expire when one of his engineers informed him that the canyon could not be worked profitably. Jackling recommended the purchase of the property to Charles MacNeill.

In June of 1903 the Utah Copper Company was formed with MacNeill as president, Wall as vice-president, and Jackling as general manager.

Jackling's idea was basically simple, as great ideas often are. Finding it unprofitable to work this ore by the usual tunnel and shaft method, he proposed to mine it with steam shovels—what is now known as strip mining. Everything dug up would then be run through mills, where the copper was separated through a flotation process and turned into a concentrate.

To make this economical, Jackling wanted to construct a mill that would handle 3000 to 5000 tons of ore a day instead of the 300 to 500 tons that was the usual capacity of such plants. By increasing the productive capacity of the mills, while keeping the overhead cost constant, the low-grade ore could be refined at a profit.

From the outset it was realized that the experiment would be costly. Stock was sold at $10 a share. The company organizers subscribed heavily but still were unable to interest the public sufficiently to get the working capital they needed. It was at this point that MacNeill talked to me of the project.

I met Jackling and liked him at once. His theory seemed sound to me. It was the mass-production idea, then in its infancy, applied to copper mining. I bought a good many shares.

With the limited capital available, Jackling could do little more than build an experimental mill and concentrator to determine what would be the most economical plan to be followed in later and larger operations. Within a year this plant was running. Eagerly we awaited word of the result. This small experimental mill showed an operating profit.

Jackling wanted to push on and build a large mill. This called for an outlay into the millions. The Utah Copper Company was searching for means to raise it when in 1906 the Guggenheims decided to take another try at copper.

The Bingham operation interested them so much that they asked John Hays Hammond to investigate it. Hammond was perhaps the best known mining engineer of the time. His reputation was based not only on his engineering ability but on his public relations skill.

While in South Africa, Hammond had been captured by the Boers and condemned to die. He was saved from the gallows by a petition from the U.S. Senate. Afterward the Guggenheims and William C. Whitney put Hammond in charge of the Guggenheim Exploration Company. In Mexico, Hammond supplemented his engineering work with rare diplomatic skill in handling Porfirio Diaz and helped build up the Guggenheim interests there.

Hammond sent two eminent engineers, Seeley W. Mudd and A. Chester Beatty, to examine Bingham Canyon. Their findings brought in the Guggenheims with badly needed cap-

ital. The venture was to give the Guggenheims a heavy advantage over other copper companies, including the Amalgamated Copper Company, which was then the big trust in the
industry. Amalgamated had clever engineers who were given
the same opportunities to study Jackling's proposition as the
Guggenheims had. But the Amalgamated people felt that
Jackling's idea was impractical. Today the larger part of the
copper refined in this country is processed by Jackling's
methods or by improvements on his process.

At the time the Guggenheims came in, a speculative wave
was beginning to gather force and money was freer than it
had been at any time since the 1903 panic. In fact, the prospects of the Utah Copper Company seemed so good that the
Utah's backers were able to get $20 a share from the Guggen-
heims for stock which had sold originally for $10 a share.

Jackling seized this new capital and threw it into his works.
Then he asked for more money and still more money. To
meet his needs, a bond issue of $3,000,000 was suggested.

The size of Jackling's expenditures frightened many persons in the company, including Colonel Wall, who had been
the first to gamble on copper in Bingham Canyon. Wall opposed the bond issue in the councils of the company. Losing
the fight there, he resigned as a director to carry his battle
into the courts. He obtained an injunction against the bond
issue but this obstacle proved only temporary. The injunction was dissolved and the bonds were issued.

While the injunction dispute was being fought out, Dan
Guggenheim asked me over to discuss issuing the $3,000,000
in bonds. I offered to underwrite it for a five-per-cent commission.

I had received assurances of subscriptions for a good part
of the issue when Charles Hayden, of Hayden, Stone & Company, came forward and agreed to underwrite the issue for
less than 1 per cent, an unheard-of low commission. Although
I thought an honorable commitment had been made to me
by the Guggenheims, I did not feel that I could hold them
to it in the face of such a bid. The issue, which was over-

subscribed, supplied Jackling with the funds he needed to complete the erection of his big mills.

At the same time I also had agreed to underwrite an issue of Nevada Consolidated convertible bonds. But this venture also was undertaken by Hayden, Stone. Charley Hayden showed considerable shrewdness in letting neither of these issues get out of his hands. Nevada Consolidated proved a fine property and was later absorbed by Utah Copper.

3

Originally it had been expected that Jackling's mill would be in operation before the end of 1906. Because of construction obstacles, it was not until the spring of 1907 that the wheels of the mill began to turn. Up to that moment Jackling had spent $8,000,000.

In March of 1907 there had been a serious break on the Stock Exchange. Shrewd hands began to shorten sail. Still no one, not even Morgan, anticipated actual panic.

By summer, though, even as Jackling's mills stepped up their activity, the general financial uncertainty increased. In October the Knickerbocker Trust Company closed and its president killed himself. This precipitated a run on New York's banks such as the city had never seen within my memory. The panic spread to the floor of the Stock Exchange; the credit structure of the country collapsed. We found ourselves in the worst financial emergency since the crisis that followed the readjustment after the Civil War.

How one man, J. P. Morgan, then in his seventy-first year, exercised the powers of a czar to stem the crisis, is a story that does not require repetition here. I cannot forbear, however, relating a personal incident in connection with what Morgan did.

To relieve the market, Morgan created a special fund to which various financial institutions were contributing. After lying awake in my bed for a long time one night, I decided to make a dramatic gesture regarding that fund.

I would go to the Morgan office, step up to the old gentleman's desk, and say that I wished to contribute to his fund. When Mr. Morgan asked how much I intended to put in, I meant to offer him $1,500,000 in cold cash. I had good reason to believe that this might be the largest individual contribution the fund would receive, unless from himself.

But on my way downtown the next morning, I found that I just couldn't bring myself to go through with this gesture. Instead I went to the Bank of Manhattan Company and told its president, Stephen Baker, to add $1,500,000 from me to whatever the bank itself was contributing. The money went over to Morgan's in the name of the Bank of Manhattan rather than in my name.

Why I decided against going directly to Mr. Morgan, I cannot explain. I am not overly modest. I also wanted to impress Mr. Morgan with my faith in his leadership and in my own ability to discern the essential soundness of the country. But I just couldn't go through with it.

Had I carried through my original plan, my later relations with the Morgans, as with the Atlantic Coast Line and Texas Gulf Sulphur, might have been different. But then, had I become a financial intimate of the Morgans, Woodrow Wilson might never have given me the opportunity to serve this country as chairman of the War Industries Board. Kingdoms have been lost for want of a nail, but sometimes the same lost nail will open to the rider an experience which might never have been his.

While the panic of 1907 was at its worst and no one could foretell whether Mr. Morgan would succeed or fail, I received an urgent request for $500,000 in cash to meet the payroll of the Utah Copper Company. Copper had fallen in price from twenty-two to twelve cents per pound and the company's shares from 39 to 13. But Jackling had to keep producing to hold his organization together, even if the metal piled up beside the railroad tracks.

It may seem strange that a company backed by the Guggenheims and Hayden, Stone would have to come to an unattached market operator without banking connections for a mere $500,000; and stranger yet that I should be able to deliver such an amount in cash at such a time. But the explanation was simple.

Like many other people I had made preparations, not for a panic but for a financial stringency. I had increased my cash balances at the Manhattan Company. Moreover, I had told Stephen Baker that I might want my money in cash at any time.

"You will get it," he assured me. "We look after our customers."

When I received the telegram from Charlie MacNeill, president of Utah Copper, I decided that sooner or later the economic pendulum would swing back to normal. The world would go on. It would need copper until some better substitute could be found. And so I went to Baker and said I wanted $500,000 in cash. That was what MacNeill needed —the currency to stuff into pay envelopes. Credit, even if he could have obtained it, would not do.

Mr. Baker sent into his vaults. The currency was counted out, put into boxes, and shipped by express to Salt Lake City.

On that day money was being loaned at 150 per cent. I told MacNeill 6 per cent would be enough and he could have all the time he wanted. He sent back the company's note, on which he made the rate 20 per cent. After that transaction I went into the market and bought many shares of Utah Copper at the depressed quotations prevailing.

Utah Copper came through the panic with flying colors, and in the first year of operation Jackling's estimates were more than realized. In the thirty years that followed, Utah Copper paid its stockholders more than $250,000,000 in dividends. The world's largest copper workings, the hole in the ground at Bingham that Jackling began to dig in 1903 is still one of the biggest man-made excavations on the face of the earth.

That Utah Copper was able to survive the panic of 1907 is worth noting by those who wonder what makes a good investment. Value in an investment is like character in an individual. It stands up better under adversity and overcomes that adversity more readily. In perfecting his process for the handling of low-grade ores, Jackling, of course, was adding a whole new dimension of value to properties which had been of dubious worth previously. When new values are created in this way they will survive even financial panic. A panic may bring a temporary collapse in the market price of an investment, but the stock is bound to recover if the company meets a genuine economic need and is under good management.

The success of Utah Copper is also evidence of the importance of individual initiative and character. Jackling was only thirty years old when he got his great idea for doubling the world's copper output. It took him five years to find financial backers and four more years to justify the faith those backers had in him.

During World War One, Jackling received the Distinguished Service Medal for building a smokeless powder plant for the government when there was grave doubt whether it could be done. The Du Ponts had set terms for building the plant which the Armed Services felt were onerous. At the end of a long morning conference on the problem, I said I knew a man who could do the job and recommended Jackling. Secretary of War Baker said he would take it up with the President.

That afternoon I telephoned Jackling at the St. Francis Hotel in San Francisco and told him, "I do not know whether they will accept you, but I would like to have you come anyhow." A few days later, when Secretary Baker asked me to get Jackling, I said, "He is already here, I will bring him in."

Before Jackling went in, I gave him one piece of advice. "Don't let them put a uniform on you," I told him. "Remember, a man in higher command can tell you where to get on and where to get off." Jackling stayed out of uniform and built the factory in jig time.

In 1933 the mining, mechanical, electrical, and civil engineering societies of the United States awarded Jackling the John Fritz Medal, the highest honor an American engineer can acquire.

But Jackling had his failures as well as successes.

During World War One he built a pilot mill which showed the steel companies that the low-grade taconite ore of the Mesabi iron range could be used after the high-grade Mesabi ores were depleted. Then he tried a third time with low-grade ores of gold in Alaska, but here he failed—to my own loss as well as his.

4

This venture—the Alaska Juneau Gold Company—represented the most money I ever sank into the ground before any came out. The main property of the company was an open-cut mine in a mountainside across from Gastineau Channel, south of the city of Juneau. It was brought to my notice by three tip-top mining men, Fred Bradley, J. H. Mackenzie, and Mark Requa, a close friend of Herbert Hoover. For a time, in fact, Hoover was interested in the mine but we beat him to it—to our own later regret.

Jackling had gone up to Alaska and turned in a glowing report on the possibilities of the Alaska Gold Mine Company, which adjoined the Alaska Juneau mine. Having great faith in Jackling's judgment, I decided to go into Alaska Juneau. In the spring of 1915, with ore reports showing a favorable gold content, 400,000 shares of stock at $10 a share were offered by Alaska Juneau in a statement which included these words:

"All stock not taken by public subscription will be taken by Eugene Meyer, Junior, and B. M. Baruch."

Never before—and never afterward—had my name been

used publicly in connection with a stock offering. The issue was oversubscribed five times. Within a few days the stock had soared to 15.

But soon it became known that Jackling had struck an unexpectedly low grade of gold content in the ore of the Alaska Gold Mine. This cast doubt on the future of Alaska Juneau as well. Its stock began to drop.

Finally, Jackling gave up and Alaska Gold decided to close up. But Fred Bradley refused to strike Alaska Juneau's flag. Since my name had been used as a sponsor of Alaska Juneau, I felt a moral obligation not to quit before Bradley did. A few others looked at it the same way. With money and public confidence gone, W. H. Crocker, Ogden Mills, whose son became Secretary of the Treasury under Herbert Hoover, Fred Bradley, Eugene Meyer, and myself put up $3,000,000 to carry on the work.

In 1916 Alaska Juneau closed at 7¾, in 1917 at 2, in 1920 at 1¾, while during the depression of 1921 it was down to ⅝. The bond holders were about to foreclose when the first glimmer of hope came in sight. In September of 1921 the mills made an operating profit of $24,000. This was not enough to pay fixed charges, to be sure, but it was a base from which to expand operations that would pay for themselves.

Gradually Bradley perfected his methods and increased the volume of operations to where ore could be handled profitably even when it ran as low as eighty cents' worth of gold to the ton. Ten years earlier the thought of tackling such rock would have been called madness. By 1930 debts had been paid off and in 1931 the first dividend was declared. That this was done was a tribute to the dogged determination of Fred Bradley.

When President Franklin Roosevelt devalued the dollar and increased the price of gold, Alaska Juneau profited, of course. However, I opposed Roosevelt's action, as did Eugene Meyer, then the publisher of the Washington *Post*, even though both of us had large holdings in gold mines.

In later years Alaska Juneau fell into trouble again as costs rose and the gold content of the ore fell. Finally, the mine itself had to be closed, although its power plant still is used.

5

What was learned from these experiments with low-grade ores is of considerable significance for our national security. One of the running conflicts we face in our foreign economic policy stems from the question of from where our raw materials should be drawn—from within our own borders even if the cost is higher, or from foreign countries where the cost may be lower.

In this conflict I have never sided completely with either the so-called "free traders" or the protectionists. As was shown in both World Wars, the ability to use domestic ores and domestic minerals is a valuable defense asset.

If it had not been for the processes which Jackling developed and later engineers refined and improved, we would have had to import most of the copper we used in World War Two. This in turn would have absorbed considerable shipping which would have had to be diverted from other war uses—at a cost in either production or fighting efficiency.

For that reason I always have felt that we should encourage experiments in perfecting methods for the more economical use of lower-grade ore bodies. However, as I learned with Alaska Juneau, there are limits to what can be wisely undertaken in this regard.

What is needed is a balance between these two alternatives, to continue to import the materials we need from the cheapest available foreign sources but to continue as well to improve our ability to develop and utilize our own domestic resources.

I do not believe in trying to become self-sufficient at all costs, as Hitler attempted before unloosing World War Two. But I also do not believe that we should sacrifice the relatively high degree of self-containment which the American continent commands merely to increase our trade abroad.

It also seems unwise to try to treat this far-flung problem as if it could be settled by proclaiming some doctrine or some fixed formula. New technological developments can give new uses to areas which might have been worthless a few years earlier.

In regard to all of these materials that are vital to our national defense, we should maintain a running inventory of both our needs and possible sources of supply. The balance that is struck between domestic production and foreign imports should reflect not only the economic cost but the relative contribution to our national security of a sure source of supply.

18. J. P. Morgan Declines
to Gamble

AN UNFORTUNATE CHOICE of a word apparently is what deprived me of an opportunity to become associated with the elder J. P. Morgan. The development in which we almost became partners proved to be the most profitable single enterprise of my money-making career. It also enabled the United States to retain predominance in the world's sulfur market. Yet I always regretted Mr. Morgan's withdrawal from this venture since his decision, which cost his house many millions of dollars in profits, also cost me the experience of working with the greatest financial genius this country has ever known.

Mr. Morgan could well do without the money his company would have earned. Actually, he cared little for the possession of money. What he strove to achieve was the economic unity and stability of the country. In my economic, industrial, and social views I was more inclined to favor the policies of Theodore Roosevelt. But I regarded Morgan as a master and teacher under whom service would have been a worth-while experience.

That I never really got to know the elder Morgan remains a source of regret to me. As a youthful runner in Wall Street I delivered securities and market reports to him personally several times. Once I saw him at a Boys' Club at St. George's Church on the lower East Side. I had been conducting an evening gym class at a Boys' Club on West 69th Street and was visiting some of the other Clubs in the city to see what they were doing. I remember Mr. Morgan standing absolutely absorbed over a boy who was cutting a jigsaw puzzle from a cigar box.

While working for Arthur Housman, I carried a report to Mr. Morgan with some quotations on Milwaukee Electric bonds. Mr. Morgan asked me what I thought. Assuming that his question related to the general financial situation, I replied that I felt we were headed for a panic.

Mr. Morgan fixed those famous eyes on me for a moment and demanded, "Young man, what do you know about panics?"

I did not know what to say in reply.

That remained the only time I had talked with Mr. Morgan until in 1909 Charles Steele of the Morgan firm asked me to investigate a sulfur dome near Brazoria, Texas, about forty miles southwest of Galveston, along the Gulf Coast. I was surprised that the Morgans should seek me out. The understanding was that, if the prospect proved worthy, the Morgans would furnish the capital, I would do the work, and we would divide the profits sixty-forty.

My first step, of course, was to get a highly qualified mining engineer. I turned to Seeley W. Mudd, who had worked for Hammond in the Guggenheim Exploration Company. Mudd, in turn, engaged a young assistant named Spencer Browne.

We went down to Texas, got a crew of drillers and started drilling some test holes.

Day after day I sat on Bryan Mound, as the property was called, watching the drillers send their shafts down and bring up cores of earth which then were tested for their sulfur content. Night after night in the little hotel in the town of Brazoria I slapped mosquitoes while I studied the facts and figures of the world's sulfur trade, trying to determine what part we might play in that trade if our prospect proved worth while.

Finally, Mudd decided that the chances were about fifty-

fifty that the sulfur content of Bryan Mound was rich enough to be mined profitably.

Back in New York, I reported this to Mr. Morgan, explaining that we could buy the whole property outright, including royalties, for $500,000. I added that I was willing to "gamble" half of this sum from my own funds.

"Gamble" was a poor choice of language. I should have said "invest."

"I never gamble," replied Mr. Morgan with a gesture that signified that the interview was over and the venture closed as far as he was concerned.

We had been together only a few minutes before I was dismissed in this cavalier fashion. He did not even give me the opportunity to present the conclusions I had reached from my study in the hotel in Brazoria of the world sulfur trade. That study showed that the time was peculiarly "right" for a vast expansion of U.S. sulfur production. For one thing, the growth of American industry was increasing the need for pure sulfur, which is the base for sulfuric acid, then perhaps the most important of all industrial chemicals.

Moreover, the technical development of sulfur mining had reached the stage where American producers could undertake to free themselves of dependence on imported sulfur.

Up to 1900 the production of pure sulfur had been largely an Italian monopoly, the island of Sicily being the source of 95 per cent of the world's output. Around 1870, an extensive sulfur deposit was discovered in western Louisiana, but early attempts to mine these deposits were frustrated by the overlaying quicksands, which were impregnated with poisonous gases. These obstacles challenged the inventive genius of Herman Frasch, a successful oil engineer, who had come into Louisiana hunting for petroleum. In 1891, after years of experimentation, he perfected a new method of mining sulfur which became known as the Frasch process.

What Frasch did was to drive into the earth a metal tube or pipe about ten inches in diameter. Within this pipe were inserted, one inside the other, three additional pipes of varying diameters. Superheated water was forced down one of these three pipes to melt the subterranean sulfur. Compressed air was then forced down a second pipe, causing the molten sulfur to rise in the third pipe. Once it had come to the surface, the liquid sulfur was carried into cooling bins, where it was allowed to solidify.

The Union Sulphur Company, which was formed to work the Louisiana deposits by means of the Frasch process, became an immensely profitable concern. But as American industry expanded, Union's output proved insufficient to meet domestic needs, which put a premium on other sources of supply.

In 1908 the basic patent on the Frasch process expired. This made the process available for use in Brazoria County, Texas, or any other place where the mining problem was similar to that in Louisiana. I had intended to recommend the Frasch process to Mr. Morgan when I was cut off by his abrupt refusal to participate in the project.

Stung by his attitude, I decided to press ahead with my own sulfur undertaking.

2

While Mudd and I were in Texas, a number of prospectors, promoters, and sundry other hopefuls had come to us with stories or offers of sulfur properties. Some of these properties we looked at quickly at the time. After Mr. Morgan washed his hands of the Brazoria project, we continued these investigations.

Mudd thought that one particular property in Texas, known as Big Dome, in Matagorda County, was very promising. It had been brought to our notice by A. C. Einstein, who was connected with one of the utility companies in St. Louis. When a test well bore out Mudd's opinion, I formed the Gulf Sulphur Company and began acquiring more property in Matagorda County.

Meanwhile, some of the people who had brought the Brazoria mound to Morgan's attention went ahead with its development under the name of the Freeport Sulphur Company. These operations proved immediately profitable. The outbreak of World War One greatly increased the demand for sulfur, which swelled the profits of the Freeport. But with both the Union and Freeport sulfur companies in production, there seemed to be no room in the market for a third producer.

All we could do was to wait on future developments. Einstein suggested that we acquire still more property in Matagorda County. I gave him authority to do so, suggesting that he invite the owners to come in with us. None of them did, however. I financed the acquisition of these properties.

By 1916, with the high wartime demand for sulfur, the Freeport Company had paid something like 200 per cent on its investment. Mudd felt that the time had come to open up our own property. To do so effectively we needed additional capital. J. P. Morgan, the elder, had died three years earlier. In view of the earlier interest in sulfur of the Morgan firm, I thought I'd see if they would share in developing the Gulf Sulphur holdings.

I approached Henry P. Davison, who turned the matter over to Thomas W. Lamont, another Morgan partner. Lamont called in William Boyce Thompson, the organizer of the Newmont Mining Company, which eventually became one of the largest mineral and oil investment companies in the world.

After studying the proposition Thompson advised the Morgans to take an interest. They took about 60 per cent. Before our development had gone very far, the Morgans sold out to Thompson for a small profit. This was done without consulting me. I considered it an unfair action and told the Morgans so.

The stock should first have been offered back to me and not to Thompson. If someone had done a thing like that to the

Morgans, they never would have forgiven him. Had they held the stock, which I allotted them at $10 per share, it would have paid them out many, many times. By the late 1920's, their original investment of $3,600,000 would have been worth $45,000,000. In addition they would have received close to $25,000,000 in dividends.

3

Meantime, with our entry into the war, President Wilson named me to the War Industries Board and, eventually, to its chairmanship. In view of my official responsibilities, I felt it my duty to give up my seat on the Stock Exchange and to sell every share of stock and every bond I owned in any enterprise that might benefit from government contracts or purchases.

Among the stocks I sold were some like Fisher Body, which would have yielded a sizable fortune in later years had I held on to them. However, I should add I never begrudged what I did. I have had all the money I needed; and no fortune, however large, could have given me the satisfaction I derived from serving my country.

A few securities I had to hold because they were not listed on the Exchange and could not be sold. Among these were my sulfur stock and my interest in a California tungsten mine. With these shares, I left my secretary, Miss Mary Boyle, standing instructions to transfer the dividends, if any, to the Red Cross and other patriotic agencies. All this was explained to and approved by President Wilson.

The tungsten mine did yield sizable dividends, all of which went to charity. But Texas Gulf Sulphur (the corporate name having been changed from Gulf Sulphur Company) did not get into production until the war was over.

Before I became chairman of the War Industries Board, the Federal Bureau of Mines asked producers of scarce war materials to increase their output and to inaugurate new production. One company the Bureau approached was Texas Gulf Sulphur, which was promised the usual accommodations in the way of priorities for construction materials and equipment.

One day I met Walter Aldridge, president of Texas Gulf Sulphur, in the corridor of the building in Washington that housed the War Industries Board. Asked what had brought him there, Aldridge replied that he was inquiring about priority orders.

Since I had withdrawn entirely from the company's management, this was the first I knew that consideration was being given to priorities for equipment for the Matagorda deposit. Immediately I informed Secretary of War Newton Baker of my interest in the company. I also asked my old schoolmate, Dick Lydon, then a director of Texas Gulf Sulphur, to insist that the company not only sell its sulfur at cost but, if its costs were not as low as the price of the lowest competitor, to sell it at a loss.

Actually this precaution proved to be unnecessary, since the war was over some four months before Texas Gulf Sulphur began to produce.

After my return from the Paris Peace Conference I became active again for a time in the affairs of Texas Gulf Sulphur. Much had to be straightened out in the industry. The abrupt end of hostilities had left the two other sulfur companies—Union and Freeport—with hundreds of thousands of tons of sulfur above ground for which no immediate market existed.

Moreover, bad feeling existed among the three companies. Union Sulphur had sued Freeport for alleged infringement of the Frasch patent. The suit was lost because the patent had expired. This probably saved us from a similar suit, because we also used the Frasch process.

The Union people attacked us from another angle, however. Owning lands next to ours, they brought suit on the ground that our wells drained the sulfur from their deposits. This suit was settled out of court, but not until there had been a good deal of unpleasantness.

One Union stockholder, a member of the Frasch family, went so far as to charge that, as chairman of the War Industries Board, I had demanded a commission of so much a ton before I would permit Union to fill government contracts. This charge was alleged to have been made by Herman Frasch. The fact is that Herman Frasch died in 1914, before World War One started. I add this in justice to his memory.

The recession of the early 1920's greatly reduced sales of minerals and metals throughout the world. The urgent need for a foreign market in which to dispose of accumulated production and the activity of foreign cartels induced Congress to pass the Webb-Pomerene Act, which encouraged American producers to unite for handling export sales. For the sulfur companies this was a timely privilege.

The Sulphur Export Corporation, jointly owned by Union, Freeport, and Texas Gulf, was formed. Shortly thereafter an agreement was made with Sicily to cover the sulfur requirements of foreign countries.

Over the succeeding five years, drastic changes took place within the American sulfur industry. In tonnage sales, Texas Gulf had reached a position about equal to that enjoyed by Union Sulphur, while Freeport had slipped to third position. Then the Union's Louisiana deposits became depleted, forcing a shutdown of its plant. The Freeport Company found that new acquisitions, upon which it had built high hopes, were much less profitable than anticipated. This left Texas Gulf Sulphur the largest and lowest-cost producer in the world.

From then until 1929 the company's history was spectacular. Shares which had cost $10 at the company's outset were exchanged for shares which, if sold, would have brought the equivalent of $320 apiece. I disposed of my personal holding of 121,000 shares before this peak was reached. When friends asked me why I was selling, I explained that the price seemed to me too high. I advised these friends to sell, as well.

Many of them, however, took this advice coldly. The price of the sulfur stock was still soaring, and many of my questioners implied that my selling showed that I had lost my grip and become a back number. But by the time the 1929 crash came, I had liquidated my sulfur holdings completely.

Repeatedly in my market operations I have sold a stock while it still was rising—and that has been one reason why I have held on to my fortune. Many a time I might have made a good deal more by holding a stock, but then I would also have been caught in the fall when the price of the stock collapsed. If I have missed some opportunities for money making because of this practice, I have also avoided "going broke," as I have seen many other men do.

Some people boast of selling at the top of the market and buying at the bottom—I don't believe this can be done except by latter-day Munchausens. I have bought when things seemed low enough and sold when they seemed high enough. In that way I have managed to avoid being swept along to those wild extremes of market fluctuations which prove so disastrous.

4

Just why do we fall victim to such madnesses as the frenzy of stock market gambling that preceded the 1929 crash? I believe it is largely a reflection of the curious psychology of crowds which has been demonstrated again and again in human history.

It was a financial reporter for the old New York *Herald,* John Dater, who first set me thinking about the strange behavior of crowds. In the early 1900's on my return from a trip to Europe, Dater interviewed me on board ship. We got to talking about panics and Dater urged me to read a book he had come across, entitled *Extraordinary Popular Delusions and the Madness of Crowds,* by Charles Mackay. Dater and I went around among the secondhand bookstores until we found a copy.

Mackay's book, which was published originally in 1841

and reprinted in 1932 by L. C. Page and Company, is a remarkable documentation of the unbelievable crazes that have swept mankind down through the ages. No nation has been immune to these frenzies. If the supposedly stolid Dutch were overcome by the Tulip Craze, the volatile French had their Mississippi Bubble, while the sturdy English had their South Sea Bubble.

As I read the accounts of these madnesses, I was tempted to shout, "This cannot have happened!" Yet within my own lifetime I have seen similar deliriums in the Florida land boom of the 1920's and the stock-market speculation that led to the 1929 crash. Something of this same crowd madness may have been at least partially responsible for Hitler's rise to power in Germany.

These crowd madnesses recur so frequently in human history that they must reflect some deeply rooted trait of human nature. Perhaps it is the same kind of force that motivates the migrations of birds or the mass performances of whole species of ocean eels. There seems to be a cyclical rhythm in these movements. A bull market, for example, will be sweeping along and then something will happen—trivial or important—and first one man will sell and then others will sell and the continuity of thought toward higher prices is broken.

"Continuity of thought"—what a wonderful expression that is. It did not originate with me. The first time I heard it was while I was operating in steel stock which J. P. Morgan was trying to accumulate. The general market was on the rise. Then, while these operations were going on, the stock of Rock Island broke. At the time I happened to be with Middleton Burrill, who remarked, "That collapse is going to break the continuity of bullish thought." I had never heard the expression before, but I saw at once that Burrill was right and even though Steel was being supported by the Morgans, I sold and took my profits.

Another strange thing about these crowd madnesses is that education and high rank is no immunization against the virus. Mackay's book is full of examples of how kings and princes, merchants and professors have succumbed to these crazes. In our own day the stock market madness of 1927 to 1929 swept through every level of society.

I can remember my own feelings in those days. From 1928 on I felt uneasy about the level of stock prices. Looking out over world affairs, I could see where a new surge of prosperity might be touched off if we could solve the problem of reparations and war debts—then weighing down as heavily on world trade as the Old Man of the Sea on Sinbad the Sailor. On the other hand I did not like the effects of the loosening of credit that the Federal Reserve had begun in 1927.

Several times in 1928, in fact, I sold, feeling that a break was imminent, only to have the market continue upward.

In August of 1929 I went to Scotland for grouse hunting. While there I received information from home of a proposed exchange of the stocks of a number of old-line companies for the stock of two newly organized holding companies. This exchange promised to raise the stock of the companies affected to a fantastic figure.

I cabled three men I knew intimately, asking their judgment of what was going on. Two of the men sent me noncommittal replies. But from the third man—who occupied one of the highest posts in American finance at that time—I received a cable describing the general business situation as being "like a weathervane pointing into a gale of prosperity." I know this man believed what he cabled me because in the crash he lost every penny he had.

Shortening my visit in Scotland, I decided to sail for home. While I was waiting in London to embark there were several times when I cabled orders to New York to buy stocks, only to follow them the next day with orders to sell. On the boat coming home there happened to be a brokerage office which was run by a charming young man who solicited my business. I gave him some orders to sell. Soon after I landed in New York, I decided to sell everything I could.

In the dark days that followed I reread Mackay and found his tales curiously encouraging. For if his book showed how baseless are man's moods of wild hope, it also showed that man's moods of black despair are equally unfounded. Always in the past, no matter how black the outlook, things got better.

Whatever men attempt, they seem driven to try to overdo. When hopes are soaring I always repeat to myself, "Two and two still make four and no one has ever invented a way of getting something for nothing." When the outlook is steeped in pessimism I remind myself, "Two and two still make four and you can't keep mankind down for long."

19. My Investment Philosophy

I HAVE HEARD attributed to Sir Ernest Cassell, who was the private banker to King Edward VII, a remark that I wish I had thought of first.

"When as a young and unknown man I started to be successful I was referred to as a gambler," Sir Ernest said. "My operations increased in scope and volume. Then I was known as a speculator. The sphere of my activities continued to expand and presently I was known as a banker. Actually I had been doing the same thing all the time."

That observation is particularly worth pondering by those who may think that there is such a thing as a sure investment. The elder J. P. Morgan could gag at the word "gamble" when I used it. Still, the truth is there is no investment which doesn't involve some risk and is not something of a gamble.

We all have to take chances in life. And mankind would be vastly poorer today if it had not been for men who were willing to take risks against the longest odds. In setting out to discover a new route to India, Columbus was taking a chance that few men of his time were willing to hazard. Again, in our own age when Henry Ford started to make the first Model T, he was embarking on one of the most gigantic speculations of all time.

Even if it could be done—and it cannot—we would be foolish to try to stamp out this willingness in man to buck seemingly hopeless odds. What we can try to do perhaps is to come to a better understanding of how to reduce the element of risk in whatever we undertake. Or put another way—and this applies to governmental affairs as well as money making —our problem is how to remain properly venturesome and experimental without making fools of ourselves.

As I already have pointed out, the true speculator is one who observes the future and acts before it occurs. Like a surgeon he must be able to search through a mass of complex and contradictory details to the significant facts. Then, still like the surgeon, he must be able to operate coldly, clearly, and skillfully on the basis of the facts before him.

What makes this task of fact finding so difficult is that in the stock market the facts of any situation come to us through a curtain of human emotions. What drives the prices of stocks up or down is not impersonal economic forces or changing events but the human reactions to these happenings. The constant problem of the speculator or analyst is how to disentangle the cold, hard economic facts from the rather warm feelings of the people dealing with these facts.

Few things are more difficult to do. The main obstacle lies in disentangling ourselves from our own emotions.

I have known men who could see through the motivations of others with the skill of a clairvoyant, only to prove blind to their own mistakes.

In fact I have been one of those men.

Let me relate two business experiences which illustrate how penetrating one's vision can be when focused on the faults of others, but how blurred and fogged it becomes when we look at ourselves.

2

As a student of human nature, I always have felt that a good speculator should be able to tell what a man will do with his money before he does it. One December afternoon in 1906, this belief was put to the test by an unannounced visit to my office of William Crocker, whose father was one of the builders of the Central Pacific Railroad in California.

Crocker had one of the most engaging personalities I have known. Erect in his carriage and meticulous in appearance, he never seemed to have a hair out of place, even in his short, pointed beard. There was a slight impediment in his speech which fascinated me, but there was no impediment in his heart or head. He was the kind of banker who did not desert his clients when things went bad. No matter how distressing were the circumstances, he never lost his good humor or courage.

Crocker had brought with him Senator George Nixon of Nevada. In his characteristic direct manner, Crocker opened the conversation by saying, "Nixon needs a million dollars and he's good for it."

Nixon had bought the Combination Mines, whose workings adjoined his Goldfield Consolidated Mines, agreeing to pay $2,578,216 in three installments. The first payment of $1,000,000 in cash was due in three weeks. Since Nixon was known to be in need of money, the stock of Goldfield Consolidated had been going down.

After a short discussion, I agreed to loan Nixon $1,000,000 for a year. He signed a note secured by Goldfield Consolidated stock.

But this only overcame Nixon's first difficulty. He had to pay the remaining $1,578,216 in two equal installments over four months, either in cash or in Consolidated stock, the choice being left to the Combination owners. For Nixon, of course, the ideal arrangement would be for the Combination owners to accept Consolidated stock rather than cash.

I told Crocker and Nixon I had a plan to get the Combination owners to do just that. Without explaining what lay in my mind, I gave Nixon a certified check for $1,000,000 and told him to follow my instructions exactly.

"When you go to the Waldorf and take a table in the café," I told him, "someone is bound to ask how you are making out. They know you need money. Take this check out of your pocket and show it to them. Then put it away and say nothing. If anyone offers to buy Goldfield Consolidated, say, 'You will have to see Baruch.'"

Sure enough, Nixon hardly had seated himself in the Men's Café at the Waldorf before he was asked about his financial difficulties. Playing his part perfectly, he pulled out the certified check. To all the questions that followed he replied simply, "See Baruch," in a tone that implied all his burdens had been lifted from his shoulders.

The next day Nixon left for Chicago to meet with the Combination creditors. Still following my instructions, he endorsed over to them my certified check, saying nothing about the two remaining installments.

One of the Combination owners left the room. Presently there came to the New York curb market an order to sell a large block of Goldfield Consolidated. Anticipating some such testing of the market, I had placed orders of my own to buy Goldfield. Instead of being driven down, the stock held to within a fraction of a point. This showed a market strength in Goldfield Consolidated that few had dreamed possible.

The rest of my plan also worked out as I had anticipated. The psychological effects of $1,000,000 cash and of Consolidated's firm tone in the face of heavy selling moved the larger stockholders of Combination Mines to ask for Consolidated stock instead of money in satisfaction of Nixon's remaining obligations. They asked for it that same day, without waiting for the later installments to fall due.

In high glee Nixon returned to New York, his financing difficulties overcome. He gave me 100,000 shares as a bonus, which I accepted because I thought I had earned them.

But before acclaiming me as a wizard, the reader should hear my second story.

I already have written of how I became rich by listening to Herman Sielcken explain how foolish the organizers of Amalgamated Copper were to try to control the price of copper. In essence, the whole copper affair had been a simple test of the validity of the law of supply and demand—even in the face of manipulation by the most ingenious speculators. One would have thought that after such an experience I never could have made the mistake of trying myself to outwit the law of supply and demand. Yet this is exactly what I did.

In 1902 the state of São Paulo in Brazil had decreed a

limitation on planting for five years, which would materially reduce the crop commencing in 1907. No one knew the coffee trade better than Mr. Sielcken. It was his judgment that these planting restrictions, along with poor weather prospects, would lead to a considerable rise in the price of coffee.

Early in 1905, I began buying coffee and bought heavily. Since I bought on a margin account, a rise of a few cents a pound would have made me a fortune.

But the anticipated upsurge did not take place. Nature ceased playing into the hands of the speculators and threatened to bring forth a tremendous coffee crop in 1906—a year before the planting restrictions imposed in 1902 would show their effect.

In the closing months of 1905, coffee, which for a year had stood around eight cents, began to drop. The Brazilian government took alarm and, after consulting such authorities as Mr. Sielcken, devised a "valorization" scheme which called for buying millions of bags of coffee and keeping them off the market. Confident that these purchases would maintain the price of coffee, Sielcken advised me to hold on. To finance these coffee purchases, Sielcken helped float loans for the Brazilian government.

But coffee prices continued to sink a fraction of a point at a time, each fraction's drop costing me thousands of dollars. Still I held on, watching my bank balances dwindle and the profits of many prosperous years vanish.

What I should have done, of course, was to sell my coffee as soon as it became clear that the 1906 coffee crop would exceed expectations. It would have meant pocketing a loss, but in the stock market the first loss is usually the smallest. One of the worst mistakes anyone can make is to hold on blindly and refuse to admit that his judgment has been wrong.

This I knew, but instead of acting sensibly I did as good a job of taking leave of my reasoning powers as any amateur caught in a market squeeze.

Many a novice will sell something he has a profit in to protect something in which he has a loss. Since the good stock usually has gone down least, or may even show a profit, it is psychologically easy to let go. With a bad stock the loss is likely to be heavy and the impulse is to hold on to it in order to recover what has been lost.

Actually, the procedure one should follow is to sell the bad stock and keep the good stock. With rare exceptions, stocks are high because they are good, and stocks are low because they are of doubtful value.

All this, as I say, I had learned. But what did I do? In 1903 I had bought large holdings of Canadian Pacific, which had risen considerably in value and which, I was sure, would go up more. Yet, I sold my Canadian Pacific to raise more margin money for coffee!

Soon all of my Canadian Pacific stock was gone and the price of coffee kept dropping. I was in the West—San Francisco, I think—when I finally came to my senses and realized that I had better get out.

That experience cost me $700,000 or $800,000. For some days I suffered from nervous indigestion. More painful than the money I had lost was the blow that had been dealt to my confidence in my fancied astuteness. I made a resolution never again to take an important risk in anything I did not know about.

When it was over I saw clearly enough that I had done everything wrong. It may seem strange that a man like Herman Sielcken, who could see so clearly the stupidity of others in trying to hold up the price of copper, should have made the same error with the commodity he knew best. But often we become carried away so much by the desirability of an end that we overlook the impracticability of its accomplishment. In such cases the more one knows about a subject—the more inside information one has—the more likely one is to believe that he or she can outwit the workings of supply and demand.

Experts will step in where even fools fear to tread.

3

Those two tales, I believe, reveal how important it is—and also how difficult it is—to approach the task of fact finding free of emotion. In relating my failures, I have hoped that others might profit from my errors. But I must confess that I am somewhat dubious how effective any advice I may give will prove.

Other people's mistakes, I have noticed, often make us only more eager to try to do the same thing. Perhaps it is because in the breast of every man there burns not only that divine spark of discontent but the urge to "beat the game" and show himself smarter than the other fellow. In any case, only after we have repeated these errors for ourselves does their instructive effect sink home.

Being so skeptical about the usefulness of advice, I have been reluctant to lay down any "rules" or guidelines on how to invest or speculate wisely. Still, there are a number of things I have learned from my own experience which might be worth listing for those who are able to muster the necessary self-discipline:

1. Don't speculate unless you can make it a full-time job.
2. Beware of barbers, beauticians, waiters—of anyone—bringing gifts of "inside" information or "tips."
3. Before you buy a security, find out everything you can about the company, its management and competitors, its earnings and possibilities for growth.
4. Don't try to buy at the bottom and sell at the top. This can't be done—except by liars.
5. Learn how to take your losses quickly and cleanly. Don't expect to be right all the time. If you have made a mistake, cut your losses as quickly as possible.
6. Don't buy too many different securities. Better have only a few investments which can be watched.
7. Make a periodic reappraisal of all your investments to

see whether changing developments have altered their
prospects.

8. Study your tax position to know when you can sell to
greatest advantage.
9. Always keep a good part of your capital in a cash reserve. Never invest all your funds.
10. Don't try to be a jack of all investments. Stick to the
field you know best.

These "rules" mainly reflect two lessons that experience
has taught me—that getting the facts of a situation before acting is of crucial importance, and that getting these facts is a
continuous job which requires eternal vigilance.

I have heard, for example, that one of the Rothschilds,
who certainly were among the wisest financiers of their day,
set out to make secure the fortune of a loved one. He decided
to invest this fortune in Austrian and German government
bonds, English consols above par, and French rentes above
par. When the story was told me many years later, this estate
had shrunk to only a fifth of its original worth. The Austrian
and German securities were completely valueless, of course,
while the others had depreciated considerably.

One cannot, in other words, make an investment and take
for granted that its worth will remain unchanged. New
sources of supply coming from hitherto untapped areas of
the world may transform the competitive position of a company, as will changes in people's habits or technological in-
novations. Often something will shrink in value because of
one discovery, as coal did in relation to oil and electricity,
only to be given new economic life by another development
such as the new chemical uses being made of coal.

Actually one can point to only a few things whose value
has resisted the change of time down through the centuries—
and even then not without fluctuations. Among these I would
list some minerals like gold, silver, and copper; precious
stones; works of art; and crop-bearing lands.

Even with these things one must add the qualification "at

least so far." The development of cultured pearls, for example, has nearly destroyed the old value of pearls. As for gold, some governments, including our own, have passed laws making its possession illegal.

This fact, that the value of an investment can never be counted upon as absolute and unchanging, is one reason why I urge everyone to make a periodic reappraisal of his or her investment position. It also explains why it is unwise to spread one's funds over too many different securities. Time and energy are required to come to a sound judgment of an investment and to keep abreast of the forces that may change the value of a security. While one can know all there is to know about a few issues, one cannot possibly know all one needs to know about a great many issues.

In no field is the old maxim more valid—that a little knowledge is a dangerous thing—than in investing.

In evaluating individual companies three main factors should be examined.

First, there are the real assets of a company, the cash it has on hand over its indebtedness and what its physical properties are worth.

Second, there is the franchise to do business that a company holds, which is another way of saying whether or not it makes something or performs a service that people want or must have.

I have often thought that perhaps the strongest force that starts an economy upward after it has hit bottom is the simple fact that all of us must somehow find a way to live. Even when we are sunk in the blackest despair, we have to work and eat and clothe ourselves; and this activity starts the economic wheels turning anew. It is not too difficult to determine the things people must have if they are to continue to live. Such fields usually open up investments which are likely to hold their value over the long run.

Third, and most important, is the character and brains of management. I'd rather have good management and less money than poor managers with a lot of money. Poor managers can ruin even a good proposition. The quality of the management is particularly important in appraising the prospects of future growth. Is the management inventive and resourceful, imbued with a determination to keep itself young in a business way? Or does it have a sit-and-die attitude? I have learned to give less weight to big financial names at the head of a company than to the quality of its engineering staff.

These basic economic facts about various enterprises, to repeat, must be checked and rechecked constantly. Sometimes I have made mistakes and yet, by abandoning my position in time, still was able to emerge with a net profit.

Early in 1904, for example, I heard that the Soo Line was planning to increase its wheat traffic by building a branch line from Thief River Falls in Minnesota to Kenmare, North Dakota, about three hundred miles westward. I asked Henry C. Davis to go West and explore the Soo's possibilities. On his return we shut ourselves up with a map. From the information Davis brought I concluded that enough wheat would come over the new rails to increase the Soo Line earnings greatly.

The Soo stock was selling at 60 or 65 and paying $4 a share, which was over 6 per cent on the investment. I began to buy the stock. Work on the Soo extension got started but soon the gossip spread through Wall Street that financial returns were a long way off and rather doubtful. I had learned that gossip of this sort often is put out to frighten people away from a good thing. And so I bought more Soo stock.

Along came a bumper wheat crop, which increased the Soo Line's revenues some 50 per cent. This jumped Soo stock to 110, nearly two thirds higher than it had been when I began to buy. All this was before the Thief River extension was even open.

Meanwhile, I had taken additional precautions to recheck my facts on the prospects for the Soo extension. I had sent another man through the Northwest and adjacent parts of Canada to plot grain movements under a variety of actual and hypothetical conditions. He came back with pages of figures which I studied long and deeply.

My conclusion was that the Thief River extension would prove a disappointment since most of the wheat would move to the head of the Lakes and then east by water. Since this was contrary to the judgment on which I had started my operation, I began to sell, mostly to Soo insiders.

By discovering my error in time, I managed to retreat from the field of battle with a handsome profit before the stock broke. This feat, may I stress, was accomplished by superior research rather than the legerdemain so often attributed to speculators.

4

Outside my old office in Wall Street there used to be an old beggar to whom I often gave gratuities. One day during the 1929 madness he stopped me and said, "I have a good tip for you."

When beggars and shoeshine boys, barbers and beauticians can tell you how to get rich it is time to remind yourself that there is no more dangerous illusion than the belief that one can get something for nothing.

Tips are most numerous, of course, when the market is booming. The tragic part of this is that in a rising market, for a time at least, anyone's tip will seem good. This only draws people deeper and deeper into the market.

The things that people will misinterpret as tips are amazing. One winter when we were living at the St. Regis Hotel in New York, my wife and I had a number of friends and relatives in for dinner. I was called to the telephone. My part of the conversation sounded something like this:

"Consolidated Gas. Yes, yes. That's good. That's good. Yes, yes. Good."

A few weeks later I arrived at my plantation in South Carolina to find a guest of that evening at the St. Regis, a charming relative, in tears. She had lost much of her money.

"But you must have lost a great deal in Consolidated Gas, too," she sobbed.

"Lost a great deal in Consolidated Gas?" I repeated in amazement.

"Yes," she said, "I bought it on your recommendation. Oh, you didn't know you were recommending it to me. I'm afraid I have been guilty of eavesdropping. But when I heard you say over the telephone, 'Consolidated Gas, good, good,' I just could not keep from going in."

What had happened was this. Suspecting Consolidated Gas to be due for a fall, I had commissioned someone to get certain facts for me. His telephone call to the St. Regis was in the nature of a report which confirmed my beliefs. In saying, "Good, good," I was merely acknowledging the confirmation of what I had expected.

Consequently I had begun to sell the stock while my relative, thinking she had a tip, was buying.

In speculation, our emotions are constantly setting traps for our reasoning powers. It is far more difficult, for example, to know when to sell a stock than when to buy. Men find it equally hard to take either a profit or a loss. If a stock has gone up, a man wants to hold on to it in anticipation of a further rise. If a stock has gone down, he tends to hold on to it until an upward turn comes along so he will at least be even.

The sensible course is to sell while the stock still is rising or, if you have made a mistake, to admit it immediately and take your loss.

Some people, after selling, bedevil themselves with thoughts of "if only I had done this." To do this is both silly and demoralizing. No speculator can be right all the time. In fact, if a speculator is correct half of the time he is hitting a good average. Even being right three or four times out of ten should yield a person a fortune if he has the sense to cut his losses quickly on the ventures where he has been wrong.

In my younger days I heard someone, I forget who, remark, "Sell to the sleeping point." That is a gem of wisdom of the purest ray serene. When we are worried it is because our subconscious mind is trying to telegraph us some message of warning. The wisest course is to sell to the point where one stops worrying.

I have found it wise, in fact, to periodically turn into cash most of my holdings and virtually retire from the market. No general keeps his troops fighting all the time; nor does he go into battle without some part of his forces held back in reserve. After my first youthful reverses were behind me, I tried never to go into any speculation over my depth—beyond my financial capacity to pay for any error of judgment. By maintaining a large cash reserve, I have also been in a position to take advantage of unforeseen opportunities as they developed.

Another common illusion some people have is that they can do anything—buy and sell stocks, dabble in real estate, run a business, engage in politics—all at once. My own experience is that few men can do more than one thing at a time —and do it well. A skilled operator in any field acquires an almost instinctive "feel" which enables him to sense many things even without being able to explain them. In a few instances, as in coffee, where I went into speculations where I lacked this "feel," I have not done too well.

Success in speculation requires as much specialized knowledge as success in law or medicine or any other profession. It never would occur to anyone to open a department store in competition with Macy's or Gimbels or to make motor cars against Ford and General Motors without prior training or preparation. Yet the same man will cheerfully toss his savings into a market dominated by men who are as expert in their line as Macy's and the auto makers are in theirs.

What of the man or woman with modest savings who is simply looking for a fair return on his or her savings and who cannot give full time to a study of investments? My advice to such persons is to seek out some trusted investment counselor.

The emergence of this new profession of disinterested and careful investment analysts, who have no allegiance or alliances and whose only job is to judge a security on its merits, is one of the more constructive and healthy developments of the last half century.

When I entered Wall Street a man had to be his own analyst. Nor was there a Securities and Exchange Commission to require the disclosure of the information that was needed to measure the value of securities. In those days secrecy was the prevailing rule. Many stories were told of how uncommunicative the titans of finance were. The head of one corporation defined his company's business as "addition, division and silence." Another story used to be told about James Stillman. On his return from Europe, he ran into George Perkins, a Morgan partner, who remarked, "I see you're back."

When Stillman remained silent, Perkins added, "Oh, you need not confirm it."

The Stock Exchange has waged a long, hard, and successful fight to get corporations to release more information about their affairs to stockholders. But in the 1890's and early 1900's not much had been accomplished in this regard. The Exchange first had to persuade the companies of the advantage of listing their stocks. Only after that battle was won could the Exchange take the next step of getting more information released to the public.

If anything, too much information may be available today. The problem has become less one of digging out information than to separate the irrelevant detail from the essential facts and to determine what those facts mean. More than ever before what is needed is sound judgment.

There are several influences, though, which make it more difficult to judge the value of securities today than it was at the turn of the century. Two such forces are the ever-present threat of war and the continuing problem of inflation.

The effect of these two threats—war and inflation—are worth intensive study because they illustrate so well the clashing motivations that impel people to invest in stocks. Some people invest in hope and confidence in the future of an enterprise; others because of fear that the value of their capital will be lost through inflation. The main reason for the unusual and puzzling behavior of the stock market in the years since World War Two has been that *both* these motivations were so active simultaneously.

Many businesses have increased enormously in value. At the same time, we have felt the cumulative effects of the inflationary government policies which have held sway for so long. Nor, at least as of this writing, has this inflation been halted.

5

In the winter of 1955, the price of securities began to rise in spectacular fashion. Immediately much alarm was touched off that 1929 was about to repeat itself with an unhealthy boom being followed by another disastrous collapse.

The Senate Banking and Currency Committee ordered an investigation and, after several months of hearings and study, published its report. By then, however, the market had settled down and the committee's investigation was all but forgotten.

There will be similar such speculative flurries and investigations in the future. When they come up it would be well to bear in mind two things:

First, the stock market does not determine the health of our economy. Largely because of the 1929 crash, the impression got built up that the stock market itself is the cause of economic booms and busts. Actually, the Stock Exchange is simply a market place where buyers and sellers of securities meet. All the market does is register the judgments of these sellers and buyers on what business is like and what it will be like in the future.

The stock market, in short, is the thermometer and not the

fever. If the country is suffering from the effects of inflation or from a weakening of the government's credit, the effect will show up in the stock market. But the causes of the trouble will not lie in the stock market itself.

This distinction between the thermometer and the fever, I repeat, is a crucial one. We face one kind of problem if the thermometer is not working properly, but quite a different problem if the difficulty is that the stock market is recording—all too accurately—the ills of our economic world.

Now, as it happens, in recent years a number of structural changes in security investment have taken place and are worth careful investigation. Among these changes are the remarkable growth of investment trusts and mutual funds, also of tax-free pension funds and tax-exempt foundations. With the change in the laws regulating their holdings, some institutions, like life insurance companies and savings banks, have purchased stocks.

The capital gains tax has made many investors reluctant to part with their holdings. Many industries have financed their plant expansions through their own earnings and tax write-offs rather than through capital from outside. No really thorough study has yet been made of how the workings of the stock market have been altered by these and other changes.

The full implications of every form of tax exemption should also be re-examined. With tax rates as steep as they are, business decisions are being determined more and more by the tax position of a company or individual. This makes tax exemption ever more far-ranging in its economic impact.

But the need to guard against possible abuses in these new developments should not be confused with the larger policy problems of the whole economy. If our general economic policies and our national defense are sound, the stock market will adjust to them and we will not need to worry about a possible collapse of the market. If we do not preserve our national security and national credit, then nothing can have lasting value.

The second illusion to guard against is that people can be protected against speculative losses through regulation. I am not opposed to regulating the stock market wherever necessary. While I was on the Board of Governors of the Stock Exchange before World War One, I always argued for stricter self-regulation. After the crash I supported additional regulation of the stock market because of the abuses that had developed.

The racketeer should be eliminated whenever possible, and we can even try to protect the weak from the strong. But no law can protect a man from his own errors. The main reason why money is lost in stock speculations is not because Wall Street is dishonest, but because so many people persist in thinking that you can make money without working for it and that the stock exchange is the place where this miracle can be performed.

In trying to regulate speculation we really are trying to regulate human nature. I supported the Prohibition Amendment when it first was enacted but soon learned that there are limits beyond which one cannot succeed in regulating human nature. As long as a man believes he can beat the game and outsmart the other fellow, there will come a time when he will try to do it.

If the government is really bent on protecting the public's earnings, it should begin at home with the purchasing power of the dollar. During World War Two millions of families were persuaded to invest in U.S. savings bonds as the patriotic thing to do. These people have seen the value of their savings slashed by the lowered purchasing power of the dollar, while others who did not heed these patriotic appeals have profited. If any company listed on the Stock Exchange had engaged in equivalent financial practices, its directors would be facing prosecution by the SEC.

20. Hobcaw Barony

IN THIS HECTIC AGE OF DISTRACTION, all of us need to pause every now and then in what we are doing to examine where the rush of the world and of our own activities is taking us. Even an hour or two spent in such detached contemplation on a park bench will prove rewarding.

The importance of such periodic stocktaking was one of the most valuable lessons I learned from my early experiences as a speculator. After every major undertaking, as I have written earlier, I would shake loose from Wall Street and go off to some quiet place where I could review what I had done. If I had lost money, I wanted to make sure that I would not repeat the same mistake. If it had been a successful operation, getting away from the clattering tickers helped clear my mind and refresh me physically for any future action.

Having acquired this habit, I naturally grasped the opportunity that came to me in 1905 to acquire a veritable Shangri-La in my native South Carolina—famed Hobcaw Barony, whose sandy beaches and salt marshes once offered the finest duck hunting in the United States, with four rivers and a bay abounding in fish; vast stretches of almost primeval forest, and—no telephone.

For years the only approach to my 17,000-acre plantation was by water from Georgetown, roughly three miles away. In 1935 a new bridge and highway were put in between Georgetown and Wilmington, North Carolina, which provided easy physical access to Hobcaw. But even then I preserved its isolation. Twice a day mail and telegrams were brought from Georgetown, and that was all the communication with the outside world I desired for myself or my guests.

When I entered public life I found that having an oasis

of serenity in which one could take refuge was as valuable as in my Wall Street days. During World War Two in particular I would urge the harried, overworked officials in Washington to get away from the atmosphere of bitterness and feuding that blanketed the capital. Many of these officials were so intent upon winning the war that they literally slept with pencil and pad by their sides and rushed to their offices in the morning without pausing to wipe the egg off their chins. They went from conference to conference, grappling with one crisis after another with never a chance to think.

Late in 1945 when General George C. Marshall, then Chief of Staff, was spending a week end at Hobcaw, I remarked to him how important it was for the top officials of government to be able to look beyond the immediate pressures of the day to the looming problems on the horizon. Nodding his head vigorously, he told me, "Early in the war I instructed every officer assigned to the General Staff to get away from Washington for a day or two each week. I didn't want tired minds making decisions that would affect the lives of millions of soldiers."

Even Franklin D. Roosevelt, overburdened with his crushing war responsibilities, learned that no man can be too busy to rest. In April, 1944, he journeyed to Hobcaw for what originally was intended to be a two weeks' visit. He stayed a whole month.

Hobcaw is said to be an Indian word meaning "between the waters." The name was given to my plantation since it covers a neck of land between the Waccamaw River and the Atlantic Ocean. This part of South Carolina, around Pawley's Island, had fascinated me from the day—I was about eight years old—when we visited my Great-aunt Samson, who lived there.

From Camden we had gone to Charleston and then had taken the stern-wheel steamer *Louisa* north to Georgetown. It was my first sea voyage and what a stormy trip it was! Old Minerva, my nurse, was on her knees asking the Lord to take her to Heaven right then. The terrors of the ocean have remained with me from that day to this.

From Georgetown we went to Pawley's Island, to my great-aunt's. It was then that I met her son, Nat, who became one of my boyhood heroes. He was the captain of a little coastwise vessel called the *Banshee*—a most piratical-sounding name. He regaled me with marvelous stories of the turkeys, deer and ducks to be found on Waccamaw Neck about ten miles away. These memories came back to me when I heard that part of Waccamaw Neck was for sale.

Hobcaw is rich in history. It originally was part of the barony granted Lord Carteret by King George II. Even before the English colonization, a Spanish settlement is said to have been attempted there. During colonial times the main coastal road between Wilmington, North Carolina, and Charleston ran through Hobcaw. The part of this road which runs through Hobcaw is now only a track through the woods but it still goes by the name of the King's Highway.

These historical details delighted President Roosevelt. He was intrigued to learn that Hobcaw had been the country seat of William Alston, whose son Joseph, a governor of South Carolina, married Aaron Burr's daughter Theodosia. One day I took President Roosevelt down to the edge of Hobcaw's woods at Winyah Bay and showed him the ruins of a fort which the British had erected during the Revolutionary War. Around it were the graves, now overgrown, of several British soldiers. I have never permitted these graves to be opened.

President Roosevelt was also surprised to learn that he was actually the second President to visit Hobcaw. Grover Cleveland was the first, and one of the choicest hunting sites on the plantation is called "President's Stand" in his honor. How "Presi*dent's* Stand"—the official local pronunciation puts the accent on the last syllable—got its name is one of my favorite stories.

It was told to me by Sawney Cains, an expert duck hunter who acted as a guide for President Cleveland. As Sawney

used to tell it, he rowed the President to the marsh, con-
cealed the boat with palmetto, and set out the decoys. Then
he escorted the President to the shooting stand. This meant
walking over a strip of oozing mud which bordered the creek
bank.

Walking on mud like this is quite an art. You must put
your foot down lightly and raise it quickly so as not to sink
too deeply. Since President Cleveland's normal weight was
over 250 pounds, one can appreciate the complications
which followed.

Sawney was lending his strength to support Mr. Cleveland's bulk when the President's arm slipped from Sawney's
shoulder and down he sank into the muddy marsh. The
thought of the President of the United States becoming mired
in mud generated superhuman energies within Sawney. It
was not easy to get a good "holt" on the President's rotund
form, but Sawney got one and gave a mighty heave.

The President's hip boots stayed where they were, but the
President himself was lifted high and dry in his stockinged
feet. By this time Sawney was nearly waist deep in the ooze.
He managed to get out, though, and to pilot the President
back to the boat, both of them pretty well plastered with
mud. After washing they changed to warm clothing, and
were "medicined," to use Sawney's tactful word.

After a few swallows of good stiff "medicine" Mr. Cleveland began to shake with laughter, at which Sawney said he
was never more relieved in his life. When he told this story
Sawney never cracked a smile. It was always a serious matter with him.

Since it was wartime, President Roosevelt's own visit to
Hobcaw was shrouded in secrecy—at least at the start. He
arrived at noon on Easter Sunday, his private train stopping
north of Georgetown so that he could get off unseen. To
avoid passing through town, the Secret Service drove to Hobcaw by a back road. As we went through the gates into my
plantation, a Negro boy whose family lived on the place
caught a glimpse of the President with a cape draped over

his shoulders. "Gee!" exclaimed the boy. "It's George Washington!"

But the identity of my visitor did not remain secret very long in Georgetown. Even before the President was seen driving in an open car, many of the townspeople had guessed what was up from the sudden appearance of squadrons of camouflaged marines on the highways, and from the fact that three White House correspondents registered at the local hotel. The President's private railroad car also stood on the siding in town. Since I would permit no telephone to be strung into Hobcaw, the car was equipped with a telephone and was used as a message center linked with Washington.

My guest's identity became known, of course, in the office of the *News and Courier* in Charleston, about sixty miles away. The editor was William Ball, who has since died. A bitter foe of the New Deal, Ball never spared his vocabulary to make clear exactly where he stood. The *News and Courier* was one of the newspapers the President got every morning with his breakfast tray. Shortly after the President's arrival editorials lambasting him began to appear daily.

When I saw how much this irritated Roosevelt, I went to Ball and told him I thought he ought to stop the editorials while the President was there. I explained to Ball that my feeling had nothing to do with his right to express his opinions, but that it was not a gracious way of treating a guest in South Carolina.

Despite this one annoyance, the President enjoyed his stay so much that he did not want to leave. He had come to Hobcaw tired and with a cough. He left tanned and in better health, as Admiral Ross McIntire, his physician, told me, than in many a year.

April is probably the prettiest month at Hobcaw. Along all the walks circling the house the azaleas are in full bloom, the green foliage of the bushes almost lost in the mass of red, lavender, pink, and white flowers. But April, unfortunately, is not the fishing season. To find out where the President might have the best fishing luck, I had the creeks and inlets scouted in advance. Finally I learned that Ralph Ford, who ran one of the leading stores in town, knew of a wonderful fishing spot a few miles out in the Atlantic Ocean. He took President Roosevelt out. A ship had been wrecked there, and each time the President's boat circled the wreck the fish would hit the lines.

Roosevelt tried to persuade me to go out to sea with him. But I knew he had always been something of a practical joker. As I explained to his military aide, General "Pa" Watson, "He knows I get seasick easily. It would be just like him to get me out there and order the captain to go where the water is roughest."

The President did a good deal of work while at Hobcaw. One day he showed me an Air Force report claiming the destruction of a sizable number of Japanese planes. "Can you count?" he asked skeptically. "If these reports are true, the Japs can't have many planes left." After V-J Day, of course, we learned that the Japanese Air Force had indeed been all but destroyed.

While the President was at Hobcaw, Secretary of Navy Frank Knox died. One day at lunch, the conversation turned to who might be his successor. When someone mentioned James Forrestal, who later received the appointment, the President remarked, "He's from New York and we already have three cabinet members from New York. Don't you think that's too many, Bernie?"

"What difference does it make where the man's from?" I replied. "We're at war. The people will want you to name the best man. You have to take someone who knows what's been going on. You can't start someone from scratch."

A number of important visitors came to Hobcaw to confer with the President. Whenever I heard that some VIP was arriving, I would leave for Washington or New York and come back a few days later. I wanted the President to feel as if Hobcaw were his own home and that he didn't have to put up with my company. On my return one day my valet, William Lacey, told me excitedly, "You know who was here today? General Mark Clark, all the way from Italy."

But the President got more rest at Hobcaw than he had had in any similar period for years before. I had given him a two-room suite on the ground floor which could be shut off from the rest of the house. He slept ten and twelve hours a day. In the afternoon he would drive over to my daughter Belle's place for a drink. In the evening he often played solitaire. Once, while Admiral William E. Leahy was waiting to go over some cabled reports with him, the President insisted on showing me the many varied forms of solitaire that he knew. He had two ways of playing the game I had never seen before.

On other evenings, "Pa" Watson, Admiral McIntire, my nurse Blanche Higgins, and I would play gin rummy in the living room. The President would wheel himself in and, sitting off to a side, dictate letters while we played. As he dictated he kept one ear cocked to catch the bantering over who was winning and losing that went along with our game. Every now and then the President would join in our own laughter.

2

The house in which the President slept is not the original manor house of Hobcaw Barony. This first structure, a spacious frame building, caught fire in 1929 during our annual Christmas gathering. My wife and three children were with me along with Dick Lydon and Senator Key Pittman of Nevada.

We managed to save some of the valuables but could do nothing to stop the flames from spreading through the building. We were standing on the front lawn, watching the flames, when suddenly Senator Pittman exclaimed:

"My gosh, Bernie! You've got a barrel of good corn licker

in the basement which will go up like a bomb when the fire hits it."

Whether it was the threat of an explosion or the prospective loss of good liquor that worried Key, I don't know, but he and Dick Lydon tied wet handkerchiefs over their faces, dashed into the basement, and came out rolling the barrel before them.

I rebuilt the house the following year. To eliminate the threat of another fire, the new structure was made of red brick and concrete and steel, but its architecture is of the Georgian colonial period. We provided for ten bedrooms, each with its own bath and fireplace although there is also a central heating system.

The house stands on a rise in a parklike setting of magnolia trees, moss-draped live oaks, rare camphor trees, and bushes of camellias and azaleas. One day as he emerged from the house and saw the Spanish moss hanging like shawls over the trees, Otto Kahn, the banker, exclaimed, "I really know for the first time why Southerners feel about the South as they do." Another guest, Ralph Pulitzer, the publisher of the New York *World*, was once inspired to write a poem about Hobcaw. Although the poem is in my files, I will refrain from printing it.

From the front porch, with its six white two-story columns, the green lawn slopes down to the yellow waters of Winyah Bay, into which flow four rivers, the Sampit, Black, Waccamaw, and Peedee. It was along the banks of these waters that rice used to be cultivated while on the higher ground behind these rice marshes cotton was grown. At one time almost a fourth of Hobcaw's 17,000 acres were devoted to these crops, but now less than 100 acres are under cultivation.

Between the house and the Georgetown highway is a four-and-a-half-mile drive, all of it over plantation grounds. Along the way one passes through an eerie cypress swamp, where weirdly shaped "knees" protrude from the water. There also are long stretches of virgin pine and wild forest, much of which had never been cut until World War Two, when the

War Production Board appealed for timber to ease the lumber shortage. Along the road one also passes through what is left of the old Negro villages. At one time there were four separate Negro villages on the plantation, but as rice and cotton growing were abandoned, the villages began to break up. When President Roosevelt visited us only one village was left, and this one has gone since.

Usually we opened Hobcaw around Thanksgiving and kept it open until April, but only rarely as late as May. Christmas Week was always largely a family affair. In our first years, of course, most of the guests were businessmen I knew in Wall Street or friends of the family. Later the visitors came to include political figures and newspapermen, some of the commanders of our armed forces, writers, actors, theatrical producers, educators, and others.

Over one week end my guests were a number of political leaders from Maryland, including the late Albert C. Ritchie, who was then governor. The discussion, as I recall it, centered around who was likely to control the Maryland delegation to the Democratic national convention. Frank Kent, then the chief political writer for the Baltimore *Sun*, was standing with his back to the blazing fireplace, voicing his own views rather definitely. Everyone in the room began to smile, which only encouraged Frank to argue even more warmly. Then suddenly Frank jumped away from the fireplace and glanced behind him. While he had been arguing his pants had caught fire!

Another less heated political discussion that I recall was one which involved raising funds for the Democratic party. One of the guests quoted the late Senator Ollie James of Kentucky, who had a habit of spicing his conversation with race-track terms. When someone suggested that he try to tap a particular individual for funds, Ollie snorted, "I would be wasting my time. That fellow is closer than a dead heat."

Winston Churchill and his daughter, Diana, came for a brief visit in 1932. They had been vacationing at Bermuda, where Diana picked up one of the earlier Calypso songs which she chanted. The weather at Hobcaw was bad. I invited in a number of Georgetown's leading citizens and other noted South Carolinians. Several times in later years Mr. Churchill would ask me about some of the people he had met. He had forgotten their names but would ask, "What has happened to that little storekeeper with the bald head?"

Unfortunately, Hobcaw's old guest books have been lost. But among the other guests I recall were Jack London, who was a friend of my brother Harty's; Edna Ferber; Deems Taylor; Franklin P. Adams; Max Hirsch, the famous horse trainer; Robert Sherwood; Harry Hopkins; Bob Ruark; Hedda Hopper; Westbrook Pegler; and Heywood Broun. When I asked Broun if he was going to join us in duck hunting, he retorted, "I do my hunting in bed." The Prince of Monaco, grandfather of the present Prince Rainier, spent several days at Hobcaw hunting rare butterflies and unusual birds.

General Omar Bradley was a particularly good shot. When Air Force General Hoyt Vandenberg and Stuart Symington came down we had long discussions about air power. Early in 1953 Senator Robert A. Taft and Senator Harry F. Byrd spent a week end in hunting and political talk. They had a high respect for one another and I sometimes have wondered what turn our politics might have taken if Taft had not been stricken with cancer.

Other friends were regular guests almost every year, like the late Joseph Pulitzer, who was the publisher of the St. Louis *Post-Dispatch;* Roy Howard and Walker Stone of the Scripps-Howard newspapers; Arthur Krock; David Sarnoff; Clare and Henry Luce; Herbert Swope; John Hancock and General Hugh Johnson, when they were alive.

When theatrical people like Walter Huston, John Golden, Max Gordon, or Billy Rose came, we often visited one of the Negro villages. If it was Saturday night, dances would be going on in the barn. On Sundays we might attend the services in the little whitewashed church.

Every New Year's Day we used to stage a big deer drive,

over which the Governor of South Carolina would officiate, and which would draw various sporting notables. These drives began while Richard I. Manning was governor and continued for many years. However, I did not enjoy deer hunting, nor did my children, who refused to pull a trigger on one. Today Hobcaw constitutes a sort of unofficial sanctuary for deer. One cannot ride far on the grounds without deer jumping across the trail almost under the nose of one's horse.

I have hunted in Scotland, Czechoslovakia, and Canada, but never in my travels did I ever come upon a place to compare with Hobcaw, when it was in its prime, for the abundance and variety of its game. Our bays and rivers abounded with sea bass, mullet, flounder, sheepshead, whiting, bluefish, and shad. In the water courses that meandered through the rice fields were brim and trout; in the marshes, oysters, clams, crabs, terrapin, and shrimp.

The woods and fields were filled with woodcock, jacksnipe, quail, and turkey. At one time the turkeys were so numerous that I often had to stop my buggy to let large flocks cross the road. I tried, without too much success, to protect them against the increasing number of foxes, possums, coons, and wild hogs which raided their nests. These wild hogs or boars were descended from domestic animals that had taken to the woods, and could be quite dangerous when molested.

In the early years when I first owned the place, we caught wildcats and otter. There were also a few bears, but they long ago disappeared.

3

But first and foremost Hobcaw was known for its ducks. A rice field is a prime feeding ground for ducks, and, earlier in the century, when rice was still under cultivation along the South Carolina coast, I believe that there was no better place for duck shooting in the whole United States. As rice planting was abandoned in South Carolina, the ducks began to vanish from Hobcaw's marshes. Another reason for their disappearance was the raiding of their breeding grounds in Canada, where millions of eggs were taken each year and sold to bakers.

The profusion of ducks at Hobcaw led to a good deal of poaching, which in turn almost cost me my life. When I bought Hobcaw, its marsh lands were under lease to a club of Philadelphia sportsmen. This gun club had been having a running dispute with four of Sawney Cains' brothers over their poaching. The Cains family had lived on or near Hobcaw for generations and claimed some vague property rights.

One day Ball Cains and his brother Hucks sailed a boat up to where a club member was shooting. Sitting in the boat, with double-barreled shotguns across their knees, they "cussed" the Northerner and told him what they thought of Yankees in general.

When I took over the plantation two of the Cains brothers, Bob and Pluty, came to work for me as guides. Ball and Hucks continued to poach. One morning I spotted Hucks on my land, not half a mile from where I was. I caught him with 166 ducks. I confronted him sternly but wound up asking if he would work for me instead of poach on me.

But I never could induce Ball Gains to quit poaching. He resisted threats and persuasions. After doing everything possible to convince Ball that I meant business, I had him and another poacher arrested and sent to jail for nine months. While Ball was in jail my lawyer looked after his wife and children, but when Ball was released, he came out looking for trouble.

One day Hucks Cains was coming in with me from duck shooting at the "President's Stand." Suddenly Hucks said to me in alarm, "Mr. Bernie, Ball is on the landing. You better be careful."

Hucks started to turn the boat. I told him to swing around and row straight to the landing, which he did. As I climbed out Ball cursed at me and swore he would send my soul to hell. He aimed his shotgun at me.

I can still see those barrels. I felt that I could have jumped into them without touching the sides. I was so frightened that mechanically I simply walked up to Ball and asked if he realized what he was doing.

Just at this moment, one of my employees, Captain Jim Powell, came running toward the landing with a big six-shooter in his hand. As calmly as I could, I said, "Here comes Captain Jim." Ball turned for a moment. I grabbed the barrels of his gun and pushed them up toward the sky.

After that my poaching troubles subsided. Powell, who was six feet four, raw-boned and fearless, became my superintendent.

It always troubled me that I had put a man in jail just for shooting ducks. The ducks themselves did not matter, but I knew that if Ball shot, everyone else would shoot, and soon my place would be a rendezvous for poachers. I would be respected neither by the poachers nor anyone else. It was as my father said when telling me of Mannes Baum—if you took an insult you were done for in South Carolina.

I was glad that I didn't have to use such drastic measures with Hucks Cains. Hucks had a wonderfully laconic sense of humor. When I offered some explanation for missing a duck, he would observe, "Well, a poor excuse is better than none."

Again early in the Prohibition era I had as guests four senators—Joe Robinson of Arkansas, Pat Harrison of Mississippi, Key Pittman of Nevada, and A. O. Stanley of Kentucky. We had had a wonderful morning and were getting into the buckboard to drive home when I remarked to our guide, "Hucks, do you know that these gentlemen are the senators who make the laws up in Washington?"

Hucks leaned on the front wheel of the buckboard and asked, "Is they really the gentlemen who make the laws up in Washington?"

"Yes, Hucks," I replied.

"Well," said Hucks, "if they don't know no more about

other things than they does about whiskey and ducks, this country is in a devil of a fix."

Hucks was an ardent follower of Cole Blease, then Governor of South Carolina and later United States Senator. Blease was a self-appointed champion of the "plain" people. Hucks never could understand why his hero railed against me. Every time Blease came to Georgetown, Hucks would argue it out with him; but that was the only flaw he saw in Blease.

"When another man speaks," Hucks once told me, "folks applauds, but when Blease speaks they sets up the hallelujahs. You can't get in the place when people hear he is going to speak. When God Almighty and Jesus Christ made a perfect man they done made Cole Blease."

Hucks also told a story about another United States senator from South Carolina who voted dry but liked his liquor. Hucks' admiration for the Eighteenth Amendment was limited to the fact that it gave him an opportunity to increase his personal revenue by bootlegging. This senator made a wonderful speech on Prohibition. Hucks was so dazzled by it all that he went up and asked, "Senator, that was a fine speech but which side is you on?"

Hucks could call a duck so well with his mouth or with a caller that neither the hunter nor the duck could distinguish the call from that of a real duck. The only person who could approach him in this respect was my son Bernard. When I asked Hucks for the secret of his success as a duck man, he would say, "Mr. Bernie, this business is like everything else —you just got to know."

In those earlier days our duck-hunting parties would be moving by four or four-thirty in the morning. We would row out sometimes in the dark, sometimes in the moonlight, with no sound except the creaking of the oarlocks, the lapping of the water against the side of the boats, and now and then a frightened quack of ducks getting up or the swish of their wings overhead. Sometimes the moon would just be going down, and the sun coming up.

To the eastward, as the sun rose, one could see tens of

thousands of ducks. At times they appeared like bees pouring out of a huge bottle. Their numbers were so great that you had to blink your eyes to be sure that you were not suffering from some illusion. As the sun mounted above the horizon, flock after flock would break away from the swamps and rice fields and come down to the marshes, flying in V formation. Nearing the marsh or hearing the call of the hunter, they would circle around and come down to the decoys. I have seen outlined in the sky the patterns of the very creeks from which the ducks rose.

There were so many ducks that I laid down the rule that no one could pull a trigger after eleven o'clock in the morning. Only on exceptional occasions did we shoot until eleven. Ordinarily we were through at nine o'clock—ready to go home by ten-thirty.

After a day of shooting, the dead ducks would be lying in a circle about us, for a distance of 120 yards. Retrievers could not be used in the Hobcaw marshes because the oyster shells cut their feet. We tried all kinds of contrivances, such as putting boots on the dogs' feet, but they never worked.

If you kept a count of the birds you shot, though, your guide would pick up practically every one. A good guide would remember where every bird shot had fallen. I have seen Hucks Cains pick up all but two or three birds when the bag was close to two hundred.

Some of the bags that have been shot at Hobcaw were truly incredible. I used to return to New York and Washington from Hobcaw with duck stories that some of my friends refused to believe. Thomas W. Gregory, Attorney General under President Wilson, would say to Jesse Jones, who became Secretary of Commerce and chairman of the Reconstruction Finance Corporation under Roosevelt, "Jesse, keep quiet. Let's sit back and hear Bernie lie about the ducks."

Back around 1912 or 1913, the Whitneys—Harry Payne and his brother, Payne—sailed their yacht into Winyah Bay for a week end of hunting. At lunch, after the first day's shooting, Harry Whitney spoke up, "Bernie, I'll give you a million dollars if you want to sell this place." He sounded serious, but since I didn't want to sell I changed the subject.

Probably the best duck hunter I ever saw at Hobcaw was Roy Rainey, a New York businessman. Hucks Cains told me that once Rainey, encumbered by a heavy coat, missed two ducks in succession. Throwing off his coat, Rainey flapped his arms to stimulate circulation and exclaimed: "Now let 'em all come." He took up his gun and killed 96 ducks without missing.

Quail shooting was another favorite sport at Hobcaw. As the woods grew thicker, however, it became more difficult to find the birds. When you did find them the undergrowth usually was too dense for shooting. Most of my quail shooting has been done on leased land near Kingstree, South Carolina, about forty-five miles inland. It is where I now spend most of my time in South Carolina and where I still shoot quail.

To conserve the quail on my property, I never permit a covey, which ordinarily runs from twelve to twenty birds, to be shot down to fewer than five birds. A covey shot down to this number will give the best results in the way of increase in the next season.

Like other game, quail will go only where there is good feeding and shelter. I arranged for careful examination of the craws of the quail we shot for a period of years. I found out that quail prefer the partridge pea, or beggar lice, which ordinarily grows wild. We learned to pick it and sow it on my land. As another means of keeping quail on my property, I had my men trap "swamp" birds—which are hard to shoot and practically immune in their thick cover—and put them on the hills.

4

The most ardent hunter I ever knew was Senator Joe T. Robinson of Arkansas. Whatever Robinson did, he did with intensity—and it was this that killed him.

As Democratic leader in the Senate, he was carrying the burden of pushing through President Roosevelt's unpopular program for the reorganization of the Supreme Court. For several years Joe had been taking digitalis to ward off anginal twinges. His doctors warned him to slow up but Joe paid no heed. Early one morning, in the middle of the fight over Roosevelt's court-packing plan in 1937, Joe was found dead beside his bed, an open copy of the *Congressional Record* by his side.

Joe was a wonderful companion, a hearty eater, and full of gusto, with enormous physical and intellectual courage. I often tried to get him out of Washington for a few days' rest. Sometimes at the beginning of a week end when I thought he was working too hard, I would call him from New York and say, "Joe, I am going down to Hobcaw tomorrow and the train passes through Washington at seven forty-five in the evening. There will be a place for you aboard."

Invariably he would say, "Sorry, but there isn't a chance in the world. I just can't get away, even for a day."

After a little conversation Joe would ask, "How did you say the shooting was down there?" I would reply, "It is fine."

Then he would ask, "What time did you say that train goes through?" knowing full well that it went through at seven forty-five. He then would wind up saying, "I will do what I can but I don't see how I can make it." Usually, the next evening, we would find him aboard.

Joe brought the same single-mindedness to hunting that characterized his legislative work. Before sunup in the morning he was out after ducks. In the afternoon he was hunting quail. In the evening he would go out to the edge of the swamp, sit there, and wait by the hour for a turkey to rise to its roost in a high tree.

Once Robinson, thinking himself alone, saw a huge bird light on the limb of a tree about one hundred yards away. From the bird's long whiskers Joe knew it was a gobbler. I do not permit anyone to shoot hens. Creeping up slowly, Joe raised his gun and muttered aloud, "Here is where I bring down Mr. Secretary Hughes."

He came in with the bird, which weighed 24¾ pounds. Pretty soon outside the house we heard a couple of Negroes talking. One remarked that it was funny about Mr. Joe. He called turkeys Secretary Hughes.

We decided to send the turkey to President Warren G. Harding. Robinson returned to Washington. Days passed and he received no acknowledgment from the President. Then Joe ran into Senator Jim Watson of Indiana, who remarked, "That certainly was a fine bird you sent the President."

To this Robinson, who always spoke his mind, replied, "Yes, and I think it's a hell of a note for the President not to ask any of us Democrats to help him eat it."

This was quickly followed by gracious and apologetic letters from the White House to all of us. Just the same I heard Joe vow that the next time he shot a twenty-four-pound turkey, he would not send it to a Republican.

As enthusiastic a hunter as Joe Robinson, but somewhat less successful as a nimrod, was Admiral Cary Grayson, who had been President Wilson's physician. Cary was a fine and gentle man whom I loved dearly. He could spend an entire day in the woods and might, as one of my guides put it, "bring home a feather." Cary's good humor never failed him, though.

One day I arranged to have Cary bring back something more than a feather. He was walking through the woods when his hunting guide tapped his shoulder and pointed out a big turkey at the foot of a tree. Cary raised his gun, fired, and rushed forward to examine his prize. As he bent over, he noticed that the bird was tied to a tree. Around its neck was a string to which a card was attached which read, "With the compliments of Bernard M. Baruch."

Cary enjoyed the joke as much as any of us. In fact it was he who told it to President Calvin Coolidge, who spread the story through Washington. If Cary had not related the story it might never have gotten out, since it was a Hobcaw rule that a guest's hunting score was never revealed.

Cary's reaction to our joke supports a conviction of mine that there is no sport like hunting which will reveal a man's character so well. I know of no other sport which will bring out the latent barbarian in a man so quickly, nor any that imposes such a strain on a man's truthfulness.

One Hobcaw rule was that the guest was always right about the number of ducks he said he had shot. All of the guides were instructed to confirm the claim of any guest, whatever number it was.

Once Pa Watson and Steve Early, President Roosevelt's press secretary, had been ribbing each other about who would get the most birds. Steve came back first, and he had shot his limit. When Pa Watson came in, Steve demanded triumphantly, "How many did you get?"

For a moment I wondered whether Pa would take advantage of the Hobcaw rule, but he grinned and replied, "Oh, a certain number."

Another Hobcaw "institution" which often proved a revealing test of human nature was snipe hunting with bag and lantern. Most of the regular visitors to Hobcaw had been initiated as members in good standing into the Hobcaw Snipe Club. But there was one gentleman who failed to pass the membership test.

He was one of a party going down to Hobcaw in Mortimer Schiff's private car. Among the other guests were James Wallace, president of the Central Union Trust Company; Howard Page, formerly of Standard Oil and then president of the Intercontinental Rubber Company; Oakleigh Thorne, a financier; John Black of Wall Street; my brother Harty; and myself.

This gentleman had never been to Hobcaw before, and he clearly was skeptical of the hunting wonders of the place, which were being described to him. We decided we had a new candidate for our Snipe Club.

One evening, with a countenance as solemn as a bishop's,

Oakleigh Thorne pulled his mustache reflectively and said, "Bernie, why don't you let us have some snipe hunting?" Thorne proceeded to explain that he knew I did not like it because it called for no great ability; but, he argued, it was a novel thing and he thought all of us would enjoy it just once.

I protested that it was a stupid sport to see a man go out and hold a bag and lantern in one hand and whistle to attract the snipe to come into the light and dive into the bag. Finally I was persuaded to consent to just one evening of snipe hunting, but no more.

Then the guests began wagering who would catch the most snipe. Soon our candidate was hooked. It sounded so easy that he offered to make a bet. Writing down all the bets, I passed the paper around the table and asked each man to initial his bet or bets as correct.

The next day we were a bit uneasy. Snipe, of course, will not fly into a bag at a whistle or at the sight of a lantern any more than any other bird, and we feared our candidate for the snipe hunt would discover this. During the day we got a succession of reports that our candidate was discussing snipe hunting with some of the servants and hunting guides. But no one gave the joke away. When our candidate asked the Negro butler what he thought about snipe hunting, the Negro replied, "It is good for dem dat likes it."

It fell to Bob Cains to take out the candidate, place him in a good stand, and show him exactly how to wield his bag and lantern, and how to whistle to attract the snipe. When Bob came back he said, "Mr. Bernie, I don't want to have to go out and git that man. He is goin' to take this mighty bad."

Already the beaters were at work making the noises which were supposed to start up the snipe. We could hear our candidate, the eminent banker, whistle as he had been instructed to do, to attract the birds toward his lantern. The louder he whistled the harder we laughed. Soon some of us were rolling on the ground or stuffing our fists into our mouths to keep from laughing too loudly.

No one had to go and fetch the candidate. Before long he

came in by himself. One glance at his face and we stopped laughing.

"That was a hell of a thing to do!" he exclaimed. "How much does So-and-So know about this?" he demanded, naming an almost equally conspicuous banker who was the president of a rival trust company. Nor was that all he said.

The roster of the Hobcaw Snipe Club numbered figures distinguished in finance, industry, law, letters, and statecraft, but our candidate of that evening lacked the qualifications to be one of the company.

21. The Negro Progresses

ONE REASON I ESTABLISHED a second home in the South was that my mother had asked me not to lose touch with the land of my forebears. She also had urged me to try to contribute to its regeneration and, in particular, to "do something for the Negro."

Her urging never left my mind, and in all my activities in the South I have always sought to better conditions there and somehow to help improve the Negro's lot.

When the town of Camden asked me to contribute to the erection of a local hospital, I laid down one condition for my support—that a specific number of beds be reserved for colored patients.

The people of Camden were talking of building this hospital with $20,000. I told them that this was not enough and that I would foot the entire cost of construction if they undertook to support it. They agreed. When this hospital burned down, I financed the erection of another and better building and of a nurses' home.

When I contributed money to colleges in South Carolina, the Negro institutions got their share. Similarly, the scholarships that I provided went to both Negroes and whites.

It was not always possible to do as much as one might want to do. Once I bought a plot of ground in Georgetown to build a modern playground for Negroes. Some nearby residents protested my action. I still intended to go ahead with the playground when Dr. J. B. Beck, the head of the Georgetown school for Negroes, came to me. Dr. Beck always came through the kitchen when he called, but I always saw that he left by the front door.

"Mr. Bernie," he pleaded, "I wish you wouldn't put up

this playground. We've had pretty good relations here and don't want trouble."

And so I bought another piece of land and had the playground erected there.

In this instance Dr. Beck was wiser than I was. In all my dealings with both Negroes and whites I have tried to treat people somewhat more generously than was the prevailing custom, hoping that others might follow my example. But I have learned that to serve as an effective example—and this applies to all human affairs—one cannot be too far ahead of the people one wants to influence.

This view may not satisfy those who would remake the world overnight. It may not satisfy those who want things kept as they are. I believe that change is part of living. But I like a pace of change that does not create more trouble than good.

When I think back to how the Negro in South Carolina lived at the turn of the century I am struck by the remarkable progress he has made. The Negroes I first knew were sons or daughters of slaves, simple, lovable, but often seemingly irresponsible. As late as the 1920's most Negroes in South Carolina were sharecroppers. Today many who live near me are in business or the professions. They own their own farms and are considered among the most reliable farmers in the region.

Recently I asked one white Southerner, who had considerable dealings with Negroes, how Negro farmers managed to hold on to their land in the face of falling farm prices. "They take it out of themselves," said this white Southerner admiringly. "Once they own a piece of land they'll make any sacrifice to keep it."

Another white neighbor I know wanted to buy an acre of swamp land from a Negro farmer. But the Negro declined to sell. To test him, my neighbor offered $500 for the acre— an astronomical sum. But the Negro farmer replied, "Sorry, Captain, I can't help you. I'm just not parting with any of my land."

The manager of my own plantation tells me that Negroes get as much out of their land as the most efficient white farmers and are just as quick to adopt the latest agricultural techniques.

2

This change is all the more gratifying when I recall the conditions under which Negroes lived when I first bought Hobcaw. In those days when a man bought a plantation in the South, a certain number of Negroes came with the place. They had been born there, as were their fathers before them. They knew no other home. They felt that it was the obligation of the owner to look after them and give them employment.

This was brought home to me rather vividly one day when my superintendent, Harry Donaldson, said he wanted to move one Negro off the place because he was lazy. Ordinarily I like to give a man full authority so he can accept full responsibility, but I had made this exception—that no Negro could be turned off the place except by me.

And so I decided to listen to what this Negro had to say for himself. One Sunday afternoon, my wife, her stepmother, and I walked out to the barn and I sent for Morris. An elderly, gray-wooled Negro appeared. Hat in hand, he bowed to the ladies and then to me.

"Morris," said I, "Captain Harry says you are lazy and won't work. He says you ought to be put off the place."

"Mist' Bernie," replied Morris, "I was born on dis place and I ain't agoin' off." He said this simply, without effrontery.

Morris walked up and down in front of us as he talked. "Mist' Bernie, I was born on dis place before Freedom. My mammy and daddy worked de rice fields. Dey's buried here. De fust ting I remember are dose rice banks. I growed up in dem from dat high." He measured with his hand.

"De strength of dese arms and dese legs and of dis old

back, Mist' Bernie, is in your rice banks. It won't be long before de good Lord take de rest of pore ole Morris away too.
An' de rest of dis body want to be with de strength of de arms
and de legs and de back dat is already buried in your rice
banks. No, Mist' Bernie, you ain't agoin' to run ole Morris
off dis place.

"I'se had big troubles," he went on. Here he turned to the
ladies and addressed himself to them. His wife had died,
leaving him a daughter to raise. He told how difficult it had
been to work all day in the rice fields and still keep an eye
on this lively girl. When he spoke of the irresponsibility of
young people of courting age, his voice sank almost to a
whisper and what he left unsaid was more eloquent than what
he said.

"De Missis will understand me," he imparted confiden-
tially to my wife.

It was a sordid yet familiar story that Morris unfolded—
of how his daughter, without having a husband, had had a
baby girl. Morris went on to tell of his efforts to rear this
granddaughter and make a home for her and retain her love.

"De Missis know what I mean," he reiterated, as if the
matter were too subtle for my comprehension.

"I'se tried to be a good nigger, Mist' Bernie," he concluded, "but if I'se a bad one sometime, it is because de Lord
done made me so. You got to take me de way He made me."

I have heard many men plead a cause or for themselves,
but never a plea more moving or better based on human
justice than that of this old Negro. He became a favorite of
the family, and the artful old fellow knew it, too.

Once I asked Morris what he would like for Christmas.
He told me he would like some "hot drawers," meaning
warm underwear. Another time I scolded Morris because he
would not raise turkeys in the barnyard according to my instructions. Morris excused himself, saying, "Dem turkeys
is just such fools dat dey raises dey heads in de rain and
drowns hisselves."

Morris also started raising chickens for me, but pip struck

them and I gave up the experiment. I tried to educate Morris and some of the other Negroes to more scientific methods of farming, but in those early days I got nowhere.

Today, however, the Negro farmers I know are as adept as the white man in picking up improved methods of farming. Take Ely Wilson, who is respected by everyone. He selects his own seeds for his 200-acre farm, uses varied types of fertilizer, and rotates his crops—vegetables, cotton, tobacco and corn. He is as expert in using scientific farm techniques as any of his neighbors. In addition, he is also known as the best bird hunter in our community.

Or take Troy Jones, who works for me in addition to cultivating his own 100-acre farm. When Troy bought his farm, much of it was uncleared land. He and his wife rooted out the stumps. Today their farm is clear of debt.

Troy is only thirty-five years old. Yet when he first started farming he used an ox. Then he got a mule, and, a few years ago, a tractor. Where Troy used to clear the grass off his land with fires, he now uses a plow.

Similar evidence of the Negro's progress can be seen in every other activity. A large coastal plantation like Hobcaw constituted an almost complete, self-sustained society as far as the Negroes were concerned. Practically all of Hobcaw's Negroes had been born on the place. The larger world outside Hobcaw held little interest for them. Some had never traveled even the few miles across the river to Georgetown. As far as I know, when I took over Hobcaw only two had ever been to Charleston.

They paid no attention to politics, although at that time all of them professed allegiance to the Republican party. Once I asked Abraham Kennedy, a man of fine character and a skilled carpenter and bricklayer, whether he voted.

"No, sah," he said, "I do not fool wid dat ting."

"Would you vote for a Democrat?" I asked.

"No, boss," replied Abraham. "When I was a chile my mammy used to take a picture of Abraham Lincoln and make me git down on my knees every night and pray before it and promise never to vote for nobody but him."

As part of a general plan to rehabilitate the plantation, which was sadly run down when I took charge, all the cabins were put into decent condition. The Negroes themselves did the work with pay. A day's labor at the prevailing wage was always available for every colored man or woman who wanted to work. They also were provided with fuel and garden plots. As far as their creature comforts were concerned there never was suffering or want.

For the old and disabled I set up a form of credit at Ford's Grocery in Georgetown, with the bills being turned in to me regularly. I suppose this might have been called an old-age pension system.

When I bought Hobcaw hardly any of the Negroes could read. We established a school which later became the particular pride of my daughter Belle. She would round up the children daily from the four villages. One day two seventeen-year-old boys failed to show up at the schoolhouse. Belle and a friend got on their horses and went looking for the two boys. They were found hiding in a swamp. Belle could not ride into the swamp so she dismounted and, much to the horror of her friend, waded in and reappeared, holding each boy by an ear.

Few of the Negroes went far in their schooling. But here again the new generation is different from the old. One man on my place has had practically no schooling. But he managed to send both his children through college to become teachers.

The Negroes I first knew, like my old nurse, Minerva, were steeped in superstition. The woods, the stream, the air, and the sky were filled with "hants." The new moon was a dangerous time to go through a wood. The Negroes always carried lanterns and you could hear them singing and shouting to keep up their courage.

Then there was the "plat eye," which was a variable sort of haunt. It could appear in the form of a witch that came in and beat old people, but usually it resembled an animal. It might be as big as an ox or as small as a cat. Most of the time it had only one great eye in the middle of the forehead.

You should always keep to one side of the plat eye. Above all, never let the plat eye run between your legs. Some of the braver Negroes would say they had kicked the plat eye, but with no result. "Your feet done go right through and you don't touch nothing."

The more intelligent Negroes seldom saw haunts. The ignorant ones saw much of them. But I doubt that any of them were absolutely certain there were no haunts.

One evening my guests were telling ghost stories at the table. The eyes of the colored boy who served us got bigger and bigger. After dinner one guest, Ed Smith, asked the boy to take a message down the road a piece. The boy tried to get out of it, but finally set out. We could hear him whistling and singing all the way to the cabin which was his destination. When he started back, still whistling and singing, Ed Smith walked out and stood behind a tree in the yard.

As the boy approached, Ed let out a ghostly sound. "Ooooo-ooo-oo-oo!"

The boy stopped and craned his neck.

"Is dat you, Mr. Ed?"

"Ooo-oo-ooo!"

"Mr. Ed," said the boy in a quavering voice, "I know dat's you, but I'se going to run anyhow."

Aren't we all sometimes like that boy?

Another innovation I introduced was regular medical care. I had a clinic built in one of Hobcaw's villages. Once a week my own doctor, F. A. Bell, would come to it and give medical treatment to Negroes who needed it without charge. Still, many Negroes preferred to take their ailments to the "root doctor," who was also believed to have supernatural powers. Many Negroes feared the "evil eye" that a root doctor could put on a person. I have even heard of instances where runaway wives or husbands returned because of fear of his influence.

Today there still are one or two root doctors around Georgetown, but they have little clientele beyond a few old Negroes who still retain their faith in potions and hexes.

3

Probably the strongest single influence on these old-time Negroes was their religion. The preacher was often the most important man in a plantation community. He christened and baptized his people, married them and buried them. We called them "broadax" preachers because they were not regularly ordained. Although few of the older generation of broadax preachers could read, they were genuine leaders of their people.

One reason religion has been so important to Negroes, I believe, is that it takes the place of a sense of history. The Negro in America has lacked a knowledge of his ancient past. He has not had these feelings of identity and pride which almost every ethnic group has for its own cultural origins.

This thought occurred to me several years ago while reading Galbraith Welch's *North African Prelude,* in which she told of the heroic exploits of Negro kings and warriors of old Africa. I felt that the full story of this heritage would be a source of pride and strength to Negroes everywhere. I wrote Miss Welch urging her to undertake such a study. Later when William Tubman, the president of Liberia, came to this country, I sought him out and suggested that he invite Miss Welch to Liberia to do such a study. This he did.

Once I thought of hiring someone to make a systematic survey of Negro folklore in the South Carolina low country, and I have always regretted not going through with the idea. Now, of course, it is too late since the old customs have passed away—and happily so.

Still, there was a warmth and richness in Negro life at Hobcaw. No holiday went uncelebrated. Births, baptisms, and weddings were always accompanied by appropriate festivities.

On Saturday nights dances were held in the barn. We gave prizes to the best dancers and to the best dressed among the men and women, boys and girls.

Practically all of the modern dances later popularized in New York, Paris, and London I first saw at Hobcaw. The "music" at these dances was furnished in part by a mouth organ, but mostly by clapping hands and patting feet which provided a rhythm which, I have been told, was much like that created by the native drummers in Africa.

This rhythm of clapping hands and patting feet was also used at church services. When we replaced the little log church in one of Hobcaw's villages with a better one, the elders asked me to dedicate the new edifice. I had considerable difficulty explaining why it would hardly be suitable for me to undertake to dedicate their church. We finally arranged to have the dedication performed by an ordained colored minister.

That little whitewashed church remained their place of worship for more than a quarter of a century. Although not given to any creed, I respect all religions and never have seen a truly religious man who was not happier for his faith. Sometimes I would take my place on one of the rude benches in our Hobcaw church and follow the service. Primitive as they were, these services were things of true beauty. The various parts of the service fitted together harmoniously in a way that made of the whole a sort of sacred chant.

A typical service began with one of the elders, who on week days was a field hand, leading a song to the accompaniment of clapping hands and shuffling feet. Some of these songs had been generations in the making and were native to Hobcaw. The leader would sing a line. The congregation would repeat it. And so it would go through many verses.

The song would end abruptly and another elder would kneel at the altar and in a loud voice begin to pray, again to the accompaniment of muffled hand claps and foot pats. He prayed for the welfare of the crops and the livestock, for good fishing and shooting and all the other things needed to make life good at Hobcaw. The congregation punctuated the prayer with interjections of "Yes, Lord," and "Amen."

After this supplication there would be another song. As emotional ecstasy filled the heart of the leader he would commence to dance. The hand clapping grew louder as other dancers took the floor. Soon a third of the congregation would be on its feet, filling the aisles and the space in front of the altar. Those who remained seated swayed from side to side. The kerosene lamps would tremble in their brackets.

Then came the sermon. My favorite preacher was Moses Jenkins, whose son, Prince, still works for me. The story of the liberation of Israel from bondage held a special fascination for Moses Jenkins. His account of the Exodus from Egypt was a masterpiece.

He would adjust his gold-rimmed glasses, which to his congregation were a sign of learning. Then he would pick up the large Bible my wife had given to the church and read those wonderful verses from Exodus:

" 'And the angel of the Lord appeared unto him in a flame of fire out of the midst of a bush: and he looked, and, behold, the bush burned with fire, and the bush was not consumed.' "

At which the congregation droned, "and-the-bush-was-not-consumed."

Moses Jenkins went on.

" 'And when the Lord saw that he turned aside to see, God called unto him out of the midst of the bush, and said, Moses, Moses.' "

"Moses-Moses," repeated the congregation.

" 'And he said,' " continued the preacher, " 'Here am I.' "

The audience echoed, "Here-am-I."

Moses Jenkins would go on to tell of Moses' audience with Phar-a-oh—as he pronounced it—and the ruler's refusal to allow the Hebrews to depart in peace. Then followed the plagues until finally Phar-a-oh said that the Jews might go, only to repent his decision and begin pursuit. Moses made this pursuit highly realistic. After World War One he added to his description a few modern touches such as, "And de rifles and machine guns was apoppin'!"

Usually Moses would end his sermon with the stirring and satisfying scene of Phar-a-oh and his men drowning in the Red Sea. But sometimes, when he was in good form, he would plunge past the flight from Egypt into the forty years of wandering in the wilderness before the Israelites reached the Promised Land. He simplified this narrative a good deal and to help himself over tight places would anticipate events a little by introducing Mary or Joseph, or Jesus and the Apostle Paul.

When Moses pitched his tent at the foot of Mount Sinai and ascended the mountain to receive the tablets of law from the Lord, he left Aaron and two others in charge. "You boys stay down here," said Moses—according to Moses Jenkins—"and keep wide awake and watch out after tings while I'se gone."

"But what do you think happened?" demanded Moses Jenkins. "When Moses done come back, he found dem tree Jew boys fast asleep!"

All through the sermon the undertone of hand clapping and drumming of feet swelled and died with the ebb and flow of the preacher's rhetoric. The sermon would be followed by more songs and more prayers. Often these services lasted until one o'clock in the morning. Then the congregation would file out into the darkness and scatter in murmuring, laughing groups, bound for the four villages.

To the Negro, of course, religion held out a promise of equality in the future which was not his on this earth. One thing that impressed me was the fortunate faculty the Negro had of making his religion meet his exact needs, accepting this and rejecting that until he found a formula that suited him. Often, as well, his native shrewdness and realism turned him into a skeptic. My friend, Admiral Cary Grayson, used to tell a story which was typical of this down to earth approach to heavenly matters.

An aging colored man, the story went, felt a desire to be

taken into the bosom of the church. He applied to the deacon, who said:

"Abraham, you must have faith to be taken into de bosom of the church. Do you believe everything in de Bible?"

"Yes, sah," replied Abraham.

"Do you believe de story of Jonah and de whale?"

"Yes, sah."

"Do you believe de story of Daniel and de lions? Dose hongry African lions what hadn't had nuthin' to eat? Daniel, you know, walks right into dere den and slaps 'em in de face, and dey don't do nuthin' to him."

"Hongry African lions, and he slaps 'em in de face?"

"Dat's what de Bible say," assured the deacon.

"Well, den, I believes it."

"And do you believes de story of de Hebrew children in de fiery furnace? De Hebrew children walked into de furnace, stepped on de hot coals, got all in de flames, and dey wasn't even singed."

"Wasn't even singed? A regular fire?"

"Dat's right. Dey wasn't even singed."

Abraham shook his head. "Deacon," he said, "I don't believes dat."

"Then you cain't be taken into de bosom of de church."

Abraham picked up his hat and slowly started to walk out. At the door he paused and looked back.

"And, Deacon," he said, "I don't believes dat story about Daniel and de lions, neither."

4

In all the years at Hobcaw only once did we have serious trouble with a Negro. Since there were not enough white children at Hobcaw to justify a school, a young woman teacher was hired to give lessons to Hucks Cains' two daughters. One day—my family and I were in the North at the time

—this teacher and her little charges were driving through the pine woods. Suddenly a Negro sprang out of a thicket and dragged the teacher from the buggy.

The children screamed. The teacher put up a terrific battle. Finally, when almost exhausted, she had the presence of mind to scream, "Oh, thank God, here comes Mr. Hucks!"

The ruse succeeded. The Negro dropped her and dived back into the woods.

News of the attempted assault spread through the countryside as swiftly as if it had been telegraphed by the drums of Africa. Men came over from Georgetown in boats. Others from farther up the Neck rode down with shotguns and rifles slung across their saddles. The woods, swamps, marshes, and water courses were soon alive with posses.

By a process of elimination, the fugitive was identified as a stranger to Hobcaw. We rarely employed "new" Negroes on the place and did not encourage their presence there.

After a search of a few hours the criminal was caught and brought into the yard of our house. There, surrounded by a sizable crowd, were the sheriff, my superintendent, Harry Donaldson, and Captain Jim Powell. The crowd was for stringing up the culprit then and there. Someone tossed a rope over a limb of one of the moss-hung oaks that shade the front lawn.

Jim Powell, seeking some way of preventing a lynching, strode into the excited throng and asked to be heard.

"Don't lynch him here in the yard," he pleaded. "Miss Annie"—referring to my wife—"and Miss Belle and Miss Renee"—meaning my daughters—"would never come back to Hobcaw again. It would spoil the place for them forever. Let's take him up the Neck."

In the confusion that followed, the sheriff got hold of the Negro, hustled him on a boat, and, before the crowd knew what was happening, had him on the way toward Georgetown. There he was locked up safely in jail. Rape and attempted rape are punishable by death in South Carolina. At the next term of court, the prisoner was tried before a jury, convicted, and hanged.

The sheriff and Captain Jim acted for the overwhelming mass of Southerners who resented the stain lynching left on the South. I once offered to provide the funds to see to it that anyone engaged in lynching would be apprehended and prosecuted. Others felt as I did and worked in their own way to eradicate lynching.

As the years passed, the Negro villages on Hobcaw began to break up. I was glad to see it happen. I missed the Negroes whom I had come to know so well, but I knew that the slow crumbling of these villages was evidence of progress.

The Negroes leaving Hobcaw were going out to newer and wider opportunities. Military service during the war gave many Negroes a new outlook on life. Among those who came back out of the Army or Navy, I noticed an improved physical carriage and a more observant attitude generally.

Still other Negroes have been moving off the land to the expanding cities in both the North and the South—a process which has been speeded by acreage restrictions under the government's farm price support programs.

Looking back over the years, it seems to me that education and economic improvement have been the keys to the progress that the Negro has made not only in the South but in the North as well. In my graduating class at City College there was one Negro, who was a fine debater and a good scholar. Some years later I happened to meet him on the street. I asked why he didn't come to our Alumni reunions.

"I thought I could lift up my race," he told me. "But it has been too much for me."

Today I doubt that any Negro college graduate would say that. A sizable part of our Negro population has climbed both the educational and economic ladder. Men like Ralph Bunche and Jackie Robinson—to mention only two—have won their place in American life, not as Negroes but as individuals competing successfully with all other Americans.

The Negro, like all of us, is caught up in the flooding river of change. The river's currents are so strong that there can be no return to the past. The passage ahead looms as a perilous one. But when I think how far we already have traveled, I feel confident the difficulties ahead will be overcome.

22. *The Years Ahead*

SOME MEN AND WOMEN start out early in life knowing what they want to be, and their lives become tales of how they made their ambitions come true. That, plainly, has not been true of my career. In my personal ambitions I have been constantly beset by conflicting desires. The turns my life took have been determined as much as anything by the rush of events.

Although I didn't realize it at the time, when I first came onto the Wall Street scene, it was at the end of one era in our country's history and at the beginning of a new one. The dominant financial figures of the day—Morgan, Harriman, Ryan, Hill, Duke, Rockefeller—were at the summit of their power and prestige.

Watching them and hearing of their exploits, I thought to myself, "If they can do it, why can't I?" I tried my best to emulate them, particularly Edward Harriman, who seemed to me to be the epitome of all that was dashing. The son of a minister, he had started from scratch, as I had. He bet on horses, races, prizefights, and elections—things I also liked to do.

In studying railroads, I had been excited by how he had taken over the Union Pacific, when it was not much more than two streaks of rust, and had transformed it into one of the finest railroads in America. My favorite Harriman story is of the time James Stillman, of the National City Bank, asked him what he most liked to do. "It's to be told that something can't be done," Harriman replied, "and jump into it with both feet and do it."

But I never was able to become a second Harriman. Perhaps I just wasn't the man. However, I think that the conditions which made possible the "robber barons," or "Lords of Creation," as they have been termed by some writers, were slipping away. That Fourth of July in 1898 when I took advantage of the imminent end of the Spanish-American War may have been more symbolic than I was aware of. For the years in which the United States emerged as a world power also climaxed the era of unrestrained individualism in American finance.

After the turn of the century, for one thing, the financial arena became too huge to be dominated by any one man or even group of men. If in 1907 a Morgan still could stem a panic, when the 1929 flood broke loose no one man could hold it back.

This change could be seen in the stock market itself. In 1898 something like 60 per cent of the securities listed on the Big Board were of railroads. This, of course, reflected the fact that the main business of America in the period after the Civil War was the physical spanning and conquest of the continent. By 1914 railroads represented less than 40 per cent of the Stock Exchange's listings, by 1925 about 17 per cent, and by 1957 only 13 per cent.

Up to World War One, almost the only financing of foreign governments done in this country had been for Britain during the Boer War and for Japan in connection with the Russo-Japanese War. Today, of course, the United States is the most important single center of foreign financing.

Another factor in the change in eras was the change in generations. Morgan and Rockefeller were more than thirty years older than I; Harriman was twenty-two years my senior, and Ryan nineteen years older. My generation was less satisfied with mere money making. In my own case, of course, I had the example of my father constantly before me, to disturb my mind with the question, "Now that you have money, what are you going to do with it?"

But the times were also awakening a sense of social responsibility in the whole country. The titans who had made vast fortunes had begun to give their money away—something they often found more difficult to do wisely than to make it. More important were the many social changes and currents of feeling which found expression in the progressive ideas of Theodore Roosevelt and Woodrow Wilson.

As I have written, I was slow to acquire a political philosophy. My first presidential ballot was cast in 1892 for Grover Cleveland. In 1896 I was so mixed up in my thinking that I can't remember for whom I voted. I went to hear William Jennings Bryan when he came to New York and was carried away by his oratory, but when I left Madison Square Garden, the farther away I got from his voice, the more its effect wore off. Everyone I knew was against him.

I had almost made up my mind to vote for McKinley when my great-uncle Fischel Cohen, who had been on General Beauregard's staff, began talking of the Lost Cause and Reconstruction. He told me that my arm would surely wither if I marked a Republican ballot. I probably voted for John M. Palmer, the gold Democrat, whom Father was for.

When Theodore Roosevelt ran, however, I voted for him because he was against the "plunderbund." I remember how restless and discontented I often felt at the end of the day. Looking out over Wall Street and Trinity churchyard from my office window, I found myself thinking of Gray's *Elegy* and wondering whether I should not have been a doctor.

One frequent late-afternoon visitor in those days was Garet Garrett, then with the New York *Evening Post* and later to become an editor of the New York *Tribune* and the *Saturday Evening Post*. He would come in after the Exchange had closed and listen to me think aloud. When he got up to leave, he would say, "I keep telling you, B. M., you don't belong in Wall Street; you should be in Washington."

2

But the real turning point in my thinking—and I believe in the thinking of American businessmen generally—was World War One. The war forced a shelving of the old *laissez-faire* tradition and thrust the government into a wholly new role. What was done in those war years was never to be completely forgotten. Afterward, whenever an emergency arose, whether it was a domestic crisis like the Great Depression or a Second World War, the country turned back to the pattern of action by the government which had first been developed during World War One.

I, of course, was one of the human instruments through which this revolution in national thinking and in the role of government was registered. It was not that I was particularly far-sighted. When World War One broke out I certainly was no global thinker. Military strategy meant little or nothing to me; nor did I have any comprehension of what needed to be done to mobilize a nation's economy for a total war.

But as the war swept on, I did begin to think of what would have to be done if the United States was drawn into the conflict. The very first time I visited the White House was when Secretary of Treasury William G. McAdoo arranged for me to explain to President Wilson a plan I had drawn up for mobilizing our economic resources for national defense.

When the Advisory Commission of the Council of National Defense was set up, I was made a member and was given the responsibility for seeing that the raw materials would be available for our preparedness program. Since raw materials enter into the manufacture of everything, I found myself concerned with every part of the economy. I quickly learned that the tasks given me could not be accomplished by business-as-usual methods.

A wholly new approach was needed, one which envisioned every factory and all raw materials, every business leader and worker as part of one gigantic industrial army.

What I learned I somehow had to pass on to other businessmen. It was no easy job. At some of our earlier meetings, whenever a labor leader spoke up he would be interrupted by the businessmen on the commission. I often found myself saying, "Please let Mr. Gompers finish. I would like to hear what he has to say."

In this new industrial army, men who were generals of finance or business often had to play the role of lieutenants and sergeants. Many of our business leaders had grown accustomed to thinking of themselves as virtually laws unto themselves, brooking no interference by the government or anyone else with how they ran their factories or plants. It was not easy to explain to such men why they had to shed their fiercely individualistic ways and take orders from the government or cooperate with their competitors.

I did not always succeed in making these business leaders adopt the larger view of the national interest. There was Henry Ford, for example. I went to see him at his hotel in Washington to explain why, since the steel used for automobiles was needed for war, the production of civilian cars would have to be curtailed.

Ford insisted that he could make cars and munitions at the same time. "Just tell me what you want and I'll make it," he declared.

Although I tried to explain why there just wasn't enough steel for both the war and civilian cars, he remained unconvinced.

But others, almost as intense in their individualism, did see the larger picture. One day I invited James B. Duke to lunch to discuss our plans for the tobacco industry. Duke protested that what we were doing was all wrong. I called in the man in charge of the tobacco section and said, "Mr. Duke is running things now." When Duke demurred I said, "You don't like how we're doing things. Show us what we should do. This is the problem we must meet."

Duke made some valuable suggestions. Although he was opposed to Wilson politically, he became one of my strongest supporters.

In the main, that was my approach to all of the mobilization problems which we faced. With the fighting going on there was not time enough to convert every businessman. But in every industry I could always find the man or men who could be relied on to tell us how best to meet our problem.

I already have related how Dan Guggenheim helped us cut the prevailing price of copper by more than one half. Later we were faced with the necessity of deciding what the government should pay for steel plates used in building ships. I went to H. C. Frick. He received me in his famous library. I asked him what price the government should pay.

"That's not a fair question to ask me," Frick protested. "I'm chairman of the Finance Committee of U.S. Steel."

"I haven't come to you as a steel man," I told him, "I've come to you as a patriotic citizen."

"Two and a half cents a pound," Frick snapped back.

At the time the spokesmen for some of the steel companies were asking four and a quarter cents for plates sold to government shipbuilders, while the black market price was eighteen and a half cents.

Many other businessmen—Andrew Mellon, Price McKinney, a Cleveland steel man, Clinton H. Crane of St. Joseph Lead Company, Alfred C. Bedford of Standard Oil of New Jersey, Edgar Palmer of New Jersey Zinc, and others too numerous to be cited here—responded in the same fashion as did Frick and Guggenheim.

If it had not been for my years in Wall Street I doubt that I would have been able to carry through my wartime duties. My financial dealings had given me an intimate knowledge of the personal character of many of our business leaders. I knew who would respond to a straightforward appeal to patriotism. With others I knew that, if we were to get the necessary cooperation, we would have to show them that the government was stronger than any individual.

When such a showdown came, I found myself fortunate in having made my money as a lone operator in Wall Street. Had my fortune rested on some specific industrial interest, I might have been subjected to counterpressures from business elements I was antagonizing. When the issue of setting steel prices came up, one member of our price-fixing committee remarked that the big steel companies could ruin a company he was interested in by taking away its business.

I told him that I would step out in front on the issue, explaining, "They can't hurt me."

There were numerous other ways in which my Wall Street experiences stood me well. In fact, I constantly was being surprised to find how many of the mobilization problems lent themselves to much the same approach I had used in my speculative activities.

I quickly learned, for example, that many shortages were really psychological. Frightened that they might not get what they needed, manufacturers would overbuy. Or thinking that prices were bound to skyrocket, suppliers would hold back their materials.

In the stock market I had learned how quickly a bull market could reverse itself once the continuity of thought behind the market trend was broken. In reducing the prices of key war materials as soon as we entered the war, one of my objectives was to break the prevailing expectation that prices were bound to rise and rise and rise.

Also, in Wall Street, I had learned that planning a successful financial operation was much like planning a military operation. Before going into action, one had to know both the strengths and weaknesses of the opposing forces.

Often we gained the cooperation of those who were reluctant by applying pressure on their weak points. At home we used the threat of commandeering or cutting off a manufacturer's fuel or railroad transportation. With foreign countries the measures we used were different, but the principle was the same.

Once during the war, for example, the British representatives took the position that they could not control the price of jute in Calcutta because India was a separate government. I went to Secretary McAdoo and asked him to withhold further shipments of silver which were needed to stabilize India's currency. We had sent a mission to London, headed by Leland Summers, and he told the British officials there that we would hold to this position even if the Bombay and Calcutta exchanges had to be closed. The British soon found a way to control the price of jute.

Probably the most critical single problem of supply we faced in the whole war was with nitrates. The demand for nitrates, which were needed for both fertilizer and explosives, exceeded any possible production. This shortage remained acute until the very end of the war. Each time a tramp steamer carrying nitrates was sunk, it was a grievous blow.

When the United States declared war, nitrate prices jumped almost overnight by a third and then doubled within three weeks. This price rise touched off an even wilder scramble for nitrates, with speculators trying to corner much of the available nitrates to hold off the market so as to force prices even higher.

About this time President Wilson called me in and made me solely responsible for solving the problem. I racked my brain for some way out—without success. A committee of munitions manufacturers came to Washington to ask how they were going to get the nitrates which were needed to fill their contracts. I assured them the nitrates would be supplied.

When the meeting broke up, Charles MacDowell, who headed our chemical division, asked me, "Chief, what are you going to do to make good on that promise?"

"I don't know, Mac," I confessed. "But I couldn't let them go out of here thinking the government couldn't do anything."

The next few days were among the most trying I ever have experienced. I couldn't sleep or eat. Even when I drank a glass of water my throat choked up. I believe I came as close to giving way to panic as I ever have been in my life. While dressing one morning I looked at my pale, drawn face in the mirror, and said aloud, "Why, you coward. Pull yourself together and act like a man."

What happened next made me wonder whether there wasn't some special Providence looking after me. I forced myself to eat breakfast and went down to my office. I had not been there long when a Naval Intelligence officer came in with several intercepted cables which revealed that the Chilean government had its gold reserve in Germany and had been trying in vain to get the German government to release this gold reserve.

At last I had something to work on. A few days later the Chilean ambassador came in. He began complaining about the troubles his country was experiencing because of various shortages and difficulties in controlling inflation. I knew that there was in Chile something like 200,000 tons of nitrates which Germans owned but had been unable to move out of the country. If Chile would seize these German-owned nitrates, I proposed to the ambassador, I would buy it all at four and a quarter cents a pound and pay for it in gold six months after the treaty of peace was signed.

As soon as the Chilean ambassador left my office, I arranged to have the necessary ships sent down to Chile so no time would be lost in getting possession of the nitrates.

Curiously, some State Department officials objected to the deal on the ground that it violated the Trading with the Enemy Act. I was astonished by their objection. "You mean to say," I demanded, "that I can't buy German nitrates to shoot the Germans with?"

The issue was taken to President Wilson, who supported my action. The upshot of the whole affair was a satisfactory arrangement which got us desperately needed nitrates and which helped the Chilean government overcome its domestic difficulties. Yet the agreement would not have been possible if we had not known Chile's need and used that as a basis for our bargaining.

Accommodation to mutual needs remains the best basis for all agreements between nations. Although this may seem like an obvious truth, the record since the end of World War Two shows that we have not yet learned how to apply this truth in our dealings with our allies. We have relied too heavily on the formal wording of treaties and have neglected to do what needs to be done to strengthen the structure of mutual interests which alone can support an enduring alliance.

One cannot buy the friendship of other nations. "Friends" acquired in such a way are quick to take offense over anything. Where there is a true basis of mutual interest, however, nations will make excuses for one another's failings and overlook one another's shortcomings.

Along with common interest, scrupulous fairness should be observed in dealing with allies. The golden rule could be paraphrased and applied to alliances—ask nothing of others that you are not prepared to do yourself.

It was Woodrow Wilson who first enunciated this principle on behalf of the United States. He insisted that whatever we bought for our own war effort should be made available to our allies at the same price that we had paid.

During a dispute over this very principle I first came to sense in Winston Churchill the qualities of greatness that were to make him so inspiring a war leader. We had proposed that England pay the same price as we did for anything bought in the United States, while Americans should pay the same price as did England for anything purchased within the Empire. Some of Britain's merchant princes opposed this arrangement. When the matter was brought up before Churchill, then Minister of Munitions, he agreed that it was the only fair way for allies to treat one another.

This identical principle was followed in allocating the nitrates being bought from Chile. I rejected all suggestions that we use our control of these nitrates for American commercial advantage. Instead we agreed to allocate them equitably among all the Allies through an International Nitrate Executive. This committee was to prove the forerunner of the Combined Boards that were used to allocate scarce supplies among the allies in World War Two.

I left the naming of the chairman of this International Nitrate Executive to Churchill. Afterward he often jokingly referred to the time I made him "Nitrate King of the world."

In the more than forty years that we have been friends, I

have never known Churchill to make a mean or ignoble proposal in his relations with the United States. Ever quick to defend Britain's interests, he has always accompanied it with a warm appreciation of American interests. During World War Two, when the United States was faced with the need to divert supplies from Britain, I heard him protest flatly to Franklin Roosevelt, "My people are living at the limit of austerity now and their food supplies cannot be cut." I have also heard him protest as warmly against slurs made by other Englishmen upon this country and its leaders.

At one dinner he gave for me in London, a number of Tories were present who disliked Franklin Roosevelt and the New Deal. One gentleman decided to amuse the company by asking me the riddle—why were Roosevelt and Columbus alike? His answer was that, like Columbus, Roosevelt did not know where he was going or where he was when he got there, or where he had been when he got back.

Rising, I replied, "Perhaps it is true that Roosevelt and Columbus were alike, since both explored new frontiers and new horizons and both brought a new world into existence to redress the troubles of the old world." Churchill banged the table in approval, crying, "Hear, hear!"

3

When the First World War was over, the American people in general and businessmen in particular tried to go back to things as they had been before the war broke out. I did not. My main reason, I suppose, was that I had found public service so much more satisfying than making money. But I could also see that the war had left in its wake many problems which could not be solved by a "let-things-alone" philosophy.

And so while many of my associates sought a revival of *laissez-faire*, I continued to grapple with the problem of what the role of government should be in modern life. President

Wilson called me to Paris to serve as one of his advisers on the economic sections of the Treaty of Versailles. I fought alongside of him for America's entrance into the League of Nations. Afterward I battled to give farmers a better share of our national income; I even tried to devise plans for reorganizing the nation's railroads and for breaking the impasse over reparations and war debts.

When I think back over these and the many other difficulties we have had to wrestle with—from the problems of the depression and a Second World War to the cold war with Russia—I am struck by the fact that most of them revolve around one crucial interrelationship—that of war and peace. Since at least 1914 this country—and the rest of the world—has been either going into a war or coming out of one. We have persisted in thinking that the rules of peacetime economics and peacetime society should fit our needs. Yet there has been hardly a single year since 1914 which could be considered as really free of the influences of war and its aftermath.

Most of our economic problems, from agricultural overproduction to financing our national debt, have had their origins in the dislocations of war. Twice in our lifetime we have had to turn our economy inside out to meet the needs of war, and then to go back to peaceful ways.

At the same time one role of war throughout history has been to accentuate and quicken whatever changes were in the making before war broke out. The splitting of the atom, for example, might still be unattained if we had not been driven by the fear that the enemy might achieve it first.

In our governmental skills we never really have caught up with the forces and problems unloosed by two world wars. Whatever has been done, more remained to be done. It has been as if we were chasing a train which we never seem able to catch.

It is my intention, in the second volume of these memoirs, to try to examine this crucial interrelationship of war and peace, drawing whatever lessons one can from my own experiences. Perhaps I should devote the remaining pages of this volume to a few thoughts on the nature of the crisis that confronts our world and how each of us can come to a better understanding of what is involved.

We must look upon the crucial trial we now face as, in essence, a test of our ability to govern ourselves. We do not suffer from any lack of material resources. The sheer power, both for constructive and destructive purposes, which man commands is unprecedented. What we lack is the ability to control and direct this power and these vast productive resources which are ours.

This test of our ability to govern ourselves is really three-fold.

First, it is a test of values, of what things we will give up in order to make other things secure.

Second, it is a test of our reasoning powers, of whether we have the wit to think our problems through to an effective solution.

Third, it is a test of self-discipline, of our ability to stand by our values and see our policies through, whatever the personal cost.

The issue of how much should be spent on our national defense provides a fairly good illustration of all three aspects of this trial. Some persons have contended that "our economy can stand only so much." But during both world wars we demonstrated that our economy could support an infinitely heavier effort than anyone has yet proposed be done in the struggle for peace. The physical resources at the disposal of ourselves and our allies exceed what the Soviets and their satellites can command. I, for one, will never concede that we cannot do as much in defense of our freedoms as any enemy may be doing to destroy those freedoms.

The limit on what our economy can stand is what we are willing to discipline and organize ourselves to do. It may not be possible to have the defenses we need and everything else we crave. But we have the resources for as large an effort as may be necessary, provided we are willing to curb the fancied wants which conflict with that effort.

The choice of what we prize most highly is obscured by the raging struggle over how the costs of defense are to be distributed among the major segments of our population. Each major pressure group has sought to push the burden of defense onto someone else's shoulders. This attitude of "control the other fellow but leave me alone" was largely responsible for the inflation that took place during both World War Two and the Korean War. It remains a major cause of the inflationary pressures that have plagued us in the cold war.

As far as meeting the costs of defense, our democratic society has failed to devise—or, where they were known, to adopt—the disciplining techniques that would compel each of us to subordinate our selfish interests to the national interest.

We have also failed to think through the proper role of government in a cold war for survival. Some people think only of reducing taxes, without realizing that only by taxing ourselves can we mobilize the necessary defenses for everything we cherish. But others keep proposing vast new programs of federal spending without realizing the limits of the taxing power in a democratic society.

The heavier the burden of taxes, the more difficult it becomes to see that this burden is shared equitably by all segments of the population. We have learned that in war it is vital for national morale that everyone bear a fair share of the national sacrifice; also that some things must be postponed so more vital needs can be met. We do not seem to realize that the existence of a cold war requires similar considerations.

The public's support for even the most important policies will be weakened if the taxing power is strained by other programs of lesser importance, or if our system of taxation and inflation is allowed to impose an unjust burden on some of the citizens. We cannot fight a cold war with peacetime standards of both economics and public morality.

I never have begrudged paying higher taxes. While I believe there is much waste in governmental expenditures which can be cut out, I would not favor a tax reduction until our defenses are made secure and the credit of the government made firm. Sound government credit, I might stress, is vital for a sound system of national defense. Without it the government is weakened in meeting any emergency that may arise.

Currently one hears much talk of the development of a new "ultimate" weapon which many people believe may solve our security needs. The intercontinental ballistics missile, once it is developed, may indeed revolutionize the art of warfare. Yet even after it has been perfected, we still will be left facing the same test of our ability to govern ourselves —of whether we can think our problems through and then discipline ourselves to put first things first.

During my eighty-seven years I have witnessed a whole succession of technological revolutions. But none of them has done away with the need for character in the individual or the ability to think.

4

Talk of the need for discipline and of the need to think may sound like old-fashioned preaching. This tendency to shrug off these old truths is another part of what troubles our society. Many of us listen to these truths and nod our heads at their verity but do nothing to put them into practice. Since we do not think through what would be required to apply these old truths, they remain mere words.

Sadly, the dominant trends in education seem to be operating to aggravate this neglect. Instead of teaching young people to think, too many of our schools assume that their task is done if students are kept interested. Curriculums have been enriched to cover every conceivable subject, while discipline has come to be frowned upon. Along with the growth of specialized schools seeking to turn out technical experts has come an illusion that the mere amassing of information is a sign of being well-educated.

But information cannot serve as an effective substitute for thinking. Let me cite an experience recent enough to be remembered by most of us. When World War Two was drawing to a close, many economists and statisticians predicted that the war's end would throw ten million or more workers out of jobs. This dire forecast was supported by an impressive array of statistical data.

James F. Byrnes, Director of Mobilization, asked me and my faithful associate, John M. Hancock, to draw up the policies which would guide our reconversion from war to peace. We saw no large-scale unemployment on the termination of hostilities. Instead, our report foresaw an unparalleled "adventure in prosperity." Soon after our report was issued in February, 1944, I went further and stated flatly that after the war ended there would be at least five to seven years of uninterrupted prosperity, no matter what anyone did.

What was that prediction based on? We made no statistical studies of purchasing power, nor of "consumer attitudes," nor of any of the other indices that economic soothsayers like to point to when speculating about the future. Mainly my judgment was based on the fact that the war would leave half the world in ruins. I felt confident that nothing could stop the rebuilding of the world. As I told my associates at the time, "men and women, peoples and governments will beg, borrow, and, if necessary, steal" but they will find a way to restore their homes and meet the needs that had gone unsatisfied during the war.

The point I am trying to make is that information without judgment and thought is of little value.

To be able to exercise sound judgment, one must keep the

total picture in focus. Our better educators are coming to realize that what is needed is not a familiarity with specialized detail but this ability to see our varied problems as parts of one interrelated whole. Almost nothing in our world stands alone. Everything tends to cut athwart of everything else. If action on any particular front is to be truly effective, usually a host of other actions are required on supporting fronts.

This struggle for the total as opposed to the piecemeal approach was the central issue in the long and, sad to say, unsuccessful fight to prevent inflation during World War Two. Congress and most of the officials in the executive branch argued that monetary controls alone would suffice or that only a few prices had to be controlled, while wages and farm prices could be left largely uncontrolled. Against this bits-and-pieces approach, I warned that a whole series of actions across the entire economy was needed, as parts of a single, synchronized mobilization of all our resources.

When World War Two ended I again took up the battle for a total approach—this time in relation to the peacemaking. Even as we had devised a global strategy to win the war, I urged that the equivalent of such a strategy be worked out to embrace every aspect of the struggle for peace so that we could employ the strength that was ours to the greatest advantage. Many officials made speeches about the need for "total diplomacy." But the painstaking task of piecing together all the many interrelationships of a unified, global strategy has not yet been carried through.

One reason for this failure is our yearning for quick and easy solutions. It has taken some time for the American public to learn that there are no short-cuts to world peace. The task of preventing a third world war will engage us through our whole lives and the lives of our children.

With every action that is proposed we would do well to ask ourselves not only how much it can be expected to accomplish, but what it is that it *cannot* do.

It is also important to make certain that our efforts are

directed at the decisive core of the problem and not on distracting side issues. The more complex the difficulties we face, the more important it becomes to bear this in mind, for it is human nature to try to evade what we cannot cope with.

How often have we been struck by the petty bickering that people engage in when confronted with the gravest sort of crisis. I doubt that this bickering reflects a lack of awareness of the seriousness of a situation. Rather I think it reflects what might be termed the law of distraction—that when men find themselves baffled and frustrated by some problem, they create some distraction to run after.

Mankind has always sought to substitute energy for reason, as if running faster will give one a better sense of direction. Periodically we should stop and ask ourselves if our efforts are focused upon the crux of the problem—the things that must be settled if there is to be a manageable solution—or if we are expending our energies on side issues which cannot yield a decision, no matter what their outcome.

This, of course, is enormously important in the struggle for peace. In the making of peace, I believe, there are two issues which overshadow all others. Unless these two issues can be resolved, no basis of enduring peace is possible.

One problem is that posed by a divided Germany and how it is to be reunited. As long as Germany remains cut in two every nation must guard against the day in the future when an attempt may be made to reunite Germany by force. This peril is the main reason why NATO forces are needed. Even if the threat of direct Soviet aggression could be removed, there would still be the danger that Soviet satellite troops might seize upon some pretext to overrun Germany as was attempted in Korea. Or some groups of Germans might use an internal "revolution" or coup as a means of "uniting" Germany by force.

If a third world war is to be prevented there must be troops on the Western side of the Iron Curtain who can hold

Western Germany against such efforts. These troops must be in readiness for immediate action, not on paper.

NATO would still be needed even if agreement could be reached by which Soviet troops evacuated Eastern Europe and American troops were withdrawn from Western Germany. Any such settlement could only be a guarded one, until a far greater measure of mutual confidence than now prevails is brought into existence.

It is also difficult to see how there can be any genuine disarmament as long as the problem of Germany remains unresolved.

The second indispensable requirement for an enduring peace is a foolproof system of inspection and control of all forms of nuclear energy, with punishment for any violation of the agreement. Once an agreement is reached no veto should be permitted to nullify it.

The plan for international atomic control which I had the honor of presenting to the United Nations on behalf of the United States government did not asume that this country would hold its atomic monopoly indefinitely. We were well aware that in time we had to expect other nations to develop atomic weapons. But whether one or sixty one nations possess nuclear weapons does not alter the unyielding fact that no nation can have effective insurance against atomic destruction unless there is a sure system of control to guard against the diversion of atomic energy for military purposes.

If anything, the need for such control will grow with the increase in the number of nations with atomic weapons. Even the Russians will come to realize this. A few days before he died Andrei Vishinsky, then the Soviet representative to the United Nations, invited me to a reception at the Soviet Legation in New York. At one point during the reception we found ourselves alone, and I told him that I thought his government had been unwise to oppose effective control of atomic weapons.

"It's getting easier and easier to make these bombs," I

warned him. "Pretty soon other countries will have nuclear weapons. Even your satellites will get them. Then what will you do?"

I went on to say that there was an old saying on our Western frontier that the Smith and Wesson revolver made all men equal. "Once the smaller nations have atomic weapons they will be able to threaten even the strongest power."

I concluded, "The problem of control is relatively easy now since only two nations have these weapons. Later, when other countries get them, you may want a system of control but it will be too late."

After that, in other meetings with high Soviet officials—Andrei Gromyko, Jacob Malik, and Dmitri Shepilov—I repeated this same point. I never learned whether it sank in, but some such consideration may have been a factor in the attitude displayed by the Soviets in the disarmament talks of 1956 and 1957.

Whatever lies behind the Soviet attitude, the choice before the world remains the same—real control or none. A ban on the testing of nuclear weapons will not meet the problem. Even if these tests are discontinued, the dread danger of atomic attack still would threaten. Nor can smaller nations be expected to accept any permanent freeze of the present situation, in which only the larger powers have these weapons. Unless they are protected against atomic attack, other countries will continue to search for the means of acquiring nuclear weapons of their own, and this in turn will require their testing of these weapons.

The grim danger of radioactive fallout would disappear if effective control could be established over all nuclear weapons. There would then be no need for any tests; the scientists of the world would be working together to expand the peaceful uses of the atom.

The scientists—and others—would do better to use their influence on behalf of truly effective control of all nuclear weapons, and not just to limit tests alone.

Bernard Baruch

Similarly, any measure that widens the range of peaceful atomic uses, such as President Eisenhower's proposal for an international atomic pool, is worthy. But whatever may be turned over to an atoms-for-peace agency, different nations still will hold back the larger part of the available fissionable material to develop atomic and other nuclear weapons. The dangers of atomic attack would not be lessened.

If the threat of atomic war cannot be chained up, it is far better that we face it with wide open eyes than to be lulled into a false sense of security by some meaningless agreement.

We should never give up our search for some means of effective control. Always we should listen to and study the proposals that any nation may make. But we should not let either our profound desire for peace or our fears of another war blind us to the realities that must be faced up to if we are to preserve our freedoms and have a genuine peace that every nation in the world—Russia included—can enjoy.

A few years ago I delivered a lecture before some college students in which I tried to sum up the philosophy that has guided me.

I pointed to the cyclical succession of wars and peace, booms and busts, enslavement and freedom that have charac terized human history. After each of these breakdowns there was always a rebuilding which lifted man to new heights of accomplishment—at least by material standards.

Today, however, we wonder whether our civilization could stand another cyclical breakdown. In place of the old averaging out of collapse and recovery we yearn for some system of sustained progress. This, I believe, is the dominant yearning of our time.

To break free of this cycle of breakdown and buildup, we must free ourselves of man's age-old tendency to swing from one extreme to another. We must seek out the course of disciplined reason that avoids both dumb submission and blind revolt.

I believe in reason not because of the wisdom that men

312.

have demonstrated in the past but because it remains man's best tool for governing himself. It is not mere chance that, whenever society is swept by some madness, reason falls as the first victim. Neither perfection nor utopia is within man's grasp. But if the frenzy of soaring hope can never be realized, we can also avoid the panic of plunging despair—if we learn to think our problems through, decide what it is that we value most, and organize ourselves—both as individuals and as a nation—to see that first things come first.

INDEX

Recommended Reading

How I made $2,000,000 in the Stock Market
By: Nicolas Darvas

Wall Street: The Other Las Vegas
By: Nicolas Darvas

You Can Still Make it in the Market
By: Nicolas Darvas

How I Made Money Using the Nicolas Darvas System,
Which Made Him $2,000,000 in the Stock Market
By Steve Burns

The Battle for Investment Survival
by Gerald M. Loeb

The Psychology Of The Stock Market
by G. C. Selden

The Science of Getting Rich
by Wallace D. Wattles

Think and Grow Rich
by Napoleon Hill

Available at www.bnpublishing.net

CPSIA information can be obtained
at www.ICGtesting.com
Printed in the USA
BVOW08s1419020218
506815BV00002B/164/P